HOW TO INCORPORATE

A Handbook for Entrepreneurs and Professionals
Third Edition

MICHAEL R. DIAMOND
*Partner in Washington's O'Toole,
Rothwell, Nassau & Steinbach
Adjunct Professor of Law,
American University School of Law*

JULIE L. WILLIAMS
*Chief Counsel
Office of the Comptroller of the Currency*

JOHN WILEY & SONS, INC.

New York • Chichester • Brisbane • Toronto • Singapore

ISBN 0-471-13912-2 (cloth)
ISBN 0-471-13913-0 (paper)

Printed in the United States of America

10 9 8 7 6 5 4 3 2 1

To Rebecca Caleff and my parents, with love,
and to the memory of Moses Caleff and A. L. and Selma Diamond.
They all contributed to this book's existence.

M.R.D.

With love to Don and my mother
and in memory of my father.

J.L.W.

CONTENTS

1

INTRODUCTION

Corporations are among the most visible and most powerful participants in our national economy. When one thinks of corporations, one often thinks of corporate giants such as IBM or Exxon, the Fortune 500, or the New York Stock Exchange. However, of the several million corporations operating in the United States, fewer than 10,000 are publicly traded in any significant way.

The typical corporation is closely held, that is, owned by only a small number of persons (known as shareholders or stockholders). The shares of stock they own are not readily transferable from person to person as are, for instance, those of IBM. Instead, the shareholders of the typical company usually know each other and often work together in the business.

Often, the corporations they established were organized and operated without the assistance of a lawyer or other professional. In most cases, that fact is insignificant in the life of the corporation or its shareholders. There are, however, many situations where the absence of professional planning and ongoing professional assistance has had serious consequences. While this book is not a substitute for such assistance, it is designed to fill part of the void between businesspersons and outside professionals who counsel them and also to highlight areas where outside assistance is particularly important.

The book deals with the organization and operation of a business corporation. It lays out the legal prerequisites to corporate existence, the choices the organizers of a corporation must make, and the practical implications of the potential choices. The book also discusses the legal and practical realities of operating a corporation, including many of the financial issues likely to be faced by the business's principals. In addition, we have added a chapter on a new and very versatile business form, the Limited Liability Company or LLC. While some of the planning choices for an LLC have counterparts in the formation of a closely held corporation, there are some important distinctions between the forms.

Stylistically, we have attempted to be straightforward and clear. There are forms, explanations, and examples to take readers through the various issues raised in the text. The appendixes are also intended to give the reader information, or access to information, which is useful in forming and running a business corporation.

Since much of corporate formation involves statutory requirements, and since states vary in their corporate statutes, we have chosen to use as a base for discussion the Model Business Corporation Act ("The Model Act"), which was originally prepared as a research project of the American Bar Foundation and subsequently updated and expanded by the Committee on Corporate Laws of the Section of Corporation, Banking, and Business Law of the American Bar Association. The Act has been adopted in whole or in substantial part by many states, and thus provides the most common link for discussion. Because of statutory variation, however, it is very important that the reader examine his or her own state's law to determine the degree of similarity with the Model Act. The comparison chart in the appendixes is designed to assist in that examination.

Once the statutory requirements are understood, the organizers must make choices both as to statutory possibilities and operational needs. We believe that knowledge and understanding of issues help in the decision-making process. With this in mind, we have attempted to shed some light on the inner workings of corporate formation and existence. We hope this information proves helpful.

2

THE CORPORATION

WHAT IS A CORPORATION?

A corporation is a legal entity comprised of other entities—human or artificial. Its unique characteristic is that it is recognized by the law as a thing separate from the entities that comprise it, and is frequently treated like a human being. For instance, a corporation is treated as a "person" and enjoys the Constitutional protections against unreasonable searches and seizures, deprivation of liberty and property without due process of law, and denial of equal protection of the law. A corporation is entitled to invoke the attorney-client privilege of confidentiality; it may sue for defamation of its corporate good name; and like an individual, it is subject to punishment if it violates the law. In such cases, it may be liable for damages or fines or could be prohibited from continuing in business.

For the purposes of federal court jurisdiction, a corporation is deemed to be a resident of the state (or states) where it was incorporated *and* of the state where it has its principal place of business. A corporation is not, however, a "citizen" within the meaning of the Privileges and Immunities Clause of the Constitution and, consequently, a state may subject "foreign" corporations (those incorporated in another state) to regulations not imposed on "domestic" corporations (those incorporated in that state).

Generally, an individual is considered to be "domiciled" in the place that he or she calls home. A corporation is considered to have two domiciles—it's "legal domicile" in the state where it was incorporated, and its "commercial domicile" where it has its principal place of business. This distinction is significant because it enables more than one state to impose its taxes on a corporation by virtue of the corporation's "domicile" within that state's jurisdiction.°

The most important characteristic of a corporation is the "limited liability" it affords its shareholders (or members), directors, and officers for wrongs committed by the corporation. In the case of a business or a "for profit" corporation, a shareholder's liability is usually limited to the amount he or she invested in the corporation. If a corporation goes bankrupt, stockholders are not liable for the corporation's debts—they lose only the money they paid to purchase their stock. If a customer slips on a banana peel in a store run by a corporation, the customer may sue the corporation. If the corporation is found to be liable for the amount sought by the customer, the customer may take the corporation's property to satisfy the judgment. If the corporation's property does not satisfy the judgment, the customer generally may not take a shareholder's personal assets (e.g., car, bank account, etc.). If a stockholder's stock has not been fully paid for, however, that stockholder will be liable to the corporation or to an outsider for the portion that is unpaid.

In a nonprofit corporation, *members* occupy a position analogous to that of stockholders in a for-profit corporation. Nonprofit corporations, however, may not issue stock and members do not "invest" in the corporation. Thus, the amount a member would lose if a non-profit corporation became bankrupt would generally be only the amount of membership dues paid or donations made. In both profit and nonprofit corporations, directors, officers, and other corporate personnel generally are not liable for corporate debts.

The exception to the usual state of limited liability occurs when the corporate form is used to perpetrate a fraud, evade the law, or wrongfully escape payment of a just obligation. In situations where it would be clearly unjust to allow the corporation to shield the individuals behind it, courts may ignore the corporation and look directly to its shareholders or directors and officers for liability for corporate debts and responsibility for corporate misdeeds. The courts also look behind the corporation or, to use the legal term, "pierce the corporate veil," when the corporation ignores corporate formalities (fails to comply with statutory requirements, such as, for example, if its incorporation is defective, if the corporation is merely a shell and is being used solely as a "front" to

---

° This should not result in a double tax. A corporation is generally subject to state income taxes only on the portion of its total activities that are carried on within a particular state. That is, if one-third of the company's activities (property, sales, and employees) take place in State X, one-third of the company's income is taxable by State X. What this does mean is that a corporation may be responsible for filing tax returns, and annual reports and for paying fees in several states.

evade personal liability, or if the corporation keeps inadequate records or follows improper procedures).

Another unique feature of the corporation is its ability to exist for an unlimited period of time. In most states, a corporation must specify in the Articles of Incorporation the period of its duration, which may be perpetual. Perpetual existence is one advantage of corporations over sole proprietorships and partnerships—the corporation is not terminated by the death or withdrawal of its stockholders or members. Of course, a corporation's existence may be limited in its Articles, and, regardless of a limitation, it may be dissolved at any time by its shareholders or members. Generally, a business corporation may be dissolved by vote of its Board of Directors and a majority of its shareholders present at a shareholders' meeting where notice was given of the vote to dissolve (Section 84 of the Model Business Corporation Act), or, in lieu of a meeting, by written consent signed by *all* shareholders (Section 83 of the Act).

A further advantage of the corporate form is the ease with which interests in a corporation may be transferred. The ownership of a profit corporation is represented by shares of stock that may be sold, traded, or given away by their owners. A shareholder generally may dispose of any portion of his or her stock, or merely the income such stock produces, while retaining voting rights, or vice versa, all without regard to how the other shareholders feel about his or her actions.

The shareholders, however, may voluntarily place restrictions on the transferability of shares. To protect a prearranged control group structure from outsiders, stockholders of a corporation may enter into a "shareholders' agreement" which may provide that any person wishing to sell his or her stock in the corporation must first offer it to the corporation for purchase, or to the other shareholders, or that upon the death of a shareholder, the corporation has the first opportunity to buy the stock from the deceased stockholder's estate. Absolute restrictions on share transfers, however, have not been sustained by the courts.

CORPORATE STRUCTURE

The control of a corporation is basically three tiered, with the stockholders or members making up the largest group in the corporate hierarchy. Nonprofit corporations are not required to have members, but if they do, these are people who are generally interested in the objectives of the corporation but not inclined to become involved in actually running it. Stockholders, on the other hand, may be absolutely disinterested in what the business corporation does, as long as it makes a profit and distributes money to them.

Stockholders (or members) generally have few powers in connection with day-to-day operations of a corporation. They usually elect the Board of Directors, have the ability to remove the Board, are often responsible for amending the Bylaws, and must ratify any amendments to the Articles of Incorporation. In a small corporation, the shareholders may want to give themselves a more significant role by including provisions in the Articles and Bylaws giving themselves broader powers and more direct control over the management of the corporation.

Generally, the Board of Directors is more intimately involved in corporate management than the stockholders. Directors are the corporation's managers. Their legal authority includes decisions of policy, personnel, compensation, delegation of authority to committees, declaration of dividends (in a business corporation), and general supervision and responsibility for all corporate activities.

Pursuant to its power to delegate authority, the Board of Directors may appoint various committees to assist it in its functions. It is possible for the Board to vest virtually all its powers in an Executive Committee composed of a limited number of Boardmembers—at least two. This Executive Committee may exercise all the authority of the Board of Directors in the management of the corporation, but the members of the Board may remain responsible for actions of the Executive Committee. (This may include potential liability for improper distributions of corporate funds, guarantees of corporate obligations, liability and fines for acting as a corporation without proper authority, fines for failure to file required annual reports, or prosecution for non-compliance with Internal Revenue requirements.)

The Board of Directors may also create other committees to perform supportive functions such as publicity, fund raising, community projects, or designing the corporation's stock certificates. Members of these committees (which do not exercise the authority of the Board) need not be members of the Board.

The officers of the corporation are generally selected by the Board of Directors and generally may be removed by the Board. Since officers may be directors, directors may select themselves as the corporation's officers. This is frequently done in a closely held corporation.

Officers carry out the day-to-day business of the corporation, frequently without interference from the Board of Directors, which concerns itself with broader policy decisions. Thus officers are often, in reality, the most powerful group in the corporation. They hire and fire employees, set policy, and make decisions that legally bind the corporation.

The most familiar corporate offices include: President, Vice-President, Secretary, and Treasurer. There may also be numerous assistants for these positions, for example, Assistant Treasurer. While the officers can be given a wide range of powers, there are some powers that are inherent in an office.

For instance, the President traditionally presides at the Board of Directors' and shareholders' meetings and may also act for and obligate the corporation in ordinary business transactions. The President may, for example, sign leases, order goods, and so forth.

The Vice-President generally does not have the power to bind the corporation, and his or her duties are usually merely to act in the place of the President should he or she be absent, disabled, resigned, or dead. The Board or the President could, of course, delegate special additional duties to the Vice-President.

The Secretary attends meetings of the shareholders (or members), Board of Directors, and various committees, keeps minutes of these meetings, sends notices, prepares corporate records, and has custody of the corporate seal.

The Treasurer is the chief fiscal officer of the corporation and is responsible for the corporate treasury, that is, for receiving and keeping the corporation's money and disbursing it as authorized, for maintaining financial records, and for reporting on the financial condition of the corporation.

PROFIT AND NONPROFIT CORPORATIONS

Whether a corporation is for-profit or nonprofit, the previously discussed concepts of the corporate entity (its limited liability and continuous existence) are equally applicable. However, profit and nonprofit corporations are not identical and there are differences that are important to recognize.

A not-for-profit corporation is defined, basically, as "a corporation, no part of the income of which is distributable to its members, directors, or officers." This does not mean that a not-for-profit corporation cannot make money. Both not-for-profit and business (for-profit) corporations may make money, but in figuring "profits," expenses are subtracted from the gross receipts the corporation takes in. In a not-for-profit corporation, the money that remains as "profits" after the payment of expenses may not be distributed to the corporation's members, directors, or officers, but must be applied to further the corporation's purposes or to expand its facilities. "Reasonable compensation for services rendered" is a legitimate corporate "expense" to be subtracted from gross receipts in order to arrive at "profits," and salaries are one way in which members, directors, or officers may receive funds from a nonprofit corporation. Another instance is if the corporation's purposes incidentally benefit members, directors, or officers as well as the other groups it serves (such as a director of a day-care center whose eligible child attends the center), or if the corporation dissolves and its assets are distributed to its members.

A business corporation is strikingly different. While a nonprofit corporation may not issue stock or pay dividends, a business corporation may issue and sell a variety of financial instruments that evidence interests in itself, and may reward the holders of these interests with a portion of corporate profits.

One type of interest in a corporation is represented by shares of stock, the owners of which are, collectively, the owners of the corporation. A for-profit corporation has the ability to offer for sale a variety of types of stock, each attractive to a different type of investor, and thus may be able to achieve broad investment support.

Stock may be differentiated into "preferred" and "common" types. Preferred stock is so called because its holders generally enjoy a preference in the form of a constant, nonfluctuating dividend payment derived from the corporation's earnings, which they receive before the holders of any other type of stock are entitled to receive any portion of profits. Preferred stock is generally considered a conservative investment because of this payoff preference.

Subject always to the Board's discretion, earnings that remain after preferred stockholders receive their dividend payments may then be distributable as dividends to the holders of common stock. The payoff to these stockholders may vary greatly from year to year, depending on the corporation's business success each year. Since preferred stockholders always receive the same fixed amount of dividends off the top of the corporation's profits, in a very profitable year there may be a large amount left over for the common shareholders to receive as dividends, while in a less profitable year, common shareholders may receive nothing. Because of this uncertainty in distributions, common stock is more speculative than preferred stock.

Within each type of stock there may be different "classes" with different purchase prices, rates of dividends, voting rights in the selection of the corporation's management, and so forth. For instance, Class A common stock could pay 10 cents a year per share in dividends but have no voting rights, while Class B common stock pays only 5 cents a year per share, but possesses full voting rights. Those who were primarily interested in financial return would be inclined to buy Class A, while people who wanted control of the corporation would be the investors in Class B.

In addition to stock, a profit corporation may issue a type of interest in itself known as a "debt security." Stock is an equity security because stockholders are considered the owners of the corporation. The corporation has no legal obligation to repay the purchase price of a shareholder's stock. The holders of debt securities, on the other hand, are regarded as creditors of the corporation, that is, the corporation *owes* them money. Debt securities are sold, like stock, for a certain price, paid by the purchaser to the corporation. The holder of a debt security is then entitled to receive interest payments from the corporation based on the value and interest rate of the debt security he or she holds. Thus, if X buys a $1,000 debt security, payable at 6% interest annually, the corporation must pay X $60 every year until the security's due date, at which time the corporation must "redeem" (buy back, pay off) the face value of the security. Since the redemption price is usually the face value of the security, X gets back his or her $1,000 and makes $60 a year until that time.

Unlike dividends, which are paid at the discretion of the Board of Directors, the obligation to pay interest on debt securities continues regardless of the corporation's financial condition.

WHY CHOOSE A PROFIT CORPORATION?

The obvious reason for organizing a business or for-profit corporation is to make a profit. A corporation is an excellent vehicle for a business venture because of the insulation it provides against personal liability for corporate debts and because of the multiple opportunities for personal gain it presents.

As mentioned previously, both profit and nonprofit corporations shield their stockholders or members from liability for corporate debts; however, it is difficult to get rich from a nonprofit corporation. In contrast, the principal motivation of a profit corporation is to make as much money as possible for distribution to its shareholders. In fact, the managers of a profit corporation generally have a *duty* to place the business interests of the corporation and its stockholders before any other considerations when making corporate decisions. Thus if undertaking a socially beneficial project was weighed against giving company stockholders increased dividends, absent other factors, it could well be the duty of the Board of Directors to forgo the good deed and attempt to maximize profits to distribute as dividends.

It is the potential for profit that motivates people to create and invest in business corporations. When a small corporation is created, shares of its stock frequently are owned entirely by the corporation's founders. These founding shareholders may provide their company with the money it needs to begin its operations by purchasing interests in it—these interests are represented by shares of stock. If the corporation does well, the founders' rewards can be very pleasant, for instance:

Three people organize Corporation A, intending to be equal owners of the business. They then decide that the corporation will have 30,000 shares of common stock. To be equal owners, each organizer must now buy an equal number of shares of stock up to 10,000 shares apiece. The price for the stock will be set by determining how much money the business needs at the outset and how much money will come from sources other than the purchase of stock. In this instance, however, let us assume the 30,000 shares are sold for 10 cents apiece. If the corporation is successful and makes a profit, the Board of Directors (elected by the shareholders who may elect themselves as directors) may declare that the company will share its profits with the shareholders. The Board will then declare a dividend of a certain amount to be paid per share of stock.

In this case, if Corporation A made a profit of $3,000 for the year, a dividend of 10 cents per share might be declared. Each of the shareholders would then receive $1,000. If the corporation is very successful, larger dividends may be declared as the stockholders' share in the business's good fortune. However, in the early years of a business's life, profits, if any, are generally plowed back into the business. In any event, corporations typically do not distribute all their profits to shareholders but retain some for growth and reserves.

As a corporation prospers, other investors may notice this success and approach the original organizers with an offer to buy their stock for $1 per share. The organizers may decide to give up their investment by accepting the offer and selling their stock for a gain of $9,000 each over their original investment. Of course, had this been a not-for-profit corporation, the organizers could not have sold their "interest" in the corporation and would have received nothing.

Returns are rarely as spectacular as in the preceding example, but stock ownership does supply a significant and steady source of income for many investors. With the ability to attract new funds by selling stock or other types of interests in itself, all with an expectation of financial return to the investor, a for-profit corporation will be able to weather financial storms more readily than a not-for-profit corporation, which must rely principally on donations for additional funds.

Small businesses, on the other hand, may have difficulty selling their stock and other interests. They are hampered by their lack of recognition, the difficulty in determining the value of their shares (since they are not traded on a stock exchange), and, ironically, by the small amounts of money they need to raise (since investors may prefer large investments because of the potential for large profits).

In summary, business corporations have financial advantages: They are usually able to raise money more easily than nonprofit corporations, and they may generously reward those who choose as their investment a business which becomes successful.

The virtues of a business corporation are not entirely financial, however, for business corporations may be more efficient than nonprofit organizations. This could stem from the desire to make as much as possible by spending as little as possible. While this could result in cheap, shoddily made goods, it might also produce more efficient use of time, streamlined work procedures, and more effective use of personnel. The desire to save money may lead to less expensive manufacturing techniques and materials and less expensive goods. The desire to make money may serve as a spur to research and the development of different, newer, and better techniques and products to outsell the competition.

The drive to make money may have an indirect social benefit as well. A business corporation is usually not content to make the same amount of money every year, but tries instead to increase its profits. Making more money may involve improved techniques and products, as discussed previously, but may also be accomplished by an increased volume of business, or both. In order to make more products or perform more services, it is frequently necessary to hire more people, buy more raw materials, and/or invest more money in new machinery and facilities. Thus a successful venture may provide additional jobs and may also contribute to the well-being of other industries by purchasing larger quantities of their products.

DISADVANTAGES OF A PROFIT CORPORATION

There are, however, disadvantages to the for-profit form. While many non-profit corporations may be tax-exempt, business corporations are not. State income taxes vary, but federal income taxes currently range from 15% on the corporation's first $50,000 of taxable income to 34% on taxable income in excess of $75,000.

The activities of nonprofit corporations are potentially more flexible than those of profit corporations. Nonprofit corporations need not be primarily concerned with making maximum possible profits, and consequently they may experiment with new products or innovative management, or they may dedicate themselves to helping disadvantaged groups—without being under pressure to make these changes result in increased revenues. Also, through membership in a nonprofit corporation, residents of particular areas may become organized and effective in dealing with community problems. Nonprofit corporations may receive local, state, or federal government grants, and people may give these groups money because they support their activities. This combination of grants, donations, and a subordinated profit motive allows nonprofit corporations to work in fields that for-profit corporations may avoid because of the high risk and/or low or nonexistent profits involved. Thus, while there is some crossover in function, each type of corporation has its own purposes and fills its own niche in society.

3

CHOICE OF FORM

There are, of course, other forms of organizing and operating a business. One may choose a sole proprietorship, a general partnership, or a limited partnership rather than forming a corporation. Each of these forms has its own advantages and disadvantages. This chapter will describe briefly their attributes and uses. In Chapter 13 we will discuss a new form of business, the Limited Liability Company.

SOLE PROPRIETORSHIP

A sole proprietorship is the simplest form of business organization. It is really nothing more than one individual undertaking some business activity in his or her personal capacity as sole owner. This does not mean the business must be made up of only one person. There may be employees, perhaps many employees. A sole proprietorship involves a one-*owner* business. The proprietor owns the business directly in an individual capacity.

The major advantage of this form of business is the lack of legal formality in its establishment and operation. A sole proprietorship may be established anywhere, anytime, by anyone. There are no requirements for filing organizational documents, or, with the exception of tax returns, annual reports with the state. If special licensing is necessary in order to engage in an *occupation* (such as law or medicine) one must obtain the license regardless of the form of business chosen (i.e., proprietorship, partnership, etc.). There is no additional license needed for a licensed attorney, for example, to set up his or her business as a sole proprietorship.

Additionally, there is administrative ease of operation. Since there are no co-owners, there is no need to hold policy-setting meetings or to report to colleagues. Moreover, there is no legal distinction between the proprietor as owner and as individual. Therefore, financial record keeping may be less formal (although as a practical matter, one should be able to account for and distinguish between income and expense from the proprietorship and income and expense from other sources if for no other reason than the tax law treats business expense differently from personal expense).

The proprietor, as sole owner, has the ability to make all business decisions and stands to benefit from business gains. On the other hand, the proprietor is also personally responsible for all business losses. There is no separate identity shielding the proprietor from such liability. Thus all of his or her personal assets may be called on to satisfy business obligations.

Similarly, there is no separate entity to be taxed. All gains or losses are attributed directly to the proprietor and are combined with the proprietor's net income from other sources to arrive at his or her taxable income. The proprietor will fill out Schedule C to IRS Form 1040 in reporting business income or loss.

Because there is no entity separate from the proprietor, the proprietorship's existence terminates with the departure, through the sale of the business, or through the abandonment or death of the proprietor. There is no continuity of life, so if a proprietor sells the proprietorship to another sole proprietor, from a legal standpoint the first proprietorship ends and a new one begins at the time of sale. The fact is legally significant because of the personal liability of a proprietor.

GENERAL PARTNERSHIP

A general partnership is defined by Section 6(1) of the Uniform Partnership Act as "an association of two or more persons to carry on as co-owners a business for profit." Thus, the most obvious (and critical) distinction between a partnership (also known as a *general* partnership) and a proprietorship is that it is comprised of more than one person; there are *co*-owners. By law, this means that each owner is entitled to a say in the partnership's affairs and is entitled to have information about the partnership's business. Often, partners will agree to let one or more (but less than all) of the partners actually run the business. As to the outside world, however, each partner retains his or her right to run and to bind the partnership.

The main advantages of a partnership include its ease of formation and the greater resources it can command. Like a sole proprietorship, there are no organizational documents that require state approval. Unlike a sole proprietorship, however, it is very useful to have a written partnership agreement, that is, a contract between the partners setting out their various rights and responsibilities. This is because there is more than one owner and responsibilities are shared and rights divided.

Again, like a proprietorship, there is no intervening legal entity. The partners stand to gain or lose, in proportion to their partnership interest, from the success of the business, and are personally liable for its obligations. They also are taxed directly for their share of the partnership's income (even if it is not actually distributed to them but instead is reinvested in the business) and may be able to deduct partnership losses from their income from other sources. The partnership pays no taxes (although it does file a partnership information return on IRS Form 1065). It then sends a Form K1 to each partner setting out his or her share of the partnership profit or loss. The partner will transfer that information to his or her Form 1040.

This array of tax forms points out the need for good financial record keeping but, again, the relationship between the assets of the partnership and those of the partners is less clear than in a corporate situation. With a corporation, even a one-person corporation, there is a need to distinguish between corporate assets and those of the shareholder. The absence of this distinction, the commingling of funds, is one of the bases on which the protection offered the shareholder by the corporate existence may be lost.

People choose the partnership form for several reasons. As mentioned previously, a partnership is easier to establish and maintain than a corporation. No documents, meetings, or reports are required (although all may be recommended). On the other hand, more capital and resources may be available to a partnership than to a sole proprietor. However, the tax advantages formerly available especially to partnerships and proprietorships (primarily the pass-through of tax write-offs directly to partners or to the proprietor) have largely been made available to corporations through the liberalization of Subchapter S of the Internal Revenue Code (which will be discussed in Chapter 12) and to Limited Liability Companies (which will be discussed in Chapter 13).

Again, since the partnership is not recognized as a separate legal entity, its existence is limited to the retention of the original partners. If one should leave or a new partner enter, the partnership is said to have "dissolved" (although its business may continue as before). When the business itself terminates, it is said to have been "wound up" or "liquidated."

Finally, as a side note, the definition of a partnership calls for "a business for profit." Thus, by definition, there cannot be a nonprofit partnership.

LIMITED PARTNERSHIP

Section 1 of the Uniform Limited Partnership Act defines a limited partnership as "a partnership formed by two or more persons . . . having as members one or more general partners and one or more limited partners." The limited partnership is a device designed to bridge a gap between the tax benefits available to partners and the liability protection available to shareholders. Subject to the Tax Reform Act of 1986, general partners can write off partnership losses against income from other sources but are personally liable for partnership obligations. Shareholders generally cannot write off corporate losses but *are* protected from corporate obligations. The limited partnership allows the *limited* partners to retain tax benefits by permitting some partnership losses to be written off against income from other sources *and* protects the limited partners from liability for partnership obligations.

In exchange for this obviously beneficial situation, the limited partner gives up his or her right to participate in the management of the partnership. This right is left to the general partner or partners who remain personally responsible for partnership liabilities. The limited partner becomes what is colloquially known as the "silent" partner. If a limited partner becomes actively involved in management, he or she forfeits the limited liability enjoyed by limited partners and becomes, at least for liability purposes, a general partner. Since this limitation is not applied to members in a Limited Liability Company, there is some likelihood that LLCs, where available, will replace limited partnerships as a form of choice in many circumstances.

A limited partnership has other similarities to a corporation. For instance, it is created by a written document that must be filed with the state. This document is like the Articles of Incorporation for a corporation but is in addition to the partnership agreement that is typically signed by the partners. In addition, the Tax Reform Act of 1986 (TRA) has significantly reduced the tax benefits available to limited partners.

Taxation is treated as with any other partnership. There is basically no taxable entity other than the partners themselves. It should be noted again, however, that much of the tax advantage that a limited partnership has over a corporation has been removed with the liberalization of Subchapter S of the Internal Revenue Code.

One remaining advantage of the limited partnership over a Subchapter S corporation is that an S corporation is limited to 35 or fewer shareholders, whereas a limited partnership may have as many limited partners as desired. Thus businesses with a need for greater capital and a need to retain individual tax benefits may prefer the limited partnership route, which permits more investors to be brought in than in the more restricted

S corporation. On the other hand, in the limited partnership there always must be at least one general partner and, as such, that partner has unlimited liability.*

The following table sets out the presence or absence of various attributes and requirements in several business forms:

BUSINESS ASSOCIATIONS

	Sole Proprietorship	General Partnership	Limited Partnership	Corporation
Associates	No	Yes	Yes	Yes
Objectives to carry on a business	Yes	Yes	Yes	Yes
Continuity of life	No	No	Yes, as to the limited partners	Yes
Centralized management	No	No	Yes	Yes
Limited liability	No	No	Yes, as to the limited partners	Yes
Free transferability of interest	No	No	Yes, limited partners' interests in capital and profits	Yes
Legal documents required	No	No	Yes, limited partners'	Yes, Articles of Incorporation
Taxed as an equity	No	No	No	Yes, unless S Corporation

* Efforts to get around this problem by establishing a limited partnership with a lightly capitalized corporation as the sole general partner have not succeeded. The IRS has established an asset-based test concerning corporate general partners. If there are insufficient net assets in the corporation, the IRS will not issue an advance ruling indicating that it will recognize the organization as a partnership. The absence of such a ruling makes it extremely difficult for organizers to attract investors.

4

PREINCORPORATION ACTIVITIES AND INCORPORATION

The first event in a corporation's history is someone's idea to start it. Before going any further, the prospective organizers of a corporation should evaluate their plan and attempt to gauge its potential for success. If the organizers are thinking of a particular type of business, they should consider the success of similar businesses in the community and the need for another such venture. (If nothing similar exists, they should ponder the need for the business in the first place.) If organizers decide that their idea has a chance of success, they may then want to begin preliminary planning and establishing business contacts.

PREINCORPORATION AGREEMENTS

Organizers frequently choose to impose additional obligations on themselves other than those of good faith and fair dealing owed to the corporation. Especially if they intend to control the corporation when it is eventually incorporated, organizers may want to enter into a preincorporation agreement to establish mutual commitments to be satisfied after the corporation is formally in existence. They may agree among themselves, in writing, as to who will act as the corporation's incorporators; who will serve on its first Board of Directors; who will purchase what types of stock, in what amounts, and for how much; or that corporate documents that have already been prepared will be adopted by the organizers when the corporation comes into existence.

This type of preincorporation agreement is helpful to establish organizers' responsibilities and to chart steps to be taken following incorporation. An agreement also can prove to be especially valuable as an incentive for organizers to fulfill their preincorporation promises.

In addition to agreeing among themselves, organizers may also enter into agreements with third parties on behalf of the corporation to be formed. Common examples include lease arrangements for space that the corporation will use when it begins business, equipment rental agreements, or agreements for the purchase of goods that the corporation plans to resell. Since some things cannot be arranged at the last minute, the organizers may find that they need to assure space, equipment, or merchandise for the corporation before the corporation really exists.

This is potentially awkward because the third party providing the goods or service is actually agreeing to perform for a nonexistent entity—the not-yet-formed corporation. If the corporation comes into being and adopts the contracts the organizers entered into on its behalf, no difficulty occurs. The new corporation, however, is not bound by its organizers' contracts, and should the corporation not be formed, or, once formed, decline to accept a contract entered into on its behalf by one of its organizers, a third party will want to recover money for the goods or services it provided or will want damages for breach of the contract. The question is—the contract with whom? The organizers or the corporation? Very often the answer will be that the contract is with the *organizers* and they are personally liable for contracts they entered into on behalf of an unformed corporation.

In practical terms, this means that organizers should be cautious in contracting for a corporation before that corporation is formally in existence (i.e., before the appropriate state official has issued its Certificate of Incorporation). A preincorporation agreement among the organizers could provide some protection against this liability if the organizers intend to remain in control of the corporation after its incorporation (as shareholders, directors, and/or officers), if the preincorporation agreement obligates them to support the adoption of the preincorporation contracts they arranged.

A more direct technique would be for promoters to have precise written agreements with all third parties they contract with on behalf of the prospective corporation. These contracts could state expressly:

1. The scope of the promoter's potential liability (complete, none, partial, etc.)

2. The promoter's rights and obligations under the contract (e.g., the right to approve the work performed, the obligation to use best efforts to form the corporation, commitment to vote for its adoption as a member of the Board, etc.)

3. The rights and obligations of the corporation (e.g., the right to approve the work performed, a requirement that it decide whether to accept the contract within a certain period of time, etc.)

4. What happens if the corporation is never formed (e.g., promoter liable, contract void)

5. What happens if the corporation is formed but declines to adopt the contract

6. What happens if the corporation ignores the contract

7. What happens if the corporation accepts benefits under the contract

8. An express statement that the corporation is not then in existence

9. A disclaimer of any implied agreements in addition to the terms stated in the contract.

PREINCORPORATION SHARE SUBSCRIPTIONS

Another possible preincorporation event is a preincorporation share subscription. This may be used when people (including the organizers) agree to purchase stock in an as-yet unformed corporation. Because the corporation does not exist and the shares are not yet issued, a preincorporation subscription is a continuing offer conveyed by the organizers to the corporation to buy a certain amount of its stock. An offer to subscribe for shares is irrevocable by the person wishing to buy stock for a period of six months unless otherwise provided in the subscription agreement or unless there is unanimous shareholder consent to the revocation of the agreement by the subscriber (Section 17 of the Model Business Corporation Act). This means that the corporation has six months from the time of the offer to accept it, and the person making the offer may not withdraw it unless he or she *expressly states* at the time of making the offer that it is only open for a specified period of time.

Organizers should require that all share subscriptions be in writing, in order to establish firmly each offer and its details, including the number of shares to be purchased and the price to be paid.

In a small corporation, the organizers could use a share subscription as a device to prearrange corporate ownership. As part of the preincorporation agreement, the organizers could promise to subscribe for amounts of stock representing each organizer's agreed future shareholding in the corporation. Working out this agreement may help determine how corporate interests will be distributed, and the contract's existence may help to preserve that allocation in the event of later squabbling.

INCORPORATION

Obviously one of the first things the organizers must decide is what their corporation will do. A corporation organized for any lawful purpose other than banking or insurance may be incorporated under Section 3 of the Model Business Corporation Act. Thus the statute allows a vast array of activities.

Organizers must also decide on a corporate name. The name must include the words "corporation," "company," "incorporated," "limited," or an abbreviation of one of them. This requirement is imposed so that people who are not familiar with the corporation are on notice that they are dealing with an entity in which no individual may be held personally liable if the business is unable to pay its debts (Section 8 of the Act).

The corporate name may not inaccurately describe what the corporation does, and to avoid confusion, the name of a new corporation may not closely resemble the name of another corporation that does business in the same jurisdiction.

If organizers have any doubt about whether the corporate name they have selected is acceptable, or if they merely want to reserve the name for 120 days so that no one else can claim it, they may file an Application for Reservation of Corporate Name with the appropriate state official. The official will notify the corporate organizers if the name is available and, if so, that it will be reserved for 120 days (Section 9 of the Act).

The next document to be filed is the corporation's Articles of Incorporation. The Articles must be signed by at least one "incorporator" and "duplicate originals," that is, two fully signed copies must be sent or delivered to the Secretary of State or other designated official, along with the statutory filing fee.

The charge for filing and indexing the Articles varies from state to state. The amount can be ascertained by checking the state's statute or by writing to the Secretary of State. In addition, an initial fee is generally imposed for each authorized share of stock. You should check with the state filing office to verify current fees before submitting Articles of Incorporation or other corporate documents for filing.

Within several days to several weeks, the corporation will receive from the filing office a Certificate of Incorporation. When this Certificate is issued, the corporation's existence officially begins.

5

FINANCIAL STRUCTURE

A business corporation may obtain money to finance its operations by issuing interests in itself that are generally known as securities. This term is used to describe all types of interests that a corporation may create in itself and offer for sale. There is nothing necessarily *secure* about a security; the term here refers to an interest or an investment in a corporation.

Securities are of two basic types: debt securities and equity securities (in fact, there are many types of securities, often being anything but basic). "Debt securities" are so called because the corporation is considered to be in debt to the person who holds this type of interest; the person has lent the corporation money and eventually the corporation will have to pay it back—with interest. An "equity security" creates no debt relationship. When a person purchases an equity security, he or she is not lending money to the corporation, but is considered to be acquiring an ownership stake in the business.

DEBT SECURITIES

A debt security generally is created when the corporation (through its Board of Directors) decides that it will attempt to borrow money, from individuals, institutions, or the public. Typical sources of borrowed money are the corporation's organizers (or their families) or a bank. If the money is lent to the corporation by such individuals or institutions, the corporation will issue its promissory note (one form of debt security) to the lender. If, on the other hand, the corporation hopes to borrow from members of the general public, it will issue and offer for sale to the public (usually through a broker) debt securities known either as bonds or debentures (which are basically the same except that a bond is secured by particular property of the debtor, while the debenture is unsecured indebtedness). These securities generally are issued in face amounts of $1,000 each. If the bond is sold for more than its face value, it is said to be "sold at a premium." If sold for less than the face value, it is "sold at a discount." Like other evidence of indebtedness, bonds have a maturity date, a specified time when the corporation must pay back the face value of the bond to its holder. The face value is the principal amount owed by the corporation. But a bond costs the corporation more than merely repaying the principal amount for the use of an investor's money. The corporation will also periodically pay an interest charge, typically calculated as a percentage of the face value of the bond.

Debt securities come in various forms. For instance, mortgage bonds are one type of debt security where the bondholders have a mortgage on the corporation's property. If the corporation fails to pay its obligations, the bondholders may foreclose their mortgage and claim the corporation's property to the extent necessary to satisfy its debt to them.

Unlike a mortgage bond, a debenture is a simpler type of debt security; there is no property to which the holder of a debenture has any special claim if the corporation should fail to pay its obligations on the debenture. Debenture holders, and other holders of unsecured debt instruments, are instead considered to be "general creditors" (as opposed to "secured creditors") of the corporation.

Status as a corporate *creditor* is one of the important features of a debt security. It means that if the business should fail, the holders of the corporation's bonds may take whatever property secures the bonds. Other creditors (such as note or debenture holders) then have first claim to the corporation's remaining assets in order to satisfy sums owed to them. The holders of equity securities (stock) are left to divide whatever is left, if anything.

This preferential claim to corporate assets makes bonds an attractive, if conservative, investment. Therefore, issuing debt securities may be one device whereby a small business can make itself more attractive to outside investors who want steady income and less risk. It also keeps voting control of the corporation in the hands of the organizers, since debt holders, as such, are generally not entitled to vote.

The corporation could make a bond even more desirable by promising bondholders that the corporation will take certain steps to insure that corporate assets will be retained and available to satisfy payments due to bondholders. For instance, the corporation could agree to limit total corporate debts, reasonably restrict dividend payments to keep a certain amount of funds always on hand, create a special corporate reserve to pay bond obligations, limit issuance of additional bonds, or restrain the corporation from incurring any *secured* debts that would have a preferential claim to corporate assets above existing bondholders.

As mentioned previously, bonds usually pay a fixed amount of interest per year; for example, 8¾% on a $5,000 bond would entitle its holder to payments of $437.50 each year. The corporation has an obligation to pay this interest regardless of its profits or losses for that year. This is in contrast to dividends on equity securities that may be paid or not (as determined by the corporation's Board of Directors) even though the corporation has sufficient funds to make a distribution.

A corporation may, however, make its obligation to pay any interest conditional on its making a certain profit, and the amount of interest paid could be made dependent on the amount of profits. For instance, in the first case, the corporation would be required to pay the stated interest only to the extent that it had profits with which to make such payments. In the second instance, the corporation would be obliged to pay a fixed rate of interest, say 8¾%, and up to an additional 4% of its earnings if it had sufficient earnings to cover the obligatory interest payment and any portion of the additional 4% payment.

Whatever the terms of payment, they should be expressed in the bond instrument. This will insure that owners of the bond have notice of these terms and cannot insist on other, more favorable terms.

At a predetermined date, the corporation must pay the bondholder the principal amount of the bond, for example, $5,000 on January 1, 2000. When a corporation is profitable it may wish to pay off its bondholders before that date. This may be done with corporate funds or by issuing new bonds at a rate more favorable to the corporation. In order to be able to do this, the corporation must include a "redemption" or "call" provision in the original bond instrument. This provision will state that the corporation has the right to buy back the bond at a certain price, usually a figure in excess of the face value at a set time before the due date of the bond.

As an additional feature to attract investors, bonds may be made "convertible;" that is, the holder of the bond is given an option to exchange it for another type of bond or for types of equity securities. Bonds that are convertible must state that they are convertible, what they may be converted into, when and at what price they may be converted, and so forth. Convertibility is considered a desirable investment feature because the bondholder has a relatively safe investment that he or she may convert into a specified different interest if that new interest becomes more attractive.

EQUITY SECURITIES

The other type of corporate security is an equity security, known as shares or stock in a corporation. Stock is called an equity security because stockholders are considered to be the *owners* of the corporation.

Shares are a function of the wishes of the organizers and of the Articles of Incorporation. A corporation's Articles must state the number of shares and the characteristics of the corporation's stock. When the Articles are approved, the corporation may "issue" all or only a portion of its authorized stock. To issue stock is actually to offer shares of stock for sale. The corporation's Board of Directors may control when and to whom the corporation's shares are offered and sold. When issued shares are actually purchased, they are known as outstanding shares and the purchaser is known as a shareholder or stockholder.

Before the corporation authorizes stock in its Articles, the organizers must decide on the types of stock they feel are appropriate for their corporation. There are several choices. Shares may be with or without "par value." They may have preferences over other classes of shares or may be common shares. These terms and their importance must be understood in the planning of a corporation.

Stock may have a par value or may be of "no par value." "Par value" is an *arbitrary* value per share assigned in the Articles of Incorporation, and does not necessarily reflect the true market value of the stock. Because the law is that par value shares may not be issued and sold by the corporation for less than their par value, it is advisable for the corporation to set a par value lower than the estimated market value of the shares (Section 18 of the Model Business Corporation Act). (Once the stock is sold by a corporation to a shareholder, sales by that shareholder to any other person may occur at whatever price the parties deem appropriate, even if it is less than par.)

No par stock allows the Board of Directors (or the shareholders if the Articles of Incorporation have granted them the power) to decide, each time shares are issued, what the price per share will be. Since there is no par value attached to the shares, they may be sold without any restriction on sales price. The Board (or the shareholders) thus has more flexibility to adjust the stock's selling price to reflect the corporation's success or lack of it. (In a very large corporation, the stock might be traded on a public exchange such as the New York Stock Exchange, in which case the public demand, and not the Board, would determine the selling price of the stock.)

Despite the arbitrary nature of par or stated value (in relation to no par stock) the concept has some very practical significance. First, and most basically, if stock is sold for less than par or stated value, the purchaser of those shares may be liable, to the corporation or to its creditors, for the difference between what was paid and what should have been paid.

The second practical consequence is more subtle. The par or stated value is used to determine the corporation's "capital account." This account, which is really only an entry in the books of the corporation, is determined by multiplying the par or stated value of the corporation's stock by the number of shares outstanding. For example: if the corporation had sold 1000 shares of stock which had a $10 par value, the capital account would be $10,000.

If no par shares are issued, the total amount received from their sale is the corporation's "stated capital." However, prior to issuance of no par shares, the Board of Directors may pass a resolution declaring that only a portion of the money received for shares will constitute the corporation's "stated capital" and that the remaining sum will be deemed "capital surplus."

The importance of these accounts is mainly in relation to the payment of dividends. Although Section 45 of the Model Act permits dividends only out of earned surplus (retained earnings) or out of recent profits (even if there is no accumulated and retained earnings), most states provide for a different formula. In those situations, the corporation may pay a dividend so long as the capital account is not "impaired" or will not be impaired by virtue of the distribution. What this means is that a corporation may pay a dividend if the value of its net assets (i.e., its total assets minus its total liabilities) is greater than the amount of its capital account (par value times outstanding shares). If net assets are less than the capital account, no dividend may be paid.

To illustrate the point, assume Corporation X has 1000 shares outstanding at $10 par value. The capital account is $10,000. Assume also that the corporation has $50,000 worth of assets and $25,000 worth of liabilities. Since its net assets ($50,000 − $25,000 = $25,000) exceed the capital account ($25,000 − $10,000 = $15,000), a dividend of up to $15,000 could be declared. If, alternatively, the corporation's liabilities were $45,000 the net assets would be only $5,000. Since this is *less* than the amount of the capital account, no dividend at all could be paid.

In those states that permit dividends when net assets exceed the capital account, the excess assets could come from retained earnings (which is the basic test under the Model Act for the legality of dividends) or from a capital *surplus* account (as distinguished from the capital account). We have already discussed the fact that stock may not be issued by the corporation for less than its par or stated value. What happens, however, if it is issued for *more* than par or stated value? For instance, shares of Corporation X have a par value of $1.00 but are sold for $10. From a bookkeeping point of view, $1.00 per share would be recorded in the capital account book, while $9 per share would be recorded in the capital *surplus* account book. From an operational point of view, the entire $10 per share may be placed in the corporation's bank account and spent (even the $1 per share in the capital account) for corporate purposes. It is only when the net assets fall below the amount in the capital account book that *dividends* are prohibited.

In addition to distinctions of par and no par value, stock may be divided into different "classes" (Section 16 of the Model Act). For instance, it is possible to create one or more classes of stock whose holders have a preference in receiving dividends over holders of other classes of stock. That is, if the Board of Directors decides to distribute a portion of the corporation's profits to shareholders, the preferred shareholders receive their dividends first (in the order of their preference) and the other shareholders receive their share from the distributable profits remaining after each higher preference has been paid (though the holders of debt securities will be entitled to their payments before any shareholder, and regardless of the corporation's financial condition).

The payment to preferred shareholders is generally a constant amount, phrased as "a preference of $_____ per share" or "a preference of _____% of par value." Thus in a year in which the corporation is very profitable, there may be substantial profits remaining to be distributed to nonpreferred shareholders (known as common shareholders).

Preferred shares may possess other attractive characteristics in addition to their payment preference. The corporation may create "cumulative" preferred stock, where the corporation is obligated to pay the shareholder a fixed payment each year. If the dividend is not paid in any year (due to a lack of income from which to distribute dividends or, even if the income is available to pay a dividend, due to a decision by the Board that it would be better to retain the money for corporate purposes rather than distribute it as a dividend), it accumulates; and the aggregate amount of accumulated unpaid dividends must be paid in full to the holders of cumulative preferred stock before the corporation may pay dividends to the holders of other types of stock with a lower preference.

A variation on cumulative preferred stock is "cumulative to the extent earned" shares. The payments on these shares accumulate only to the extent that the corporation had profits from which it could legally have paid dividends, and the holders of these shares are not entitled to dividends from years in which the corporation had no profits to distribute.

Preferred stock may also be "participating." If it is (as established by the Articles of Incorporation), shareholders receive their preferential distributions and then, when all preferences have been paid, are allowed to share with the holders of common stock in the pool of money remaining. This can be very advantageous, since the preferred shareholders get a constant payment and than a second opportunity to share in corporate profits. It is possible to curtail this benefit by specifying that the common and preferred stockholders divide the profits remaining after the first fixed payment to the preferred shareholders on a 2:1, 3:1, 4:1, and so forth basis, in order to assure the common stockholders the better portion of the remaining profits. Of course, preferred stock need not be participating and would only be made so if the organizers felt it was necessary in order to be able to sell the preferred stock to investors.

Stock that does not possess a dividend preference is known as common stock. Common stock generally is the base of all shareholder power. It typically includes the broadest (often the only) voting rights and the potential for the largest financial gains (although it is also the least secure of the various investments one may make in a corporation).

As with preferred stock, the corporation is not required to distribute its profits to common stockholders, but when the Board of Directors exercises its discretion to distribute profits, the amount available for common stockholders' dividends is determined only after preferred shareholders, if any, have received their distributions. The common stock dividend is usually phrased in the form of "$_____ per share," and is established by the Board rather than by the Articles. The Board of Directors, in its discretion, may vary the amount from time to time, for instance, taking account of the funds available for distribution and of the corporation's need to retain the money.

In addition to the distinctions between preferred and common stock, stock may also be classified according to other characteristics (Section 16 of the Model Act). In the event of a corporate liquidation (when the corporation winds up its operations and distributes its assets, or their value in cash, to its shareholders), one or more classes of stock may be given a preference in the distribution of the corporation's assets (or their value). One class could be granted the exclusive right to receive all the assets. All classes could be allowed to divide them equally, or a class (or classes) could be granted a preference—a right to receive a certain value before the holders of any other class of stock receive any payments in liquidation.

Voting rights may also differ among classes. One class may be given the exclusive right to vote at shareholder meetings for the election of the corporation's Board of Directors. Other classes could be empowered to vote only on extraordinary corporate matters such as merger or dissolution, or all classes could be given equal and complete voting rights. Many corporations do not give voting rights to preferred shareholders. This may be in recognition of the fact that preferred shareholders receive preferential distributions of the corporation's earnings, while the size of distributions to common stockholders depend on the size of the corporation's profit and thus are tied more closely to the skill of the corporation's management. It may seem appropriate, therefore, that the common stockholders are the group responsible for selecting that management.

Classes of stock may also be made "convertible" into stock of another class; that is, the shareholder has the option to swap his or her shares, at a predetermined ratio set in the Articles, for shares of another class of stock or, perhaps, for a bond (Section 18 of the Model Act).

Classes of stock are also divisible into "series" (Section 16 of the Model Act). Shares of a class may be divided into and issued in a series as provided in the corporation's Articles of Incorporation or as authorized in the Articles with the details established by a resolution of the Board of Directors. Different series could pay dividends at different rates, have different redemption rights, terms, and prices, possess varying provisions for liquidation payments, or be convertible at different ratios. For instance, Class A preferred stock may have voting rights and exclusive liquidation privileges. There may be Class A Series A, and Class A Series B, which differ in that Series A pays twice the rate of dividends as Series B.

Whatever the organizers' choices as to the types of shares that the corporation will issue, each share certificate representing stock should state the precise characteristics of the stock it represents. This provides each shareholder with clear notice of the rights, duties, and characteristics of the shares he or she owns.

THE CHOICE BETWEEN ISSUING DEBT OR EQUITY

A small business corporation almost certainly will not utilize all of the securities that have been described. Nevertheless, corporate organizers should consider the characteristics of all types of securities and then select the features most appropriate for their financial needs and anticipated corporate structure. For instance, if the organizers intend to remain in charge of the corporation, they should arrange to control the stock possessing the power to select the corporation's Board of Directors (which, in turn, is empowered to select the corporation's officers).

If there is a need for more investment than the organizers alone can provide, preferred stock with a good dividend and/or liquidation preference may attract outside investors. Assuming these shares carry no voting rights, they may be issued without diminishing the organizers' control of the corporation's Board.

Bonds also may be attractive conservative investments, and holders of debt securities generally have no say in the management of the corporation's affairs. Debt securities can be complicated, however, and for small businesses, they may be very difficult to sell to outsiders. An easier alternative is probably to seek long-term loans from a local bank or an individual.

Why should a corporation want to go into debt when it can issue such an attractive variety of equity interests, and thus raise the money it needs through equity financing? Surprisingly, there are certain advantages to debt.

When a corporation pays *interest* to the holders of its debt securities, it may take a tax deduction in the amount of interest paid, and thereby reduce its taxable income. (Internal Revenue Code, Section 163(a).) On the other hand, it may not take deductions for dividends paid to its shareholders.

This favorable aspect of debt securities invites corporations to take advantage of them, particularly when the shareholders are also the lenders. As might be guessed, though, there are restrictions on the tax benefits available through disproportionate debt financing. When the ratio of total debt to total equity exceeds 4:1, for example, when the corporation is $4,000 in debt (which is owed to the shareholders) and has issued only $1,000 in shares, the IRS may regard the debt as a disguised form of stock and attempt to disallow the corporation's tax deductions for "interest" payments. A corporation may try to avoid such a disallowance by maintaining a healthy margin below the 4:1 borderline.

There is another advantage to debt financing that is known as "leverage." In an economic sense, this means using borrowed money to finance the business. If the company does well, the leveraged financing can significantly increase the rate of return the owners get on their equity investment.

Assume a business requires $100,000 to get started and the organizers put in a full $100,000 out of their own pockets. Also, assume the business's operations net a $20,000 profit in the first year. The organizers' rate of return is 20% (they received $20,000 profit on a $100,000 investment).

If, in the same situation, they had used leverage, the results are much more dramatic. Assume that instead of putting in the full $100,000 out of their pockets, they put in only $20,000 and were able to borrow the remaining $80,000. They conduct their business with the same total cash input, $100,000, and they make the same profit, $20,000. This time, however, they have an additional expense, the interest on the borrowed money. Assume for simplicity's sake that they borrowed at 10% per year. This would result in an interest charge (tax deductible) of $8,000 (10% of $80,000) per year. When the $8,000 is subtracted from the $20,000, a net profit of $12,000 remains.

At first glance, this looks less favorable than the $20,000 earned without borrowing. On closer examination, however, it is clear that the $12,000 was earned on an equity investment—by the organizers—of only $20,000. This works out to a 60% rate of return, far higher than the 20% rate in the absence of leverage.

Thus in many cases where the organizers are able to put in the full amount needed, they *choose* not to. Assume the organizers had $100,000 cash. On a leveraged basis as described in the example, they could buy five companies worth $100,000 each or a larger company worth $500,000.

In each case, they would put in 20% of the needed cash and borrow the rest.

Nevertheless, there are serious drawbacks to leverage. The first is practical. The organizers of a new business cannot always find people or institutions willing to lend them or their business the needed money. If the loans are available, they may be at high interest, carry heavy collateral, and/or require the personal guarantees of the organizers. Any of these factors could put a damper on leveraging.

The second drawback is financial. Just as leverage can increase the rate of return when the company does well, it can be devastating when the company does not do well.

Using our original example, assume the corporation makes only $5,000 profit. If the organizers put in the full $100,000, they still have a 5% rate of return. If they borrowed the $80,000 they still must pay the interest of $8,000, which not only wipes out their profit of $5,000 but creates a $3,000 actual (as opposed to paper) loss.

SELLING SECURITIES

When a corporation sells its bonds or stock, it is subject to certain requirements concerning the value it must receive and the type of payment it may accept for their sale.

As mentioned previously, par value stock may not be sold by the corporation for less than its par value; however, once a shareholder has purchased stock from the corporation, he or she may sell it to a third party for whatever price he or she wishes. On the other hand, the purchase price of no par stock, when initially sold by the corporation, is generally set by the Board of Directors (or the shareholders if the Articles of Incorporation has given them this power) and may be adjusted from time to time (as with par value stock, once a shareholder purchases no par stock from a corporation, he or she may sell it for whatever price he or she can obtain). No par stock may not be sold by the corporation for *less* than the stated value assigned to it by the Board. However, since the Board sets that stated value at the time of the sale, this should never be a problem.

Whatever the selling price, the corporation is restricted as to the form of payment it may accept in the sale. For stock or bonds, it may receive only money, property, or services actually rendered to it. "Money" means cash, including a check. "Property" could be tangible physical property (land, machinery, a car, etc.), or could be intangible property (stock in another corporation, patent rights, etc.); however, "property" does not normally include a promissory note. "Services" refers to services that have already been performed (not a promise to perform future services) for the *corporation* (generally *not* preincorporation services).

When the corporation receives property or services in exchange for its stock, the Board of Directors has a duty to ascertain the value of the property or services and to determine that the corporation is receiving something of value at least equal to the par or stated value of the stock that will be issued for it. If the value of the property is less than the aggregate par or stated value, the stock is said to be "watered," and if the corporation should ever be unable to pay its creditors, the holders of watered stock may be liable to the creditors for the corporation's debts to the extent that their shares are watered (Section 25 of the Model Act). For example, if land worth $25,000 is exchanged for stock having a par or stated value of $100,000, the shareholder receiving that stock could be liable for up to $75,000 in corporate debts.

This situation can be avoided if the Board of Directors (or the shareholders, if they are responsible for fixing the price of shares), carefully investigates the value of property or services received for the corporation's stock. If the Board determines in good faith and without fraud that the consideration received is equal to the value of the stock, that stock would not be considered "watered" even if it ultimately turns out that the Board was wrong in its valuation (Section 19 of the Model Act).

An additional question concerning corporate finance is that of shareholders' "preemptive rights." A preemptive right gives an existing shareholder the right to purchase new shares (of the same class as he or she currently holds or of securities convertible into such shares) being issued by the corporation, before such shares are offered to other purchasers (Section 26(a) of the Model Act). The right allows the shareholder to buy shares from the new issue in proportion to his or her present holdings of that class of corporate stock. For example, Jane Doe holds one-fourth of the common stock of Corporation X. Corporation X is planning to issue 1000 new shares of such stock. Therefore Doe has a right to buy 250 (¼ of 1000) shares before they may be offered to others. If Doe does not have money to purchase the shares, or does not want more shares of stock, the corporation is then free to offer the shares to others.

Preemptive rights are controlled by statute. Some states require preemptive rights while some states prohibit them. Other states leave it up to the Articles, with statutory formulations such as "there shall be preemptive rights unless the Articles state the contrary" or "there shall *not* be preemptive rights unless the Articles state the contrary."

6

DIVIDENDS

A key feature of a business corporation is its ability to issue shares of stock and to distribute corporate earnings and profits to the holders of these shares. Such distributions are known as dividends. Business corporations are authorized to pay dividends, but may do so only pursuant to statutory guidelines (Section 45 of the Model Business Corporation Act). Even where it is legally permissible for dividends to be paid, the decision whether to distribute them or to retain profits is within the reasonable discretion of the corporation's Board of Directors. Dividends are not mandatory simply because they are legally possible. There may be other important uses for the corporation's profits which persuade the Board against a distribution. The Board, however, may not unreasonably withhold dividends from the corporation's shareholders.

TYPES OF DIVIDENDS

A corporation may distribute three types of dividends: (1) a cash dividend, which is a payment of money—in cash or by check; (2) a stock or share dividend, which is a distribution of additional shares of stock in the corporation itself—usually a fraction of the stock already held by each shareholder (e.g., for every 10 shares of stock already owned, a dividend of one additional share is declared)—which may be of the same or of a different class or series than the stock already owned by the shareholder; or

(3) a property dividend, which is one other than a cash or stock dividend and could include a distribution of tangible property such as the corporation's inventory or portions of its land, or it could consist of shares of stock in another corporation. These are known as "in kind" distributions.

FINANCIAL CONSIDERATIONS

Regardless of the type of dividend the corporation would like to distribute, it may not distribute dividends if it is insolvent, or, in some jurisdictions, if its net assets are less than its stated capital. In any case, it may not distribute an amount that would render the corporation insolvent or, in the stricter jurisdictions, reduce its net assets below its stated capital (Section 45 of the Model Act).

The concept of "insolvency" is relatively simple. "Insolvent" means that the corporation is unable to pay its debts as they become due in the usual course of its business. Therefore, a corporation may not pay dividends if it cannot pay its debts or if the payment of dividends would render it unable to pay its debts.

The concept of "stated capital" is more difficult. It means: (1) the par value of all shares outstanding having a par value, and (2) the value received by the corporation for all shares without par value, except any part thereof which the Board of Directors has elected to allocate to the corporation's "capital surplus." For example: Corporation X issues 1000 shares of Class A common stock which the Articles of Incorporation specify shall have a par value of $1.00 each. X also issues 1000 shares of Class B common stock, of no par value, but with respect to which the Board of Directors resolved that 50 cents received from the sale of each share should be allocated to the corporation's stated capital with any remaining money received allocated to capital surplus. Both classes of stock are then sold for $1.00 each.

The account books would have entries that look something like this.

	Stated Capital	Capital Surplus
Class A	$1,000	—
Class B	500	$500
	$1,500	$500

Corporation X may take the $2,000 received and use it to finance its business operations; however, it may not pay dividends to its stockholders if it does not have "net assets" worth at least $1,500, or if the payment of dividends would reduce its net assets below the value of $1,500. Net assets means the value of the corporation's assets (property, cash, and so forth) minus the amount of its liabilities. Thus the corporation must have money or property in excess of the sum of its liabilities plus the amount of its stated capital if it wants to pay dividends. If the corporation is successful and makes profits, this requirement should pose no problem.

When paying a property (or in kind) dividend, a corporation is considered to be making a distribution equal to the current value of the property it is distributing. With share dividends, the amount corresponding to the par value of all par value shares, or the stated capital value of no par shares, is the value of the dividend. In either case, the corporation must have net assets sufficient to cover the amount of its stated capital *plus* the value of the distribution. Also, after a share dividend is distributed, the corporation's capital account is increased by the par (or stated capital) value of the shares making up the dividend, while one of its surplus accounts is reduced by the same amount.

Any director who is present at a Board of Directors' meeting and who votes to distribute a dividend that violates these restrictions may be liable to the corporation for the portion of the dividend in excess of the amount that properly could have been distributed. A director may avoid this liability if he or she enters his or her dissent to an improper dividend distribution decision in the minutes of the Board meeting, files a written dissent at the end of such meeting, or after the meeting promptly mails a written dissent to the Secretary of the corporation. This does not allow a director to *change* his or her vote after the decision has become final, however. A director also will not be held liable if he or she voted for the dividend in good faith, relying in determining the propriety of the dividend on a balance sheet asserted to be correct by the corporation's President, Treasurer, or a certified public accountant.

Where directors are subject to liability, they are said to be "jointly and severally liable." This means that any one director who voted for the distribution may be held liable for the entire amount of an improper distribution, or that all directors who voted in favor of it may be held collectively liable. If any director is found liable for an amount greater than his or her pro rata share, however, he or she may sue the other directors to cause them to contribute their portions of the total amount (Section 48 of the Model Act).

Since dividends are an important attribute of a business corporation and improper dividends (or the improper withholding of dividends) can result in substantial liabilities for corporate directors, it is important for organizers to understand the legalities in this area. It is an area that calls for caution. If any difficult questions arise, especially if there are dissident shareholders, it would be wise to consult an attorney or accountant.

It is also wise to remember that the legalities are only one of many considerations in dividend policy. There are also questions of business judgment (Is a distribution of cash in line with the business needs of the corporation at this time?) and practical realities (Do the shareholders expect a distribution now and what action will they take if it is not made?).

There are, in addition, tax consequences to a distribution (or non-distribution) of cash dividends. Dividends distributed to shareholders are taxed to those shareholders at their marginal tax rate. This imposes a second tax on corporate earnings. For example, assume Corporation X had $100,000 of taxable income (which, for this example, we will assume is equivalent to its profit for the year). This amount would be taxed at the corporation's normal tax rates (15% of the first $50,000, 25% of the next $25,000, and 34% for amounts over $75,000). This would leave the corporation with $77,750 of post tax income profit. The Board decides to distribute $25,000 of this amount to its shareholders. Shareholder A receives $1,000 of this distribution. Assume A is a 28% taxpayer. This $1,000 will be taxed to the shareholder at 28% leaving A with $720 ($1,000 − $280). This scenario would be repeated for each shareholder, thus reducing the amount left in his or her hands. Remember, this same pool of money—the corporation's profits (from which this distribution came)—was first taxed at the corporate level. At the shareholder level, it is taxed a second time. (See Chapter 11 for a further discussion.)

STOCK SPLITS

In addition to dividends, a corporation may make another type of distribution to its shareholders through a "stock split" whereby the corporation splits each share of stock into a larger number of shares, usually in order to lower the price per share and thus make its shares more marketable. For example, Jane Doe holds 10 shares, then selling for $40 each. The corporation decides that it will split its stock at a 4:1 ratio. After the split, Doe has 40 shares, (i.e., 4 × 10) worth $10.00 each. The total value of her holdings has not changed (10 shares @ $40 each was worth $400; 40 shares @ $10 each is still worth $400). Neither has her relative position of ownership changed. Assume there were originally 100 shares outstanding. Her 10 shares represent 10% ownership. If all those shares are split 4 to 1, she now owns 40 shares of the 400 outstanding, still a 10% interest.

Because a stock split is only a process whereby the same corporate interests are represented by a greater number of shares, the problems of calculating stated capital and the needs for a reserve of net assets or cash are not present. A corporation generally may split its stock regardless of its financial condition.

7

CONSIDERATIONS OF CORPORATE CONTROL

As mentioned in Chapter 2, a corporation is basically a three-tiered creation consisting of shareholders, directors, and officers. Each of these groups possesses unique characteristics that can be important when corporate organizers are shaping their organization's management structure.

SHAREHOLDERS

A corporation "authorizes" the issuance of its stock in its Articles of Incorporation. Its Board of Directors then determines how many shares of stock will be offered for sale. When these shares are purchased they comprise the corporation's "issued and outstanding" stock. For example: in its Articles of Incorporation, Corporation X has been authorized to issue 10,000 shares of stock at $10 par value. It decides that it does not need the full $100,000 which it would receive if all the shares were sold, but that it does need $50,000 to begin business.* Therefore, the Board of Directors

---

* It is important to keep in mind here that a corporation may sell its stock for *more* than its par value (although it may not sell it for less). We have equated the par value and sale price in this example merely for convenience.

votes to offer for sale only 5,000 of the 10,000 shares. When purchased, these 5,000 shares are the corporation's "issued and outstanding" stock.

Especially in a small corporation, shareholders have a potentially significant role in corporate management—the election of the corporation's Board of Directors. The Board determines corporate policy and selects the officers who carry out this policy on a day-to-day basis. Shareholder power to remove directors, adopt and revise corporate documents, and to ratify extraordinary corporate events such as merger, consolidation, or dissolution may be reiterated in the corporation's Articles or Bylaws. Shareholders may also be granted additional powers that involve them more intimately in the management of the corporation.

Unless the Articles of Incorporation provide otherwise, each share of stock possesses one vote. Organizers may want to deviate from that arrangement, however, in order to protect or accommodate particular aspects or needs of the corporation. For instance, to prevent an excessive concentration of voting power, the Articles could take the drastic step of providing that no individual may own more than a certain number of shares or a certain percentage of the corporation's voting stock, or that despite the number of shares a stockholder owns, he or she is limited in the number of votes he or she may cast. In order to implement a restriction of this type effectively, it is advisable that all the shareholders execute a shareholders' agreement containing the limitation and that such restriction also be noted on each of the corporation's share certificates. This will discourage any shareholder from making a transfer that would result in a prohibited accumulation of shares. It would also put any buyer of the shares on notice of the restriction.

Cumulative Voting

Another device used to affect voting rights is "cumulative voting." Many states statutes require or permit this device when voting for the election of directors while some states prohibit it (Section 33 of the Model Act). This type of voting is basically a protection for minority stockholders and provides each share with as many votes as there are vacancies on the Board to be filled. The shareholder may distribute these votes among candidates as he or she sees fit. This allows the holders of minority share interests to cumulate their votes in their attempt to elect representatives (although not a majority) to the Board. For example, assume Jane Doe owns 10 shares of stock and there are five positions on the Board to be filled. With cumulative voting, Doe would have 50 votes that she may cast however she chooses.

For instance, if Doe owned 10 shares and Mary Smith owned the remaining 15 shares of a 25-share corporation, Smith would, in the absence of cumulative voting, always elect the entire Board. If there were five directors to be elected, she would cast her 15 votes for each of her five choices while Doe casts her 10 for each of her five choices. *With* cumulative voting, however, Doe would have 50 votes and Smith 75 (15 shares times five directors to be elected). The important feature is that Doe can use her 50 votes however she chooses. Therefore, she might cast 25 each for only two candidates. If she does this, she is assured of electing two Board members because no matter how Smith divides her votes, she *cannot* mathematically have more than three people with as many or more votes than Doe's two people. If she gave any candidate 26 votes, she would have only 49 left for remaining candidates. If she gave a second candidate 26 votes, she would have only 23 votes left. Doe's two candidates would *have* to be among the top five vote getters. Of course, Doe could miscalculate and give a greater number of candidates fewer votes each, but if she does so she minimizes her chances for representation on the Board.

Algebra has produced a formula for maximizing representation. That formula is:

$$X = \frac{(S \times N)}{D + 1} + 1$$

where *X* equals the number of shares needed to elect a certain number of directors

S equals the total number of shares which will be voting (in person or by proxy) in the election

N equals the number of directors a shareholder wishes to elect

D equals the total number of directors to be elected in the particular election

Plugging the numbers in our hypothetical situation into this formula, we see that the number of shares Doe needs to elect two directors is:

$$X = \frac{25 \times 2}{5 + 1} + 1$$

$$\text{or} \quad X = \frac{50}{6} + 1$$

$$\text{or} \quad X = 9.3$$

Since Doe has 10 shares, she can elect her two directors. If she wished to elect three directors, the formula would indicate the impossibility unless Smith misapplied her votes. To elect three directors, a shareholder would need

$$\frac{25 \times 3}{5 + 1} + 1$$

or $\quad \dfrac{75}{6} + 1$

or $\quad 13.5$

shares, more than Doe controls.

It is important to remember that cumulative voting, if available at all, is *only* used for the election of directors and not for other issues that may be brought before the shareholders for a vote.

Classes of Shares

If a corporation has more than one class of stock, its Articles may provide for "class voting." In class voting, each class of shares votes separately and elects representatives to the Board of Directors. For instance: Class A, Class B, and Class C stock are held, respectively, by the three organizers of the corporation. Since each class has the exclusive right to elect one member of the Board, each organizer is assured that he or she will always have a seat on the Board of Directors. This is *class voting for directors*—to be distinguished from *classes of directors*. The latter means that some directors have different powers or varying terms of service, or so forth.

Another use of class voting is to allow a certain class to elect proportionately more directors than another class. For instance, the organizers might want to provide Class A stock with rights to elect seven directors out of an 11-person Board, with Class B electing the remaining four directors. This could be true even if there were more Class B shares than Class A. If the organizers want to insure that they retain managerial control (assuming the absence of cumulative voting), all they need do is buy a majority of the Class A stock, thus assuring the election by them of a majority of the Board. Of course, if capital must be raised by the sale of shares to outsiders, the outsiders' willingness to invest in a situation such as we have described would be a consideration. The shares must be made marketable.

Class voting may also operate as a veto if the Articles require unanimity among the classes for shareholder actions. For instance, if a particular action needed a majority of Class A *and* a majority of Class B shares, the smaller class could stop corporate action even though a majority of the total shares supported the action. This is a drastic method of protecting minority interests and has the disadvantage of possibly paralyzing shareholder action altogether.

It is also possible to provide for a class of stock with "contingent" voting rights, that is, shares with voting rights only under special circumstances. A corporation may limit the voting powers of shares of any class. Thus shares could, for instance, be entitled to vote only when the corporation had not paid them dividends, or if sales fell below a specified level. At any given time, however, at least one class of shares must have voting rights so that the corporation's directors may be elected and other shareholder functions may be performed.

Disproportionate voting rights may also be used to allocate corporate power. This may be appropriate, for example, when two or more classes of stock exist and the stockholders have paid different amounts to purchase their shares. The more expensive class of shares might, for instance, be given multiple votes where every share of that class counts as two votes while the other classes enjoy only one vote per share. Or the system could be used to assure that a particular group of shareholders, usually the corporation's organizers, maintain control. The organizers could issue the multiple voting stock to themselves, and sell the other types of shares to outsiders, thereby obtaining disproportionate voting strength. As already mentioned, the outsiders might be less willing to invest under these circumstances and thus the ability to market the shares *must* be considered by the organizers in making decisions about the attributes of shares.

It is also possible to create classes of nonvoting shares. This type of stock might be intended to attract investors and could pay larger, more secure dividends to compensate for its lack of voice in corporate management. Most forms of preferred stock fit this mold.

Classes of shares may also be used to equalize voting rights and still reward shareholders who contribute extra money to the corporation. Although voting rights of all shares could be equal, the class of stock issued to a large investor could pay dividends at a more favorable rate, or an investor could be issued another, separate class of nonvoting stock that pays dividends. In the latter case, the shareholder's economic interest in the corporation would accurately reflect the amount he or she had invested, but his or her ability to control the corporation (through voting power) would not outweigh that of any less affluent organizers. It should be understood here that these examples are intended to be illustrative only. The organizers may create any share structure that fits their needs, is acceptable to investors, and complies with the laws of their jurisdiction.

Quorum and Vote Requirements

Minority shareholders' interests may also be protected by fashioning shareholder quorum and voting requirements to guard against oppression of minority interests. A quorum is the number of shares that must be present at a shareholders' meeting in order for that meeting legally to transact business. The purpose of a quorum is to prevent a small number of shares from deciding corporate questions in the absence of a more representative number of shares. Usually, it is required that the holders of a majority of the corporation's outstanding shares be represented, whether in person or by proxy, at a shareholders' meeting in order for the meeting to be properly constituted and able to take valid and binding action. If a quorum is not present, any actions taken at the meeting are subject to attack by disgruntled shareholders—who could seek to have a court declare those actions were invalid.

To protect minority interests, the quorum requirement could be increased to two-thirds or three-fourths or other majority level. Minority shareholders could then purposely absent themselves from, and thus prevent a quorum at, a shareholders' meeting scheduled to vote on matters they opposed. A less drastic method would be to provide that a greater-than-majority vote is required for passage of shareholder motions. This would allow the shareholders to have a quorum, yet would enable minority shareholders to cast enough votes to prevent a matter from passing unless a large majority exists. This type of greater-than-majority vote requirement must be specifically authorized in the corporation's Articles of Incorporation or Bylaws (Section 32 of the Model Act).

Both greater-than-majority quorum and vote requirements have the potential for producing shareholder deadlock. A high quorum is probably the more dangerous, however, since a stubborn shareholder could block all shareholder action by preventing the presence of a quorum and thus the legality of a meeting. A greater-than-majority vote requirement at least allows the shareholders to confront each other, discuss their differences, and pass on to other matters.

Shareholder Agreements

Another method of obtaining shareholder cooperation, one which should not cause shareholder paralysis, is for shareholders to enter into a shareholders' agreement. This is a contract pursuant to which the shareholders bind themselves to do, or refrain from doing, certain things. Among them may be an agreement as to the election of directors and, often, a dispute-resolution mechanism. In addition, there is often a share-transfer restriction, which is intended to allow remaining shareholders to be able to choose any new colleagues. Reasonable restrictions on share transfers preserve an established corporate shareholder group and management structure and protect against intrusions by new shareholders and interests with the ambition to take over the corporation.

An absolute restriction on the transfer of shares is considered to be against public policy and will not be enforced by the courts, but many nonabsolute restrictions have been held to be valid. The most common restriction requires a shareholder wishing to sell his or her stock to offer it first to the existing shareholders in proportion to their current stockholdings and/or to the corporation. If neither the corporation nor the existing shareholders choose to purchase the offered shares, then the selling shareholder could sell this stock to outsiders.

To assure representation of each shareholder on the corporation's Board, a shareholders' agreement also generally provides that shareholders will vote to elect certain persons as directors and will continue voting for them as long as they can properly perform their duties to the corporation. In a small corporation this could take the form of the shareholders promising to elect each other to the Board.

Finally, a shareholder's agreement can provide for a dispute-resolution mechanism. This is a valuable device, since it allows shareholders to set a procedure for dispute resolution *before* a dispute arises and each side seeks a mechanism favorable to themselves. Among the common choices is third-party mediation or giving a third party one share with which to break a tie.

Notice of the existence of a shareholders' agreement should be placed on share certificates held by the parties to such an agreement. This puts any potential buyers on notice of restrictions, including transfer restrictions, attached to those shares, and helps to prevent claims that stock is owned by a new shareholder in violation of a share-transfer restriction.

Voting Trusts

Voting trusts are another form of control device that consolidates shareholders' voting power in one person or a small group of persons who vote the shares of all the shareholders participating in the trust (Section 34 of the Model Act). Any number of shareholders may form a voting trust by executing a written voting trust agreement, transferring their shares to a voting trustee or trustees, and receiving in return voting trust certificates representing each shareholder's interest in the shares held in trust. The voting trust agreement contains terms that confer upon the trustees the right to vote the shares held by the trust, frequently in a designated manner (such as the names of certain persons to be selected for the corporation's Board of Directors), and usually provides that the shareholders are entitled to continue to receive dividends and other corporate distributions, except stock dividends. The voting trustee keeps a record of the holders of the trust certificates and provides the corporation with a copy of the agreement, including the names and addresses of all the parties to it.

If the terms of the trust do not instruct the trustee(s) how to vote on a particular matter, he or she may vote the shares held by the trust according to his or her own best judgment.

Voting trusts are an effective way to concentrate power in a few individuals; however, this result is somewhat at odds with the public policy of encouraging broad participation in corporate control. For these reasons, voting trusts are typically valid only for a specified period of time, often not more than 10 years. After the 10-year period, a voting trust is unenforceable—but the trust may be renewed for successive 10-year periods if the shareholders who participated in the trust sign another voting trust agreement (Section 34 of the Model Act).

Another common use for voting trusts is to protect creditors of a corporation from having management make decisions that put the creditors' loans in jeopardy. Under such a scenario, the creditor demands, as a prerequisite to making a loan, that a majority of the corporation's shares be placed in a trust with a nominee of the creditor named as trustee. The trust instrument normally leaves general management to the Board, but allows the trustee to act on fundamental financial questions.

DIRECTORS

Directors are the corporation's managers and are elected by the shareholders. They are responsible for determining corporate policy and insuring that such policy is properly carried out by the corporation's officers. Directors' responsibilities may also include determining a corporation's products, services, personnel, prices, salaries, corporate finances, and dividends. In larger corporations, these powers are not usually exercised by the Board except in the most general way. The day-to-day decisions on these issues are typically delegated to officers and managerial employees.

In smaller corporations there is often a greater overlap of owner, worker, and manager. This means that shareholders often work in the business and manage it. When a company has more than one shareholder, each of whom wants a say in the company's affairs, problems may arise between majority and minority interests. The result could be that the majority attempts to exclude minority participation on the Board.

There are several devices that could assist minority shareholders in thwarting any such effort by the majority. One is a provision, if legally available, for cumulative voting. Another is a shareholders' agreement committing shareholders to elect certain persons to the Board. The first two were discussed in preceding sections of this chapter. A third device is the classification of directors.

The Model Business Corporation Act (Section 16) permits shares to be divided into classes. The Articles of Incorporation could establish these classes based on the right of each class to elect one or more directors. This would mean that if there are three shareholders, three classes of shares would be established, one for each shareholder. Each class would be entitled to elect a specified number of directors. All the other rights and obligations of shareholders could be equivalent and all directors would have the same power and responsibility. This device, however, would guarantee equal (or proportional) representation for each shareholder.

As an example, suppose John Carpenter owned 100 shares of Corporation X while Mary Smith owned 75 shares and Jeffrey Jones owned the remaining 25 shares. They had decided among themselves that, despite the differences in share ownership, they each would have equal voice on the Board. If they chose the classification method to accomplish their goal, they would draft Articles of Incorporation creating three classes of stock. Each shareholder would obtain stock of a different class from the others and each class would be entitled to elect one director. Thus, Carpenter would vote his 100 shares of Class A stock for his choice as director. Smith and Jones would each vote their Class B and Class C stock, respectively, for their choice as directors. Each would have one director and equal representation.

Suppose, in this example, the group had decided that Carpenter, due to his greater number of shares, should have more representation on the Board. The Articles could be drafted to give Class A shareholders the right to elect three directors, while Class B could elect two directors, and Class C one director. This could be designed to maintain on the Board the proportion of interest each shareholder has in the stock of the corporation or to create any representational system the shareholders deem advisable.

Just as minority shareholders may feel the need for protection from the majority, the minority directors (chosen by the minority shareholders) may want some assistance as well. One means of protecting minority interests on the Board is a greater-than-majority quorum and vote requirements—the same device that can be used to protect minority shareholders. With respect to directors, a high quorum will protect a "minority director" (a director representing minority shareholding interests) by allowing him or her to block unfavorable decisions by being absent from Board meetings and preventing the presence of the quorum required for the meeting to transact business. On the other hand, the absence of a director for the purpose of defeating a quorum has negative implications relative to that director's duty to the corporation as a whole.

If the organizers choose a high-quorum requirement for Board meetings, it should be coupled with a requirement that directors be given notice of the proposed agenda of each meeting. Thus absences may be strategically planned rather than being indiscriminate.

A greater-than-majority vote requirement is another method to protect minority directors. Such a provision could simply state that a three-fifths, two-thirds, three-fourths, and so forth vote was necessary to carry a motion at a Board meeting. If minority directors muster enough votes to prevent that mark from being reached, they may block Board decisions unfavorable to them.

Both high-quorum and high-vote requirements risk a Board of Directors' stalemate that would be detrimental to the corporation, but these provisions are nevertheless an effective way to force directors to be responsive to all the interests represented on the Board. A greater-than-majority vote requirement is probably the safer feature, however, since it at least allows directors to appear and debate issues, giving them the opportunity to decide uncontroversial questions and compromise on others.

It may also be important to preserve an agreed-upon Board composition by preventing a majority faction of shareholders from increasing the number of directors and filling the vacancies with their own selections. To block "packing" the Board, the number of members may be established by a provision in the Articles of Incorporation or Bylaws, which may be made subject to amendment only upon receipt of a higher-than-majority (two-thirds, three-fourths, etc.) vote of the shareholders. Also, whenever the Board has a vacancy caused by the resignation, death or incapacity of a director, the power to fill that position could be vested exclusively in the shareholders acting by a greater-than-majority vote. If directors were elected by classified shares, the vacancy could be filled by the class of shares that elected the previous director.

Another safeguard of minority interests is a Bylaw provision that directors may be removed only by a greater-than-majority vote of the shareholders and then only for "cause," that is, for conduct that is detrimental to the best interests of the corporation. This protects against removals for purely personal reasons. However, even purely personal reasons may interfere with the smooth operation of a corporation and so removal without cause may be appropriate.

OFFICERS

A corporation's officers are responsible for carrying out its day-to-day affairs and are selected by the Board of Directors. Some states allow the shareholders of small, closely held corporations* to select the corporation's officers directly, instead of requiring officers to be selected by the Board.

A device that would protect incumbent officers is greater-than-majority quorum and vote requirements where the Board of Directors votes whether to dismiss an officer. Requiring a greater-than-majority vote would make a hasty dismissal difficult to obtain. (However, consider whether the officer may deserve to be banished as soon as possible.)

Employment contracts with the corporation are further protection for officers. Each officer could be hired by the corporation pursuant to an employment contract specifying standards of performance, salary, and grounds for dismissal. The contract could not prevent the Board of Directors from dismissing an officer, but if the Board did so without adequate grounds, the officer would be able to sue the corporation for damages and, perhaps, reinstatement.

---

* A closely held corporation is defined as a corporation owned by only a small number of shareholders whose shares are not traded publicly and, in fact, are generally subject to rather broad transfer restrictions.

8

ARTICLES OF INCORPORATION

A corporation is created by the filing of its Articles of Incorporation, which define its essential characteristics and basic structure. The Articles must be submitted to and approved by a designated state official, often the Secretary of State, before the corporation's legal existence begins. Section 54 of the Model Business Corporation Act sets forth the required contents of the Articles. The ordering and numbering of the paragraphs in the pages that follow, however, is for illustrative purposes only. It is the content rather than the form that is important.

HEADING

The Articles of Incorporation should begin with a heading such as:

ARTICLES OF INCORPORATION
OF
_____

TO: The (Secretary of State)
(Jurisdiction of incorporation)

The undersigned acting as incorporator of a corporation under the Business Corporation Law of the State of _____, adopts the following Articles of Incorporation for such corporation:

FIRST ARTICLE—NAME

The organizers must set out the name of the corporation in the first section of the Articles. This name must include the word "corporation," "company," "incorporated," or "limited," or an abbreviation thereof, and may not inaccurately describe the nature of the corporation. The name also may not closely resemble the name of another corporation doing business in the jurisdiction. The organizers can check on this latter point by inquiring of the office of the Secretary of State whether another corporation of the same or a similar name already exists in the jurisdiction. As mentioned earlier, organizers may reserve a chosen name by filing an Application for Reservation of Corporate name with the Secretary of State.

SECOND ARTICLE—DURATION

The second section must declare the period of the corporation's existence. The organizers may select any duration, but unless circumstances are very unusual it is best to designate a perpetual existence. When the duration is perpetual, there need be no worry that the corporation's authority to do business will lapse while it is still active. Should that occur the corporation could be fined or otherwise sanctioned for operating after the expiration of corporate authority, and would be forced to reincorporate and incur additional expenses. It is also possible that the shareholders would be exposed to individual liability during the interim period.

Selecting a perpetual existence does not, however, mean that the corporation *must* go on forever. It may dissolve at any time by recommendation of its Board of Directors and either written consent of *all* its shareholders, or by the *vote* at a shareholders' meeting of two-thirds of its shareholders entitled to vote.

THIRD ARTICLE—PURPOSE

This section must express the purpose or purposes for which the corporation is organized. A business corporation may be organized "for any lawful purpose or purposes, except for the purpose of banking or insurance" (Section 3 of the Model Act).

If the purpose of the corporation involves any restriction concerning the making of maximum profits, that should be expressed in this section of the Articles, particularly where the corporation intends to combine business with a more altruistic purpose, for example, on-the-job training of unskilled workers. Expressing a unique motivation of this type helps to define the scope of the business and the results considered important. Also, because outside investors will probably assume that a corporation's only motivation is to make money, the inclusion of this type of purpose may serve to warn outsiders that they are dealing with a corporation concerned with goals other than making maximum profits.

FOURTH ARTICLE—STOCK

This section should describe the corporation's stock. It must state the number of shares, their classification (if any), the preferences or other rights and authorized number of each class of shares and the par value (or that the shares are without par value) of all the stock the corporation authorizes.

In a small corporation, there may be no need for a large number of shares or division of shares into classes. For instance, four organizers of a corporation may decide that their corporation will issue 100 shares, all of the same class (having voting rights), and that each organizer will buy 25 shares to represent his or her one-fourth ownership interest. If the organizers intend to remain in control of the corporation and expect no one else to become an owner, there would be no need to authorize additional shares or another class of shares to be offered to outside investors. However, it is generally wise to plan for contingencies, including the possibility that more capital will need to be raised through the sale of shares. Therefore, the organizers might authorize 1000 shares even if they will only buy 25 each. The authorized but unissued shares (the 900 remaining shares) are not "owned" by anyone and are not voted or entitled to dividends until they are sold. Whether and when such a sale takes place is in the control of the Board of Directors, which in our example comprises all the preexisting shareholders.

An important decision in a closely held corporation is how much the corporation's shares will cost. Generally, a corporation should sell its stock for a price that, in the aggregate, equals at least the amount of money the company needs to begin business, including reserves but less any money borrowed by the corporation. In the previous example, if the corporation needed $10,000 equity to purchase assets and pay expenses, it should offer ("issue") its stock for a total price of no less than $10,000, for example, $100 per share if there were 100 shares. Each of the four organizers would then have to pay $2,500 to the corporation, transfer $2,500 worth of property, or perform $2,500 worth of services for it in order to acquire his or her one-fourth ownership interest.

If the organizers were unable to supply enough money or property for the corporation to begin business, they may increase the number of shares the corporation offers for sale and offer the additional shares to outsiders. (As noted previously, if this happens, the organizers must carefully consider whether federal or state securities laws are applicable.) Since the organizers' voting power would be diluted if outside investors bought and held the same type of stock as the organizers, an outside offering would make sense only if the organizers did not require 100% control of the corporation. (The organizers would normally not lose control of the corporation if, as a group, they retained 51% of the voting stock, especially if they entered into a shareholders' agreement promising to elect each other to the Board of Directors.)

When additional money is needed but dilution of control is a problem, a corporation could issue a second class of stock, financially attractive to outside investors, but with no voting rights to endanger the organizers' control of the corporation. A class of preferred stock, or nonvoting common stock, could fill this need. The corporation could also seek loans to satisfy its need for funds. As discussed earlier (in Chapter 5), there are several advantages to this route, assuming it is available, but also some drawbacks.

If the organizers intend to divide the corporation's stock into classes, this must be stated in this section of the Articles. As described in the previous chapter, classification of shares may be used as a device for assuring each organizer a role in the corporation's management, as well as for accommodating outside investors without granting them too much power. That is, the corporation could issue as many classes of stock as there are organizers planning to remain active in management of the company's affairs, each organizer could buy all the shares of one class, and the Articles of Incorporation could then provide that each class shall elect one director to the Board of Directors. Thus each organizer is assured that he or she may elect a person (usually himself or herself), to represent his or her interests on the Board. It should be noted, however, that such elaborate devices are not common and have tax consequences that will be discussed later (Chapter 12).

Finally, the organizers must decide whether their corporation's stock shall be of par or no par value. The significance of setting a par value is that stock may not be initially sold *by the corporation* for less than its par value. Shareholders, however, may transfer stock (par or no par) between themselves and others at whatever prices they choose. A par value is basically an arbitrary value assigned to the stock in the corporation's Articles and does not necessarily equal the market value of a share or even the amount of money actually paid for the share. Rather, the par value (which, if it is used, must be stated in the Articles) is used to determine the corporation's capital account.

No par shares are more flexible than shares with a par value because the corporation's Board of Directors, or the shareholders if they have been granted this power in the Articles, may determine the selling price of no par stock from time to time to reflect the corporation's success, or lack of it. That is, if the corporation is not doing particularly well but needs additional capital, the Board (or shareholders) may reduce the corporation's selling price for no par shares to the point where the shares are salable. Par value stock, on the other hand, may not be sold by the corporation for less than its par value. Thus if the market value of the shares (the value an independent third party would pay for the shares) is less than par, the corporation has an obvious problem in its attempt to raise new capital.

FIFTH ARTICLE—CLASSES OF SHARES

If the corporation has divided its shares into classes, this section must name each class and describe its preferences, voting powers, limitations, restrictions, qualification, and special or relative rights with respect to the other class(es) of shares. This is important because unless the Articles of Incorporation provide otherwise, all shares enjoy equal rights to corporate dividends, to assets on the corporation's dissolution, and to vote. Thus, if the organizers prefer a different distribution of power, they must express it in the Articles.

A frequent distinction is that one class of stock possess a preference to dividend payments. This may be expressed as a "preference of $_____" or "_____% of par value" per annum (payable yearly, semiannually, quarterly, etc.). A preference entitles the holders of the preferred stock to dividend payments of a certain amount before the holders of any other stock with a lower priority (preference) may receive any dividends on their stock.

In addition, preferred stock may be "cumulative" or "cumulative-to-the-extent-earned." Normally, a dividend is declared on a yearly basis. If it is not declared in any year, it generally is lost forever. Thus, if the corporation earned money that could have been used for a dividend but the Board decided not to declare one, the shareholders would not retain any right to receive payment for that year's dividend. On the other hand, if the dividend were cumulative, the right to payment would not be lost. Rather, the amount of the unpaid dividend would be added to the next year's dividend and the holders of cumulative preferred stock would have to be paid all accumulated dividends before holders of lower priority shares would receive anything.

Cumulative-if-earned stock is similar but has one major difference. The difference is that if the corporation has earned money from which a dividend could be paid but is not, the unpaid dividend is cumulative. If there are not sufficient earnings in a particular year to declare the dividend the dividend is lost for that year (but not for the others). Therefore, cumulative preferred stock may make a very attractive investment for some shareholders. However, because no other shareholders may be paid dividends until the accumulated unpaid dividends from past years have been paid to the holders of cumulative preferred stock, the lower preference (including common) stockholders could suffer a long spell without dividends.

Preferred stock may also be "participating" or "nonparticipating." Nonparticipating preferred stock receives no dividends beyond the amount of its dividend "preference." "Participating preferred" receives its preferential dividend and then, once other preferences have been paid, may share the remaining portion of available funds with the common stockholders in whatever proportion is established in the Articles. This may also make a very attractive investment, since these stockholders get a constant dividend payment before dividends are paid on any other shares, and are also able to share in additional corporate profits.

If a class or classes of shares is to enjoy a preference to the assets or proceeds upon dissolution and liquidation of the corporation, the Articles must also provide for this preference. This may be phrased as "a preference of $_____," "_____% of par value," or "Class 'A' will get twice (three, four, five, etc.) times per share the amount of Class 'B.'" Thus, if the corporation dissolves, sells all its assets, pays its debts, and distributes the remaining proceeds, a certain portion of the money received will go to the holders of shares with a "liquidation preference," and what money remains after all preferences have been paid will be equally distributed among the holders of the common shares.

Unless the Articles provide otherwise, all shareholders have the same voting rights. The organizers may want to alter this situation by providing for class voting for directors to insure representation of various interests on the Board (e.g., to assure representation of minority interests on the Board). In addition, there are other voting right variables such as contingent voting rights (perhaps contingent on not being paid dividends), or classes of stock with no voting rights at all (in fact, preferred stock frequently does not possess voting rights).

Class voting might also be weighted according to classes; for example, Class A shares count as two votes on any issue while Class B and C shares count as only one vote each. This is another method of allocating power to the holders of a certain class or classes of stock. Similar to this device is a provision whereby one class elects proportionately more directors than any other class; for example, Class X elects five directors out of a sevenperson Board, Class Y elects the remainder.

There are also financial considerations in the configuration of shares. For instance, after the corporation is established and has accumulated an amount of money, it may be desirable for it to buy up its preferred shares, retire them, and issue common shares or new preferred shares that pay shareholders at a lower rate. In order to do this, there must be a redemption provision in the Articles allowing the corporation to buy back its own preferred shares from their owners whenever the corporation chooses to do so (Section 54 of the Model Act). The Articles must include a redemption price, for example, "$_____" or "_____% of par value" (110%, for instance), specify if there is a time limit on the corporation's exercise of its redemption privilege, and prescribe the procedures for accomplishing the redemption. A corporation may not redeem any of its shares, however, if the payments would reduce the corporation's net assets below an amount sufficient to pay all its debts and known liabilities, or below the aggregate amount of liquidation preferences payable to shareholders.

Similarly, if one type of share may be converted into another type or into a debt security, the details of this privilege must be included in the Articles. The Articles must specify what, if any, shares are convertible, into what other shares or debt securities, at what ratio (e.g., 1:1, 2:1, etc.) and subject to what time limitations.

As discussed in Chapter 5, convertibility is an attractive investment feature, since it holds out the possibility that investors may exchange their shares for shares of another series or class, or for debt securities (or vice versa), whenever those other interests become more attractive to them than the stock they currently own. Organizers should be aware, however, that if shares or loans held by outside investors are convertible into a type of stock with voting rights, the outsiders could convert themselves into voting power. At the least, the allocation of voting power established among the organizers could be disrupted if one security holder converted another type of security he or she held into stock with voting rights.

Debt securities, bonds, debentures, notes, and so forth do *not* have to be specifically authorized in the corporation's Articles of Incorporation. They do, however, have to be authorized by the corporation's Board of Directors.

SIXTH ARTICLE—SERIES OF CLASSES

It is possible for the corporation to issue classes of stock in "series"; that is, the Articles may provide that a portion of a class of shares may be issued with a certain dividend rate, redemption privilege, liquidation preference, conversion privileges, and so forth, and that another portion of shares of the same class may be issued with a different dividend rate, liquidation preference, and so forth (Section 54 of the Model Act). The corporation need not sell each series at the same time. The details of each series could be specified in the Articles of Incorporation, or the Articles may authorize the Board of Directors to issue shares in specified series, and leave the details of each series to be determined at a later date in a Board resolution. The latter method provides more flexibility, since the Board is not bound by features of a series until it establishes the features and records them with the Secretary of State.

SEVENTH ARTICLE—PREEMPTIVE RIGHTS

Unless the Articles provide otherwise, the corporation's shareholders possess (or do *not* possess, depending on state law) "preemptive rights" (Section 26 of the Model Act). A shareholder's preemptive right is his or her right to buy a percentage (corresponding to the percentage of his or her current shareholdings to the total number of outstanding shares) of any new stock of the same class authorized and issued by the corporation. Only if he or she is not interested in purchasing or does not have the money, may the corporation offer the shares to other investors. If there are not preemptive rights, the corporation may offer new shares to whomever it chooses. Where the corporation has issued different classes of stock with different voting, dividend, liquidation, and so forth, rights, there may be difficulties apportioning preemptive rights to new stock.

To the extent preemptive rights are available, Section 26 of the Model Act limits their application, *except* as the Articles provide otherwise, in the following situations:

1. When shares are issued to officers, directors, or employees pursuant to shareholder's vote or to a plan previously approved by shareholders; or

2. When shares are issued for other than cash (i.e., property, shares of another corporation, etc.). Moreover, there is an absolute ban, under the Model Act, on preemptive rights for holders of preferred or nonvoting common shares to acquire *any* shares or for the holders of common shares to acquire preferred shares (unless those preferred shares are convertible into common shares).

State law often provides that, even if there are preemptive rights, a corporation may issue and sell new shares to its employees without the new issue being subject to preemptive rights, if two-thirds of the corporation's shareholders have previously approved the plan. It is also generally recognized that preemptive rights do not apply with respect to (1) originally authorized stock; (2) stock issued in exchange for property or personal services provided to the corporation; (3) stock purchased by the corporation itself (treasury stock) and subsequently resold by it; (4) shares issued in connection with a merger or consolidation, (5) and share dividends. In a small corporation, the organizers may want to provide in the Articles that preemptive rights exist even in some of these instances.

Another method of protecting shareholders' proportionate interests is to authorize only that amount of stock that will actually be purchased by a corporation's organizers. To create any more stock would require an amendment to the corporation's Articles, and many states' laws provide that amendments to Articles of Incorporation require the approval of two-thirds of the corporation's shares. (Although the Articles may impose a higher percentage requirement.)

To protect the proportionate interests of shareholders who may not have enough money to purchase the stock made available through their preemptive rights, or to protect against a majority of shareholders authorizing new stock and providing an unreasonably short period of time during which the stockholders may exercise their preemptive rights (thus making it more difficult to raise the money needed to buy the stock), the Articles could impose a very high-vote requirement for amendments to the Articles, or a high-vote requirement specifically for amendments increasing the number of the corporation's authorized shares. These devices would help preserve the proportionate interests of a shareholder who was unable to muster enough money to exercise his or her preemptive rights but who might be able to muster enough votes to prevent an amendment necessary to authorize additional stock. The converse, of course, is that such a requirement could prevent the corporation from raising needed new capital.

EIGHTH ARTICLE—SPECIAL PROVISIONS

This section is optional and may include special provisions for the regulation of the corporation's internal affairs, including: authorization for cumulative or class voting; imposition of greater-than-majority quorum and/or voting requirements for shareholders' and/or directors' meetings; permission for shareholders to determine the selling price of the corporation's no par shares; provision for filling vacancies on the Board by vote of the shareholders and any other important or, perhaps, unusual features of the corporation's internal affairs.

This section could also include a provision for indemnification of the corporation's directors, officers, and agents for any liability to which they may be subject as a result of the performance of their duties on behalf of the corporation. This is an important protection for corporate representatives who may find themselves subject to claims because of actions they took on behalf of, and pursuant to authorization by, the corporation.

The reason for including these provisions in the Articles is to give notice to the public of the corporation's special management features, thereby precluding an investor from later complaining that he or she was unaware of, and not bound by, these rules. It also makes it more difficult for these protections to be removed, since it would require going through the entire amendment procedure to make a change.

NINTH ARTICLE—REGISTERED OFFICE AND AGENT

This section must provide the address—including street and number of the initial registered office of the corporation, which need not be its place of business—and the name of its initial registered agent at such address.

The corporation must always maintain a registered office and a registered agent at that address in the state of incorporation. The first such office and agent must be specified in the Articles of Incorporation (Section 12 of the Model Act). The basic purpose of the agent is to receive service of process and other official correspondence in the name of the corporation and to forward such communications to appropriate corporate officers or directors. The agent may be an individual, who must be a *resident* of the state of incorporation, a domestic corporation, or a foreign corporation authorized to do business in the state of incorporation. A corporation may thereafter change its registered office or registered agent by filing a notice of the change with the state.

TENTH ARTICLE—BOARD OF DIRECTORS

This section must state the number and give the names and addresses of the members of the corporation's initial Board of Directors. The organizers may choose any number of directors to constitute the initial Board, but there must be at least *one* (Section 54 of the Model Act) although many states require a minimum of three directors. The initial directors (or any other directors) do not have to be residents of the state of incorporation, nor must they be 18 years of age or older or shareholders of the corporation, unless the Articles state otherwise.

The organizers should probably list themselves as the initial directors since they will then have managerial control from the outset. This can be important, particularly in controlling to whom the corporation's shares are offered for sale. Occasionally, however, to disguise who really controls the business or because there are only one or two organizers, there may be people who serve as directors as an accommodation and take no active part in the corporation's management. Accommodation directors are still subject to directors' duties and potential liabilities.

ELEVENTH ARTICLE—INCORPORATORS

There must be one or more incorporators who may be either "natural persons," or another corporation, domestic or foreign (Section 53 of the Model Act). Incorporators need not be residents of the state of incorporation.

Because incorporators sign the Articles when they are submitted for filing, they are responsible and potentially liable if they have made any knowing misstatement of fact in the Articles. Other than this, incorporators, *as* incorporators, have no responsibility to, or authority over, the corporation.

9

BYLAWS

Bylaws are the internal rules and regulations chosen by a corporation's organizers to govern the company's internal affairs. Bylaws need not be filed with the state and consequently are never "approved" by any official or agency. While Bylaws are more specific concerning corporate affairs than are the Articles, the authority of the Bylaws is not unlimited. They must be consistent with the state's corporation laws and with the corporation's Articles of Incorporation. Inconsistencies are resolved in favor of the statute and the Articles in that order.

The responsibility for adopting, amending, and repealing Bylaws is vested in the Board of Directors unless the Articles of Incorporation expressly grant the power to the shareholders (Section 27 of the Model Business Corporation Act). In a small corporation, the organizers may want the shareholders to be so empowered so that they will be able to maintain more control over the corporation's management.

Bylaws describe power in the corporation—where it is, who has it, how it is used, and how it is controlled. For that reason, an organization should not adopt a form set of Bylaws but should develop Bylaws that fit its structure and method of functioning. Since Bylaws are not hard to prepare, it is worth the time to tailor them to the specific needs and circumstances of each corporation. The following discussion will trace the contents of, and relevant considerations involved in preparing, a set of Bylaws. Again, the ordering and numbering of these paragraphs is optional.

SECTION ONE—OFFICES

This section may describe the location of the corporation's offices. A corporation must maintain a registered office in the state of incorporation, but its principal place of business need not be in that office or even in that state (Section 12 of the Model Act). Therefore, this section could state the location of the corporation's principal office, the location of its registered office, and that it may maintain additional offices as determined by the Board of Directors.

SECTION TWO—SHAREHOLDERS

Generally, this section describes the corporation's shareholders—their meetings and their voting procedures.

Shareholders' Meetings

Meetings of shareholders (to exercise those powers conferred upon them by law and the Articles of Incorporation) may be held either within or without the jurisdiction of incorporation. If the Bylaws do not specify a location, the statute provides that shareholders' meetings shall be held at the corporation's registered office (Section 28 of the Model Act).

Shareholders generally meet once a year to elect the corporation's directors. The time and date for this gathering may be provided in the Bylaws, preferably expressed as "the first Tuesday in June," rather than "June 1 of each year" (for instance), in order to avoid selecting a date that falls on a weekend or holiday. The specific time is a matter of corporate convenience, but many corporations schedule their annual meeting shortly after the close of their business (fiscal) year. This allows the shareholders' meeting to review a completed year's activities.

It is also possible for shareholders to hold "regular meetings," that is, to gather at specified intervals, monthly, quarterly, semiannually, and so forth to exercise their powers and keep in touch with corporate affairs. This type of meeting is optional, and in most corporations such meetings are not held since the shareholders have few powers. Also, in a small corporation where the shareholders are also the directors and officers, it would seem superfluous to convene the same group of people as shareholders when they meet regularly in their other capacities and are well aware of what is happening in the corporation. If shareholders are empowered with significant managerial duties *as shareholders*, it would make sense for them to meet frequently in order to exercise their powers effectively.

A "special meeting" is an unscheduled meeting occasioned by an unexpected event requiring the shareholders' response such as, for example, the resignation of the entire Board of Directors, the corporation's consideration of a merger with another company, and so forth. Such a meeting may be called by the Board of Directors or the holders of at least one-tenth of the corporation's outstanding shares or by such other persons as are empowered to do so in the Articles of Incorporation or Bylaws (Section 28 of the Model Act). These other people might include the President, the Chairperson of the Board, the Executive Committee, the Treasurer, any member of the Board, two (three, four, etc.) members of the Board, and so forth. The more people who have the power to call such a meeting, the more likely the shareholders can be legally mobilized to respond to emergencies. It is also more likely that meetings will be called for less important purposes. The organizers should weigh the competing elements carefully.

Notice
In order for shareholders to be aware of shareholders' meetings, the corporation must give notice of these gatherings. Unless the Bylaws express different provisions regarding the *period of* notice, Section 29 of the Model Act states that *written* notice of shareholders' meetings, describing the date, place, and time of the meeting, and the purpose in the case of a special meeting, *must* be given to each shareholder of record entitled to vote, not less than 10 nor more than 50 days before the date of each shareholders' meeting.

The majority of states require such notice even for annual (or regular) meetings, the date, place, and time of which are expressed in the Bylaws. This reinforces a strong policy in favor of active shareholder participation in the general direction of a corporation. This is particularly true in those small corporations where all shareholders do not have daily contact with the business. Therefore, the organizers may want to provide for special types of written notice, such as by telegraph, fax, or computer. Moreover, the notification period established in the statute probably need not be so far in advance for a locally based and owned corporation. A much shorter period, a few days perhaps, should suffice.

Who Is Entitled to Vote?
Obviously, persons who own shares are stockholders. The Bylaws, however, may specify a time within which a person must be listed as a stockholder on the books of the corporation in order to be entitled to notice of, and the opportunity to vote at, a shareholders' meeting. This cutoff may also apply to other shareholder matters such as which shareholders are entitled to receive dividends (that are paid as of a certain record date). The problem arises when shares are sold or otherwise transferred from one

person to another. In large corporations where this happens frequently, the corporation needs some method of deciding which persons may act as shareholders on corporate matters. The method developed is that of the "record date." This is the last day prior to some proposed shareholder action that the corporation will recognize a buyer of shares as a shareholder for the purpose of that action.

For instance, assume a shareholder vote is to be held on March 15. The corporation may say that all shareholders of record, that is, shareholders listed as such in the corporate records, as of February 15 may vote. If X bought stock from Y on March 1, Y, the seller, would be entitled to vote on March 15, not X. To cure this problem, X might demand, as part of the purchase, that Y give X an irrevocable "proxy" (which is defined below) to vote the shares.

Section 30 of the Model Act provides that a corporation's Board of Directors may "close the stock transfer books" for a period not to exceed 50 days; that is, the Board may halt stock transfers on its books within that time in order to determine those stockholders entitled to notice, eligible to vote, or qualified to receive dividends. If the books are closed in order to determine who are stockholders who are entitled to vote at an upcoming shareholders' meeting, the books must be closed at least 10 days prior to such meeting.

If no provision is made by the Board for either closing the books or setting a cutoff date, the date when notice was mailed will be considered the date for determining which shareholders are entitled to vote. It is therefore possible for new shareholders to be recognized up until the moment of the vote—if notice was delivered personally rather than by mail. Absent a contrary provision in the Bylaws, or a resolution by the Board, shareholders listed as of the time the Board declared a dividend are eligible to receive that payment.

The organizers may want to designate one of the corporation's officers, usually the Secretary, to maintain a record of shareholders. In a corporation with few shareholders, this is a simple task. If the number of shareholders is large enough that they are difficult to keep track of, however, it may be worthwhile to record transactions concerning the corporation's stock more closely. This is often accomplished by the use of a professional "transfer agent," usually a bank or other financial institution with sophisticated record-keeping systems.

Quorum

A quorum is the number of *shares, not shareholders,* that must be present at a shareholders' meeting before the meeting may properly transact business. Unless a quorum is present, the shareholders are powerless to take action except to adjourn the meeting until a quorum can be assembled. Any other action taken is invalid. If the Articles of Incorporation do not specify what constitutes a quorum, Section 32 of the Model Act provides that a majority of the corporation's outstanding shares having voting power, represented in person or by proxy, shall constitute a quorum for a meeting of shareholders.

It is important to name a realistic quorum, because a quorum requirement that is too difficult to attain may result in the shareholders never having a proper meeting. If there are many shareholders, perhaps a smaller percentage such as one-third of the shares with voting rights (Section 32 of the Model Act forbids a percentage smaller than one-third) may be indicated. On the other hand, if there are few shareholders they are probably more intimately involved in the corporation's management and a quorum of greater than 50% would be feasible, since the shareholders would be more likely to attend meetings. In addition, where the shareholders are also the corporation's directors and officers, a high quorum results in attendance by a broad base of shareholders with a management perspective, which could foster better coordination between management and shareholders.

Also, a high-quorum requirement helps to protect the interests of minority shareholders since these shareholders could absent themselves from a meeting that was scheduled to consider actions unfavorable to them, thereby preventing the quorum needed to do business. There is also an obvious negative aspect to high quorum requirements; a minority of shareholders could deadlock important corporate action.

Vote

Section 32 of the Model Act also provides that the affirmative vote of a majority of the shares entitled to vote, represented in person or by proxy at a shareholders' meeting, shall carry a motion, unless a greater number is required by statute or by the Articles of Incorporation. The section also allows the Articles to require class voting, which would supersede the majority-vote language.

Proxies. A *proxy* is an authorization from a shareholder who is absent, to another person who will be present at a shareholders' meeting, to vote the absent shareholder's stock. A proxy is not necessarily an absentee vote. The person with the absentee's proxy may be given discretion to vote however he or she wishes to vote, or the absent shareholder may indicate how he or she wants the shares voted on particular issues. Section 33 of the Model Act expressly authorizes shareholder voting by proxy. The proxy must be in writing and signed by the shareholder or the shareholder's duly authorized attorney in fact. The proxy, unless it specifies otherwise, is valid for 11 months from the date of its issuance. The solicitation of proxies is governed, for the most part, by state law. For large, widely traded corporations, proxies and their solicitation are regulated by federal statutes that, in those cases, supersede local law.

In deciding whether to allow proxies, the organizers must weigh the importance they attach to personal attendance, versus the possibility that a shareholder may be unable to attend, but still wants to vote.

Informal Actions.   Section 145 of the Model Act provides that any shareholders' action may be taken without a meeting, if a written consent, setting forth the action taken, is signed by *all the shareholders* entitled to vote on the matter. For the sake of convenience, the Bylaws could restate this provision so that the corporation's internal regulations clearly state that this procedure may be used. Many corporations with a small number of shareholders operate almost exclusively by unanimous written consent and rarely have actual shareholder meetings. This eliminates worries about the adequacy of notice of meetings and logistical problems of assembling all the shareholders at the same time. A consent resolution, or different copies of the same resolution, may simply be passed around to all the shareholders for their signature.

Cumulative Voting.   As discussed in Chapter 7, cumulative voting is a system of voting for directors whereby each share possesses as many votes as there are directors to be elected. For example, Jane Doe has 10 shares and there are three seats on the Board to be filled. With cumulative voting, Doe would have 30 votes to cast as she chooses, either all for one candidate or distributed among as many candidates as she likes. This type of voting helps minority shareholders to elect some representatives to the Board of Directors, instead of being completely outvoted by the holders of 51% of the corporation's stock. For instance, if, in our hypothetical corporation, Doe had 10 shares and Mary Smith had 15, Smith would, in the absence of cumulative voting, be able to elect all three directors. She would simply vote her 15 shares for each of her three favorite candidates. Doe would vote her 10 shares for her three candidates. Since each of Smith's candidates received 15 votes to only 10 for Doe's candidates, the Smith candidates would be elected.

With cumulative voting, each shareholder could divide his or her votes in any way he or she pleases. Doe would have 30 votes (10 shares × 3 directors) and Smith 45 (15 × 3). If Doe casts all her 30 votes for one candidate, mathematically she is assured of that candidate's election. No matter how Smith divides her votes she cannot have three candidates all having more votes than Doe's one.

In a small corporation, increased shareholder involvement in management functions may be desirable, and cumulative voting is one system for achieving this. Cumulative voting is most effective the larger the number of places to be filled on the Board. Thus one way for the effects of cumulative voting to be diluted is for only one or two directors to be scheduled for election at any one time.

Cumulative voting varies among the states. Some require it, some forbid it, and others leave it to the Articles of Incorporation with formulations such as "cumulative voting is not available unless it is provided for in the Articles of Incorporation" or "cumulative voting is required unless the Articles provide to the contrary." The provision may be restated in the Bylaws, but in those permissive states inclusion of some provision should be in the Articles. In any case, cumulative voting is available *only* in the election of directors. It is not available for *any* other purpose.

SECTION THREE—DIRECTORS

The Board of Directors is the body responsible for managing the corporation. It makes basic policy decisions for the corporation and selects the corporate officers to implement these decisions. The Board, however, must act as a whole, collectively, and not through its individual members. Thus a single director has no legal power, where there are other directors, to determine corporate policies. Of course, when there is only one director, this point is moot.

Unless the Articles or Bylaws indicate otherwise, there is no requirement that the directors be residents of the state of incorporation, shareholders of the corporation, or of any particular age (Section 35 of the Model Act). Section 36 requires that there be at least one director, but Section 35 allows the management authority of the Board to be transferred, in whole or in part, by the Articles to any other person or persons. Thus, while one director is still required, the position may be stripped of power by the Articles of Incorporation. In either case, the initial director(s) must be named in the Articles of Incorporation, but these directors could hold office only until the first meeting of the shareholders, at which time they could be reelected or replaced, by vote of the shareholders, with the parties who will operate the corporation.

Powers

The Board generally has the power to manage the business and affairs of the corporation. As mentioned previously, this includes the power to make policy decisions and to choose the people who will carry out these decisions. However, with such broad powers also come extensive duties.

Directors must always use their best efforts to manage the corporation's business and earn profits for its shareholders. The standard to which directors are held in making their managerial decisions is that of the diligence, skill, and care that a reasonably prudent person would exercise in similar circumstances. Directors must act within their authority, as defined in the Articles, Bylaws, and applicable provisions of the statute, must avoid conflicts of interest with the corporation, and may not compete with its business or usurp a corporate business opportunity for their personal benefit.

If a director falls below these standards, he or she may be sued by a shareholder to recover—on behalf of the corporation—any damage caused to the corporation by the director's misconduct. Such a lawsuit is known as a "stockholder's derivative suit" because the shareholder is suing for a harm done to the corporation, not one done directly to the shareholder. If the shareholder is successful, any recovery goes to the corporation, not to the shareholder.

To protect themselves from liability for authorizing improper actions, directors should attend and participate in Board meetings and keep abreast of the corporation's affairs. Then, if the director believes that the Board has voted to approve an improper action, that director should register his or her protest on the record in the minutes of the meeting or file a written protest with the corporation's Secretary immediately after the meeting (Section 48 of the Model Act). This will confirm the director's dissenting vote and will help shield him or her from liability. This procedure may not, however, be used by a director to change, after the fact, his or her original vote in favor of an action.

Number, Tenure, and Qualifications

The Bylaws should state how many directors the corporation will have. The organizers should keep this number manageable. In a small corporation, the number of directors may be determined by the number of organizer-shareholders. In such a corporation, there could be as many directors as there are shareholders who intend to be active in the management of the corporation's affairs.

As discussed previously, the Board of Directors is elected by the corporation's shareholders (Section 36 of the Model Act). This election may be accomplished at the shareholders' annual meeting, or by the shareholders acting by unanimous written consent. Generally, directors elected at an annual meeting hold office until the next annual meeting, at which time they may, in the absence of a Bylaw provision to the contrary, run for re-election. If no new election of directors is held, the incumbent directors simply continue to serve on the Board. The Bylaws *could* limit the number of terms that a director may serve. In a small corporation, however, where the shareholders also run the business, that type of restriction is not advisable since it would disqualify the investors from management after a few years.

The organizers may want to create different *classes of directors*—distinguished by the length and termination date of their terms. If the number of directors is nine or more, the Articles of Incorporation may provide for two or three classes of directors, with "each class to be as nearly equal in number as possible." After the first election of directors, the first class would serve for one year, the second for two, and the third for three years (Section 37 of the Model Act). Then, when the first term of each class expires, the newly elected directors in that class would serve for three-year terms (or two-year terms if only two classes were established). This staggers the election of directors so that all directors are not up for election at the same time. The goal is to provide some continuity on the Board, although critics suggest that continuity is accomplished by shareholder inertia leading to the reelection of incumbents, regardless of the classification of directors. Moreover, classes of directors may be unnecessary and superfluous if provision has been made for election of directors by classified shares, or if a shareholder's agreement assures certain persons (usually the shareholders) places on the Board.

Meetings

In order to perform their managerial duties, the Board of Directors must meet or take action by unanimous written consent. If they choose to meet, their meetings may take place either within or outside of the state of incorporation, as provided in the Bylaws or by resolution of the Board.

Although it is not required by statute, the Board may want to hold an annual meeting to review the year's business, and the Bylaws could list the date, time, and place of such a meeting. A convenient date would be the date of the shareholders' meeting, with the directors convening immediately after the shareholders have adjourned.

The Board may find it necessary to meet on a more regular basis than once a year. To provide for other meetings, the Bylaws could list the date, time, place, and so forth of "regular" meetings of the Board. For instance, "regular meetings of the Board of Directors shall be held at 8:00 P.M. on the first Tuesday of every month, at the corporation's principal office (Section 43 of the Model Act).

The organizers must decide how frequently these regular meetings should be held. This will depend on the nature of the corporation, the attention its activities demand, the willingness of the directors to gather frequently for meetings, and the feasibility of taking certain Board actions pursuant to unanimous written consent. Many corporations hold Board meetings once a month, and if the organizers feel the corporation will need periodic, in-person review, the Bylaws could provide for a monthly directors' meeting.

Instead of a Bylaws provision, a "standing resolution" could announce a regular date and time for Board meetings. A standing resolution also should alleviate notice problems since the resolution would be part of the minutes of the Board meeting that would be provided to all directors, and would set a regular meeting time far in advance. A simple resolution passed by the Board which announces only the details of its next meeting may create practical notice problems if many directors are absent from the meeting at which the resolution was passed and these directors are not made aware of the resolution in time.

Because there can be no guarantee that regularly scheduled meetings will coincide with unexpected problems that may require the immediate attention of the Board, the Bylaws should contain a mechanism for calling meetings to respond to unanticipated events. A provision for "special meetings" of the Board will accomplish this (Section 43 of the Model Act).

A provision for special meetings should list the persons empowered to call such meetings and the type of notice required. The Chairperson of the Board would be a logical choice to call meetings, as would be the President of the corporation, or a certain number of directors (one, two, three, etc.).

Notice, which should be defined in the Bylaws, may be personal, by telephone, telegraph, mail, or any other method the organizers feel is effective (Section 43 of the Model Act). (Note the difference between the notice for directors' meetings and the notice required for shareholders' meetings—the latter must be in *writing*.) The period of notice should be brief—a day or two—since this type of meeting may be called to respond to an emergency.

Quorum

Before the Board of Directors may take any valid actions, a certain percentage of the directors must be present at the Board meeting. Section 40 of the Model Act states that a majority of the directors shall constitute a quorum unless a *greater* number is required by the Articles of Incorporation or the Bylaws; thus the quorum may not be *less* than a majority of the directors.

The statutory provision of a majority quorum applies only if the Articles or Bylaws are silent on the subject. A majority quorum is a common choice, but in a small corporation there may be sentiment that no decisions should be made without a broader representation of the Board present. In such case, a higher quorum (three-fifths, two-thirds, three-fourths, etc.) would be appropriate and may act as a protection for minority directors just as a high quorum for shareholders' meetings protects the interests of minority shareholders.

Manner of Acting

The Bylaws should also reflect the organizers' decision on the margin of vote required to carry a motion of a Board meeting. Again, the common choice is that the vote of a majority of directors present at a meeting with a quorum carries an issue, and this percentage is established by Section 40 of the Model Act, if the corporation does not require a greater percentage in its Articles or Bylaws.

Greater-than-majority vote requirements are a means to protect minority interests on the Board, just as greater-than-majority quorum requirements deter actions unfavorable to minority directors. In the context of greater-than-majority *vote* requirement, minority interests could be present at a Board meeting, vote on uncontroversial issues, debate others, and, if difficulties were not resolved, the minority directors could try to muster enough support to prevent the majority from achieving the margin of vote required for taking action.

Action without a Meeting.   Section 44 of the Model Act allows the Board of Directors (as well as committees) to act by unanimous written consent, in lieu of actually meeting together. Action by consent is very convenient since it avoids the logistical difficulties of assembling a quorum of directors. Instead of meeting, all the directors simply sign a consent that describes the actions they agree to take. The consent document need not be signed by all directors at the same time, nor must directors physically sign the same piece of paper, as long as they all sign copies of the same document.

Proxies.   Directors may not vote by proxy. This is implicit in Section 40 of the Model Act, which speaks of the vote requirements at directors' meetings as a majority of the directors present. This is also supported by case law which gives the rationale that directors must exercise their personal judgment on corporate issues and that this can only be done by their presence at the meeting.

Vacancies

Section 38 of the Model Act provides that vacancies on the Board of Directors caused by resignation, removal, death, and so forth may be filled by vote of a majority of the remaining directors, even though less than a quorum. The Model Act says that the vacancy or vacancies *may* be filled by the remaining directors. This is because many cases have held that the shareholders retain an inherent right to fill vacancies on the Board regardless of the fact that the Bylaws give a similar right to directors. Similarly, where the vacancy results from an increase in the number of directors the corporation is to have, the Model Act says that the Board may fill it and, again according to the cases, so may the shareholders. Where each class of classified shares elects a representative to the Board, only the class that elected the director is eligible to vote to fill the vacancy.

Removal

Section 39 of the Model Act provides that directors may be discharged by vote of the shareholders for "cause"—that is, conduct detrimental to the best interests of the corporation—or without cause—that is, the shareholders may decide they no longer wish to retain a particular director. This latter provision could result in discharges for personal and private disputes and affords little protection to directors representing a minority of the corporation's shares. Thus the Model Act permits removal only after a meeting of shareholders called expressly for the purpose of considering removal. It is advisable for the Bylaws to provide, as many cases require in removal-for-cause situations, that the director be given written notice of the charges against him or her and an opportunity to present a defense before the shareholders vote. This clarifies the dispute and is fair to the challenged director. The Bylaws could also provide that the Board of Directors itself may remove a director from office for "cause." Some cases hold that this power does not exist unless it is stated in the Bylaws.

Resignation

Because directors may want to resign, resignation procedures should be defined. The Bylaws could state that directors may resign at any time by delivering a written resignation to the Board of Directors, Chairperson of the Board, President, Secretary, or to any other party or parties that the organizers feel is appropriate. The resignation should be effective on the date stated in the resignation or on its receipt by the appropriate party.

Compensation

Section 35 of the Model Act states that directors may establish compensation for themselves for serving as directors unless the Articles provide otherwise. The organizers may want to echo this provision in the Bylaws in order to clarify that directors may receive salaries. If the organizers feel directors should not be paid salaries as directors (although they could still be paid for serving as officers, for instance), the prohibition or distinction must be included in the Articles or else the statutory provision will prevail and directors will be eligible to receive salaries.

SECTION FOUR—OFFICERS

This section describes the corporation's officers and their duties. Traditionally, officers are selected, and can be removed, by the Board of Directors. They derive their powers from the Board, which delegates authority to the officers to carry out the Board's policies. Actually, the officers are probably the most powerful group in the corporation since they direct the corporation's day-to-day affairs, subject to policy directives from the Board.

The Model Act provides that each corporation must have a President, one or more Vice-Presidents, a Secretary, and a Treasurer (Section 50). The corporation may also create other offices such as Chairperson of the Board, Vice-Chairperson of the Board, Chairperson of the Executive Committee, Executive Vice-President, Senior Vice-President, Comptroller, Assistant President, Assistant Vice-President, Assistant Treasurer, and Assistant Secretary.

The Act, however, imposes no special qualifications for a person to be eligible for corporate office. Of course, the Articles or Bylaws may impose such qualifications, including whether officers need be residents of the state, of any particular age, or shareholders in the corporation.

The Model Act also states that two or more offices, except those of President and Secretary, may be held by the same person. Thus a corporation must have at least two individuals serving as its officers. Typically, the fewer the number of shareholders, the fewer the number of officers a corporation will have.

The Bylaws should specify the titles and duties of the corporation's officers. The usual choices are President, Vice-President, Secretary, and Treasurer, with a provision that the Board or the shareholders may create any other offices they feel are necessary.

Choosing officers from among the directors tightens the Board's control of the corporation and may also make the corporation more responsive to the shareholders—since shareholders elect the directors from whom the officers are selected. Thus, if the shareholders were dissatisfied with an officer's performance, they could fail to reelect him or her as a director, precluding him or her from serving as an officer. (Of course, this device would not be available if there was a shareholders' agreement which provided that the shareholders would elect certain persons to the Board.)

A small corporation probably does not need many officers because its day-to-day affairs are not likely to be complicated. If the corporation wants to reward its supporters with titles, however, it is certainly possible to create numerous Assistant Vice-Presidents, and so forth. But the organizers should consider carefully how many officers are really needed. It is not advisable to create unneeded officers since outsiders might erroneously assume that they are in positions of power and may attempt to do business with them.

The Bylaws should provide the manner by which officers are selected. Most corporations have their Board of Directors elect the officers at the Board's annual meeting. Although in a few states officers may be selected directly by the shareholders of a small corporation. Section 50 of the Model Act provides that the President, Vice-President, Secretary, and Treasurer shall be elected by the Board in a manner and at the time as provided in the Bylaws. Additional officers may be selected by other methods, however, including election by the shareholders.

The length of officers' terms should be specified, and any provisions that prohibit officers from serving any number of consecutive terms (more than two, three, etc. consecutive terms) should also be spelled out.

If officers must meet certain qualifications, these should be expressed in the Bylaws. Must an officer be 18 years of age or older, a shareholder in the corporation, a director? Residence in the metropolitan area is another possible qualification, especially where officers' duties require their day-to-day attention.

Removal

The corporation should be able to dismiss a misbehaving officer and, therefore, some provision for dismissal of officers should be included in the Bylaws. If the Bylaws fail to deal with the issue, Section 51 of the Model Act provides that an officer may be removed by the Board of Directors when, in its judgment, the best interests of the corporation will be served. The section goes on to say that such removal will not affect any contract rights the officer may have. The mere fact of appointment as an officer does not, according to the Act, *create* contract rights. If there is a contract, however, the Board must consider its terms before deciding to remove the officer.

In a closely held corporation, this removal procedure imperils the shareholder/director/officer identity. If there is any concern about one party attempting to freeze out another party by removal, the organizers could require a higher-than-majority margin by the Board when it votes on a removal.

Resignation

Provision should also be made for officers' resignations. The Bylaws could state that officers may resign at any time by delivering a written resignation to the Board of Directors, Chairperson of the Board, President, Secretary, or to any other party or parties that the organizers feel is appropriate.

Vacancies

Since the Act requires that the President, Vice-President, Secretary, and Treasurer shall be elected by the directors, it seems clear that the directors are responsible for filling these offices if they become vacant. Vacancies in other positions could be filled by vote of the body that filled that office.

Chairperson of the Board

The Chairperson's duties obviously include presiding over Board meetings and could include presiding at stockholders' meetings. The section might also say that the Chairperson shall perform such other duties as assigned by the Board.

Vice-Chairperson of the Board

Generally this person performs the duties of the Chairperson in that person's absence, and other duties as may be assigned by the Board.

President

The President is the chief executive officer of the corporation and has general responsibility for managing its business and affairs. The President implements policies established by, and is responsible to, the Board, uses his or her discretion in running the organization's day-to-day affairs, and has general supervisory duties and, in many cases, the ability to "bind" the corporation. Thus, for instance, the President may sign contracts on behalf of the corporation or obligate the corporation on a debt. What is more, the President has the power to do so even in some cases where the Board has not delegated to the President the authority to act as he or she did.

Depending on the nature of the corporation, the organizers may feel it important to set out other presidential duties, for example, discretion in choosing projects, power to hire and fire employees, and so forth. Details are a matter of choice for the organizers. If there are specific duties unique to the President's job, however, these should be expressed in the Bylaws.

Vice-President

The Vice-President generally acts for the President in his or her absence, and performs other duties assigned by the President or the Board. The Vice-President generally does not have power to bind the corporation unless he or she is delegated specific authority on a particular point.

Secretary

The Secretary is responsible for giving notice of shareholder's and directors' meetings, receiving and sending corporate correspondence, recording stockholders on the corporation's books, keeping minutes of stockholders', Board, and Executive Committee meetings, filing reports and statements as required by local law, certifying corporate documents, and performing any other duties assigned by the Board or the President.

Treasurer

The Treasurer is responsible for corporate funds and other corporate valuables. He or she keeps accounts of receipts and expenditures, oversees deposits of the corporation's money and valuables in banks designated by the corporation, renders accounts on request to the President or the Board, and frequently makes disbursements and signs checks.

Other Officers

If there are to be Assistant Vice-Presidents, Assistant Secretaries, Assistant Treasurers, and so forth, their positions and responsibilities could also be briefly listed and described in the Bylaws.

Because certain officers are responsible for certain duties does not mean that they have to perform such duties personally. They must, however, see to it that the tasks are properly performed by whoever has been delegated responsibility for actually doing the work.

Salaries

Officers may receive salaries for their services to the corporation as officers, and the Bylaws could contain a provision reaffirming this. If the organizers want to set or to prohibit salaries for officers, for instance, so that shareholder-officers are rewarded largely or solely through their portions of corporate profits received as dividends, that restriction should be included in the Bylaws.

SECTION FIVE—FINANCIAL MATTERS

The contents of this section clarify various corporate financial transactions such as contracts, loans, checks, and bank deposits.

Contracts

The Bylaws could require that all contracts on behalf of the corporation be authorized by the Board of Directors, or could specifically delegate the authority to enter into contracts to particular officers. In a small corporation, the former provision has some attraction, since all the directors would then have an opportunity to review a contract; however, delegation of authority is more convenient, and unless otherwise stated the President generally has implicit authority to execute ordinary contracts on behalf of the corporation. Extraordinary contracts remain subject to Board approval.

Loans

The Bylaws may provide that no loans shall be made, or debts incurred, in the name of the corporation unless authorized by the Board. Since directors could potentially be liable to the corporation if these actions were taken improperly, it is appropriate that the Board first consider and approve all borrowing. It is also a safety feature for Board members who thereby have an opportunity to examine corporate activities that might be harmful to the corporation.

Checks

The organizers must decide who will manage the corporation's money. The President and the Treasurer are logical choices, but other persons could also be designated. A possible Bylaws provision would be that two persons must always sign the corporation's checks and notes, one person being the President, and the other being any one of a group including the Treasurer, Secretary, Vice-President, or Chairperson of the Board. As a practical matter, the bank where the corporate checking account is maintained will have given the corporation a "signature card" that includes a standard Board resolution establishing the number and identity of permissible signatories. The Board will then choose the signatories, fill out the signature card, and return it to the bank, which will keep it on file. Those listed will be the only signatories the bank will honor unless the Board amends its resolution, fills out another signature card, and files it with the bank.

Deposits

The Bylaws may provide that the corporation's monies shall be deposited in banks selected by the Board, the President, the Treasurer or duly authorized persons. In addition to a conveniently located bank, the corporation should consider such factors as availability of loans, banking services offered, planning assistance available, and whether the bank has experience servicing businesses of a similar size and type.

SECTION SIX—SHARE CERTIFICATE

A share certificate is a piece of paper that evidences a shareholder's interest in a corporation. It may be a simple typewritten instrument containing the vital information regarding the interest it represents, including the name of the corporation, the number of shares represented by the certificate, who owns them, the class of shares, and its par value. The corporate certificate may also be a printed or engraved document. Blank share certificates, with space for appropriate information to be filled in, may be purchased at business stationery and legal supply stores. In fact, an entire corporate kit including share certificates, sample Bylaws, common resolutions, sample minutes, and a stock transfer ledger may be ordered from many legal stationers.

Pursuant to Section 23 of the Model Act, share interests must meet the following requirements:

1. Share interests must be represented by some form of written share certificate.

2. These certificates may be signed by the corporation's President *or* Vice-President *and* Secretary *or* Assistant Secretary.

3. The certificates must contain the corporation's seal. This can be merely a label or could be a corporate stamp that is impressed on the paper. (The latter is available from many printing companies and is generally included in the corporate kit.)

4. Every certificate representing shares issued by a corporation that is authorized by its Articles to issue shares of more than one class or series must state the designations, preferences, limitations, and relative rights of the shares of each class authorized to be issued, and the variations and preferences between shares of each series within a class, or that the corporation will furnish these details.

5. Every share certificate must state that the corporation is organized "under the laws of [the jurisdiction of incorporation]."

6. The shareholder's name must appear on his or her share certificate(s).

7. The certificate must express how many and what class of shares the certificate represents.

8. Each certificate must state the par value of the shares it represents or that the shares are of no par value, whichever is appropriate.

9. Certificates may not be issued until the shares they represent have been paid for.

10. While it is not required, it is wise to include a notation on any shares subject to a shareholders' agreement the terms of that agreement or a summary of the terms.

The Bylaws could include these provisions, and may also establish other rules regarding the corporation's shares, for example, that certificates bear the address as well as name of the shareholder, or a provision that the corporation may require a deposit or bond from a shareholder who loses a certificate and wants the corporation to replace it.

Finally, this section of the Bylaws could describe the procedures for transfers of the corporation's shares, such as notation in an official stock book, proof of stock ownership prior to allowing transfer, physical presentation of the stock certificates, and so forth.

SECTION SEVEN—FISCAL YEAR

This section may state the corporation's fiscal year, or may provide that the fiscal year shall be established by resolution of the Board of Directors. A fiscal year could be the calendar year, January 1–December 31, or any other 12-month interval. If the corporation has a period of greater activity than other times (seasonal, Christmas, etc.), the fiscal year could end just after that period. This allows the annual report and annual meetings to reflect and discuss the results of this period of peak activity.

SECTION EIGHT—CORPORATE SEAL

The corporation is not required to have a formal corporate seal but if it decides to adopt a seal, the seal may be described in the Bylaws, (e.g., "The corporation's seal shall consist of a round figure with the corporation's name written around the circumference") or the Bylaws may provide that the corporation's seal shall be adopted by resolution of the Board of Directors.

SECTION NINE—NOTICE REQUIREMENTS

A general summary of the requirements for notice of various corporate meetings could be included in the Bylaws. In addition, a provision concerning waiver of notice could be included. For instance, the Bylaws could state:

> Whenever any notice is required to be given under the provisions of the law, the Articles of Incorporation, or these Bylaws, a written waiver thereof, signed by the person or persons entitled to said notice, and filed with the records of the meeting, whether before or after the time stated therein, shall be deemed to be the equivalent of such notice. In addition, any stockholders who attend a meeting, in person, or by proxy, without protesting at the commencement of the meeting the lack of proper notice thereof to him or her, or any director who attends a meeting of the Board of Directors, or any member of any committee

who attends a committee meeting, without protesting, at the commencement of the meeting, such lack of notice, shall be conclusively deemed to have waived notice of such meeting.

SECTION TEN—PROCEDURES FOR AMENDMENTS

The procedure for amending the corporation's Articles of Incorporation is prescribed by Section 59 of the Model Act. This procedure requires that:

(a) The Board of Directors shall adopt a resolution setting forth the proposed amendment and directing that it be submitted to a vote at a meeting of shareholders, which may be either an annual or a special meeting.

(b) Written or printed notice setting forth the proposed amendment or a summary of the changes to be effected thereby shall be given to each shareholder of record entitled to vote at such meeting within the time and in the manner provided in this chapter for the giving of notice of meetings of shareholders. If the meeting be an annual meeting, the proposed amendment or such summary shall be included in the notice of such annual meeting.

(c) At such meeting a vote of the shareholders entitled to vote shall be taken on the proposed amendment. The proposed amendment shall be adopted upon receiving the affirmative vote of the holders of at least a majority of the outstanding shares entitled to vote, unless any class of shares is entitled to vote as a class in respect thereof, as hereinafter provided, in which event the proposed amendment shall be adopted upon receiving the affirmative vote of the holders of at least two-thirds of the outstanding shares of each class of shares entitled to vote as a class in respect thereof and of the total outstanding shares entitled to vote.

(d) Any number of amendments may be submitted to the shareholders, and voted upon by them, at one meeting.

In addition, the Bylaws should describe how they themselves may be amended or altered. Pursuant to Section 27 of the Model Act, the Bylaws may be amended by majority vote of the Board of Directors, unless that power is granted to the shareholders in the Articles of Incorporation. Vesting this responsibility in the shareholders is one way for the shareholders of a small corporation to keep a rein on the corporation's management; however, if there are many shareholders, granting the shareholders the power to amend the Bylaws may be unworkable. If the organizers decide that the Bylaws may be amended by the Board, they should specify whether an amendment requires a greater-than-majority vote (e.g., two-thirds, three-fifths, etc.). As with other high-vote requirements discussed earlier, a greater-than-majority vote requirement for Bylaws changes would tend to preserve the existing Bylaws and the management structure they produced.

SECTION ELEVEN—COMMITTEES

The Model Act recognizes two types of committees, those exercising the authority of the Board of Directors in the management of the corporation, and those with lesser responsibilities. The former type of committee is called an Executive Committee. Provision for an Executive Committee in the Articles or Bylaws is optional; however, if the organizers envision that the Board may want to delegate some or all of its duties to a smaller (and perhaps more efficient) group of directors, the Articles or Bylaws must contain a provision allowing the Board to pass a resolution approving the delegation of power to an Executive Committee. A delegation may be particularly useful when there is only one or two organizers, but a statutory requirement of three directors. The one or two organizers must operate with others in order to comply with the three-director requirement. If the organizers do not want an outsider to interfere with running the corporation, the Articles or Bylaws could provide for the possibility of an Executive Committee that will exercise the authority of the Board in the management of the corporation. Then the Board, by majority vote, must pass a resolution that creates the Committee and delegates authority to it.

The one or two organizers/directors who want to maintain control of the corporation may then designate themselves as the members of the Executive Committee and run the corporation virtually unmolested by the other director or directors.

Any committee exercising the Board's authority *must* be *selected by* and be comprised of directors. The Article or Bylaw provision authorizing such a committee could state the following:

> The Board of Directors, by resolution adopted by a majority of the Board, may appoint an Executive Committee consisting of at least one director who shall exercise such powers and functions of the Board as provided in the resolution of the Board establishing such Committee.

If the Board delegates its authority to an Executive Committee, it is not thereby relieved of its responsibilities nor are directors who do not serve on the Committee relieved of their responsibilities and potential liabilities as directors (Section 42 of the Model Act). It may, therefore, be wise for the Board to reserve some control over the Executive Committee. For example, the Board might retain the power to dissolve the Committee at any time, the power to limit the areas in which the Committee may act, or the power to veto any Executive Committee decisions.

The Bylaws may express the manner of selection of Executive Committee members, the authority of the Committee, the term of office of members of the Committee, and any operating procedures that the organizers wish to impose on the Committee—including quorum requirements, the percentage of vote necessary to carry a motion, procedures for filling vacancies on the Committee, whether meetings by phone or action by written consent are permitted, and who will preside at Committee meetings. All or part of the foregoing may also be contained in the resolution of the Board that establishes the Committee. The procedural details could even be left to the Committee to determine once it comes into existence. However, an Executive Committee is a powerful group, and the Board or the organizers may want to define its operations specifically before it goes to work.

Common choices concerning quorum and vote requirements for Executive Committee actions are that a majority of the Committee constitutes a quorum and that a motion is carried by majority vote of the committee members present at a meeting at which a quorum is present. If the Executive Committee has been delegated all or much of the powers of the Board, however, especially where there is a large Board, there may be reason to impose a high-quorum and/or high-vote requirement, since under the majority-quorum, majority-vote procedure, the following is possible:

Twenty-one-person Board delegates its authority to a five-person Executive Committee. Three members of the Committee constitute a quorum, therefore two members voting together could carry the vote. Thus, the 21-person Board could be subject to, and potentially liable for, the decisions of two Executive Committee members.

The preceding situation could be avoided by increasing the quorum for Executive Committee meetings, the vote requirement, or both, or requiring a majority (two-third, three-fourth, etc.) vote of the *entire* committee to carry a motion. (These considerations are not relevant, however, if the *purpose* of the Executive Committee is to centralize control to prevent a certain director or directors from interfering with the organizers' management of the corporation.)

The differences between creating a committee that exercises the authority of the Board, and creating any other type of committee, are significant enough to reemphasize. If any committee is to possess the authority of the Board, the Bylaws must permit its existence, that is, say that the Board *may* create such a committee. Then if the Board later decides to implement such a committee, a majority of the entire Board must pass a resolution creating the committee. This resolution could include the power of the Board of dissolve the Committee, the right of the Board to veto Committee decisions, the power of the Committee to act *only* during intervals between meetings of the Board, the procedure for selecting members of the Executive Committee, and so forth.

Committees that do not exercise powers of the Board do not require prior authorization in the Bylaws. To create such a committee, the Board need only pass a resolution designating the committee and appointing its members. The Bylaws may, but need not, state that the Board has the authority to create this second type of committee.

These committees may be either "standing" or "ad hoc." Ad hoc committees are created in response to one-of-a-kind situations, for example, the Ad Hoc Committee on Merger with Company X. Standing committees are continuing committees created to deal with areas of continuous concern to the corporation, for example, advertising, investment, charitable contributions, and so forth. While ad hoc committees disband after dealing with the situation that motivated their creation, standing committees remain to deal with continuing issues that arise in their areas.

It is also important to remember that a committee exercising the Board's powers may be comprised only of directors, while outsiders may serve on the other types of committees. The Bylaws *could* require these other committees to comprise only directors, or shareholders, but such a restriction would exclude some useful experts, who, although they were not directors or stockholders, nevertheless could be very helpful to the corporation (lawyers, accountants, etc.). Since any decisions by such committees are only recommendations to the Board, there is not a delegation of policy-making authority to nondirectors.

10

CORPORATE OPERATIONS

The preceding chapters have examined many of the legal requirements and legal alternatives applicable to corporations and their principals. This chapter will deal with some of the more practical aspects of corporate existence and, where appropriate, the legal implications of those realities. The assumptions for the following discussion are that the corporation is (or the planned corporation will be) a closely held corporation and that the principals are (or will be) directly involved in its management and, in many cases, with the product or service provided by the corporation.

In such cases, there is a natural tendency for the owners to treat the corporation's business and property as if they were their own. That is, they use corporate property in their personal activities; they commingle corporate and personal funds; they add money to, or take money from, the corporation without appropriate authorization or record keeping; and they fail to document important corporate decisions or activities. In fact, record keeping of any kind is often neglected.

While it is true that in many cases such conduct does not lead to dire consequences, there are several significant problems that may arise. They involve the government, fellow shareholders, and third persons dealing with the corporation.

GOVERNMENTAL RELATIONS

Problems with government take several common forms. Perhaps the most common is the failure of the corporation to file annual reports. Most states require corporations organized in that state or licensed to do business there to file an annual report with the Secretary of State (or other official). The report typically requires the corporation to inform the state of who its directors, officers, and occasionally, major shareholders are. It may also require such information as the number of shares outstanding or the name and address of the registered agent. There is usually a small fee connected with the filing.

The report form is usually mailed well in advance of its due date to the registered agent of the corporation at its registered address (both as listed with the state by the corporation). The registered agent should then, if he or she is a principal, fill out and return the form. If the agent is not a principal, he or she should forward the form to an officer of the corporation who should complete and return it. The failure to file the form generally carries with it a cash penalty and, often, after successive failures, an automatic revocation of the corporate charter. While the charter may be reinstated retroactively, there is some question of individual liability during the period of revocation.

There is also a problem concerning the proper licensing of "foreign" corporations.* Unlike individuals (or partnerships or sole proprietorships), corporations cannot travel from state to state without being subject to restrictions. Each state may legally close its doors to foreign corporations or severely restrict them. In fact, this does not occur and all states allow foreign corporations in. The procedure is for a foreign corporation to file with the state where it wants to do business a document very similar to Articles of Incorporation.

Among other things, the foreign corporation must list a registered agent and registered office in the new state. Once filed, the foreign corporation receives a certificate of authority for a foreign corporation which entitles it to do business in the foreign state. To keep that authority current, the foreign corporation must file an annual report similar to the one filed by a domestic corporation. This is in addition to filing a report with the state of incorporation. Failure to file results in penalties, including a revocation of authority to do business. A foreign corporation which never had authority, or has had its authority revoked, yet continues to do business in the foreign state, subjects itself to civil and sometimes criminal penalties and may subject its principals to personal liability.

---

* Corporations incorporated in a state, but doing business in a different state are said to be foreign corporations in the second state. They are "domestic" corporations in the state of incorporation.

Another potential difficulty with the government that is raised by inadequate record keeping concerns taxation. In order to arrive at a corporation's tax liability, it is necessary to list items of income and deductible expense. If records are not adequately kept, merely determining the appropriate figures will be difficult. Of perhaps greater concern, however, is a challenge by the Internal Revenue Service or the state tax department to the figures used. In these situations, the disallowance of a deduction or credit will result in higher taxes, interest, and perhaps civil penalties. In extreme cases, criminal sanctions could be imposed. Therefore, it is critical for principals to keep, or instruct corporate employees to keep, good records and to document important transactions. This support is necessary to justify any challenged item.

RECORD KEEPING

Similarly, decisions and activities, financial and otherwise, must be documented to protect minority interests from overreaching by the majority. Meetings must be held; notice of these meetings must be given, as required by statute or Bylaws, or notice must be waived; minutes must reflect decisions made and should reflect the discussion leading to those decisions; and minutes and supporting documents should be kept in an orderly way and in a safe and accessible place.

The value of good record keeping also comes up in buy-sell situations between shareholders. These situations may be the result of a formal shareholders' agreement or of a more informal desire of one (or more) shareholder who wishes to get out of the corporation or of another shareholder(s) who wishes to have a larger stake in the corporation. Either of these might arise in friendly or hostile circumstances.

In the friendly situation, negotiations may have moved along to the point of determining a formula for the price of the purchase or sale of shares, but the books, due to inadequate record keeping, do not accurately reflect the value of the corporation. In the hostile situation, it may be that the lack of record keeping is the cause of the demand to be bought out.* A minority shareholder may feel that the majority shareholder is running the corporation for personal benefit and in disregard of minority concerns. In such a case, the lack of records may be designed

---

* It should be noted that, in the absence of a shareholders' agreement to the contrary, a minority shareholder has no right to be bought out. Conversely, a majority shareholder is not obligated to take a minority shareholder out of his or her investment. So long as the minority shareholder is not being oppressed, a buy-out depends on the voluntary agreement of the parties.

to mask the true state of affairs of the corporation and itself could be a basis for a lawsuit by a dissatisfied minority shareholder.

PIERCING THE CORPORATE VEIL

In addition, the lack of corporate formality, including the lack of good record keeping, could in some extreme circumstances remove the corporate protection against individual liability from the principals. This process, known as "piercing the corporate veil," arises when a claimant against the corporation finds the corporation's assets insufficient to meet his or her claim. The claimant will then ask the judge in a lawsuit against the corporation and its shareholders and directors to disregard the corporation's existence and hold the principals individually liable for what appears to be a claim only against the corporation. The basis for this request is that since the principals have not treated the business as if it were a corporation, they should not have the protection of limited liability. Among the things the claimant will want to point to are the lack of corporate meetings, minutes, financial documents, and records, the use of corporate assets for personal purposes, and the commingling of corporate and personal assets.

While it is rare for a court actually to "pierce the corporate veil," the risks are sufficiently serious so that shareholders should beware. Since it is relatively simple to prevent a piercing, being forewarned is, indeed, being forearmed. All that is necessary is to comply with the state's legal requirements concerning corporate formation and operation, keep adequate records, and maintain a separation between personal and corporate activities. If there is to be some overlap in this area, be sure it is done with full disclosure to other directors/shareholders, with majority (or, if necessary, super-majority) consent and with a written record of the decision.

11

TAXES

FEDERAL INCOME TAXES

Since a corporation is recognized by the law as an individual entity apart from those who make it up, it stands to reason that a corporation will be taxed as an individual. Section 11 of the Internal Revenue Code (IRC), indeed, imposes an income tax on corporations. In many ways, the corporate tax is similar to that imposed on individuals but there are differences. Among the most important differences are the rate structure and the items that may be deducted. The Tax Reform Act of 1986 (TRA) highlights many of these differences through several changes in the law. This chapter and the next will explain some of federal tax law as it applies to corporations and their shareholders. It should be kept in mind, however, that the Internal Revenue Code is enormously complex with implications and ramifications not always readily observable, even to the practiced eye. These subtleties have been exacerbated by TRA. Therefore, while tax planning is an undertaking of great importance, it should not be undertaken without experienced, professional assistance.

To begin with the basics, Section 63 of the Internal Revenue Code defines the taxable income of a corporation as its "gross income minus the deductions allowed [by the Code]." This means that in determining how much tax a corporation has to pay, one must first determine its total income. From that amount may be subtracted allowable "deductions," that is, amounts actually spent or otherwise allowed pursuant to the Code, particularly Parts VI and VIII (Sections 161–194 and 241–250, which include deductions for interest paid, rental payments on business property, salaries paid, depreciation, bad debts, etc). Once the deductible amounts have been subtracted, you are left with "taxable income." It is against this amount that the tax rates are applied. It is here that one of the major changes wrought by the TRA appears, generally to the benefit of the small corporation.

The benefit comes from the reduction in corporate tax rates. The highest rate has been reduced from 46 to 34%, effective for tax years *after* June 30, 1987.

Essentially there are three corporate tax brackets: for taxable income up to $50,000, the rate is 15%; for taxable income in excess of $50,000 but not more than $75,000, the rate is 25%; and for taxable income over $75,000, the rate is 34%. (Some of this benefit is reduced for corporations with taxable income in excess of $100,000. For them there is a 5% surtax phased in from the $100,000 level to $335,000. At that point, the benefit of the graduated tax has been eliminated and the corporation is paying at a flat 34% for all of its taxable income.) There is an additional surtax of 3% (up to a maximum additional tax of $100,000) for corporations with a taxable income in excess of $15,000,000.

The way the corporate tax works may best be understood by a simple example. Assume Corporation X provides a service, for example, gardening. In its tax year, it receives $175,000 for performing its gardening services and also $10,000 interest on its bank account. Therefore, its income is $185,000. From this, it may deduct (among other possible items) salaries it paid to employees—$60,000; rent for its office and its equipment—$15,000; and insurance, phone, and utilities—$5,000. This total deduction of $80,000 must be subtracted from the $185,000 income leaving a taxable income of $105,000:

Income	$185,000
Deductible Expenses	−80,000
Taxable Income	$105,000

The corporate tax rates are then applied to the taxable income of Corporation X. For the first $50,000 of taxable income, the rate is 15%—giving a tax of $7,500. The next $25,000 is taxed at 25% for a tax of $6,250. The next $30,000 is taxed at 34%—for a tax of $10,200. Finally, there is a 5% surtax on everything over $100,000 (up to $335,000). In this case, the surtax is applied to $5,000—giving a tax of $250. The tax for each of these brackets is then added up to arrive at Corporation X's tax liability. Again, a short chart may be helpful in summarizing:

Corporation X's Income		Corporate Tax Rate	Corporation X's Tax
First	$ 50,000	15%	$ 7,500
Next	25,000	25%	6,250
Remaining	30,000	34%	10,200
Excess over $100,000	5,000	5% (surtax)	250
	$105,000		$24,200

It should be noted that the total tax to be paid does not correspond to any of the marginal tax brackets. In fact, the amount owed is just a bit more than 23% of the taxable income of the corporation. This is because of the "graduated" element of the tax structure. This means that corporations, like individuals, are taxed on *brackets* of income. If Corporation A had only $50,000 of taxable income, it would pay the same tax on that $50,000 as Corporation X paid on the *first* $50,000 of its $105,000 taxable income.*

Returning to our example of Corporation X, it has a tax liability of $24,200 on taxable income of $105,000. Assuming, for this example, that the taxable income is synonymous with pretax profit, Corporation X had $80,800 after-tax profit ($105,000 − $24,200 = $80,800). Assume further that the corporation needed to retain some of that profit for corporate purposes and wished to distribute the rest as dividends to its shareholders. Therefore, the Board decides to keep $50,000 and to distribute $30,800 to the shareholders. Each individual shareholder receiving a portion of that distribution is required to report it to the Internal Revenue Service (IRS), thereby subjecting it to tax as part of his or her personal income. Thus the same pool of money that was taxed as part of the corporation's income is taxed again as part of the shareholder's income. This is known as "double taxation" and is a drawback to incorporating. Despite this fact, many people believe that the advantages of incorporation far outweigh this disadvantage. In addition, there are ways of avoiding or minimizing the effect of double taxation and these will be explored in Chapters 12 and 13.

* Again, it should be noted that the 5% surtax has the effect of reducing and, eventually, eliminating the "graduated" feature. Once a corporation reaches $335,000 of taxable income, the 5% additional tax on everything over $100,000 (i.e., $235,000) results in that corporation paying, as a practical matter, 34% on all its income.

First	$50,000 at 15% = $ 7,500
Next	25,000 at 25% = 6,250
Remaining	260,000 at 34% = 88,400
Excess Over	100,000 at 5% = 11,750
$335,000	$113,900 = Total Tax
	Total Tax is 34% of income

TAX PROCEDURES

Besides its obligation to report and pay taxes on its income, a corporation must fulfill several other requirements of the Internal Revenue Code. As a taxpayer, for instance, a corporation must obtain a taxpayer's ID number, which is the corporate equivalent of a Social Security number. It is obtained by filing IRS Form SS-4. In addition, a corporation is responsible for filing a corporate income tax return every year on Form 1120 (or, for a Subchapter S corporation, on Form 1120S). If the corporation has chosen a business year of January through December, its tax return must be filed on or before March 15 following the close of its business year. If any other business year has been chosen, the return must be filed on or before the fifteenth day of the third month following the close of that business year.

If the corporation's income tax is not filed within the prescribed time (and if no extension has been granted), a penalty tax is imposed for *each month* the return is overdue.

Estimated Tax Returns

In addition to filing an annual tax return, a corporation may be required to make periodic payments of its estimated taxes during the tax year. The IRS publishes a worksheet, Form 1120-W, "U.S. Corporation Worksheet for Computation of Estimated Income Tax," which is an aid to computing these estimated tax payments.

If the corporation must make estimated tax payments, these payments must be deposited in specially designated commercial banks or Federal Reserve Banks, accompanied by Form 503, "Federal Tax Deposit, Corporation Income Taxes."

Reporting Dividends Paid

If the corporation pays dividends during the year, it may have to file a Form 1099-DIV for each shareholder who received $10 or more in dividends. The key to this reporting requirement is whether the dividend was paid out of the corporation's "earnings and profits." Generally this means that if the dividends were derived from profits of the current tax year, or from profits accumulated from previous years, the corporation must report using Form 1099-DIV. If the dividends are not paid from the corporation's "earnings and profits," but are paid out of the corporation's capital surplus, the corporation must report these using "Corporate Report of Nontaxable Dividends Schedule A," Form 1096. These dividends are not taxable because they are *not* income. It is as if the shareholder is getting back part of his or her capital contribution. The result is a reduction of the shareholder's basis in his or her stockholding.

Employment Taxes

A significant tax obligation, and one that apparently causes small businesses constant difficulty, is the collection and payment of "employment taxes." The corporation's first step along this line is to apply for an "Employer Identification Number," on Form SS-4. This number will then be the corporation's ID number for all its contacts with the IRS, not only those relating to employees.

If the corporation has one or more "employees," it may have to withhold their federal income taxes from their wages. An "employee" as opposed to an "independent contractor," is a person who performs services and who is subject to the will and control of an employer, both as to *what* shall be done, and *how* it shall be done. If there is a question whether a person is an "employee," the corporation may file a Form SS-8 for a determination of that individual's status.

There are two basic types of taxes that the corporation is responsible for in connection with its employees. The corporation must withhold a portion of each employee's wages for payment of the employee's own income taxes, if the amount of his or her wages received during each payroll period exceeds the amount of the employee's "withholding allowances" for the same period. "Withholding allowances" are exemptions from what the employer would generally have to withhold from a particular salary. The exemptions are based on such factors as the employee's marital status, the number of dependents he or she has, and so forth.

In order to discover how many withholding allowances each employee is claiming, the corporation should have each employee complete a Form W-4, "Employee's Withholding Allowance Certificate," when the employee begins employment.

The corporation is also responsible for withholding Social Security and Medicare taxes from every employee's wages. *Both the corporation and the employee must pay a Social Security and Medicare tax on the employee's wages.* This tax is calculated as a percentage of each employee's salary, up to a certain maximum salary figure—with the salary in excess of that figure not subject to Social Security tax but still subject to the Medicare tax. The corporation must file quarterly returns on Form 941 to report on its withholding from employees' wages and its own payments of these taxes.

Generally, the corporation must deposit the income and Social Security and Medicare taxes it withholds, together with those taxes it pays on behalf of each employee, with an authorized commercial bank or Federal Reserve Bank. Each deposit should be accompanied by a "Federal Tax Deposit," Form 501. How frequently the corporation must make deposits is determined by the amount of taxes owed.

On or before January 31 of each year, the corporation must also file an "Unemployment Tax Return," Form 940, and pay an unemployment tax. This is a corporate tax and may not be withheld from an employee's wages. This tax may also be payable in quarterly installments, depending on the total amount of the tax due.

These employment-related taxes are very important and, as mentioned previously, it is the corporation's responsibility to see that they are paid and that the proper sums are withheld and paid from employees' wages. If the corporation fails to collect and deposit these taxes, it subjects itself and, potentially, the corporate official or officials responsible for payment of tax obligations, to liability for the entire amount owed—including the portions that should have been withheld from *employees'* wages. If the corporation has not collected taxes properly for several years, this could amount to a huge sum. If the corporation does not pay what it owes, the IRS may seize the assets of the corporation and sell them in order to satisfy amounts due.

The IRS publishes a "Circular E, Employer's Tax Guide"; a "Business Tax Kit," Publication 454; and a "Tax Guide for Small Businesses," all of which are helpful and explain in greater detail the tax obligations and procedures discussed above.

In addition to the payment of federal taxes, many states impose income, real and personal property, and sales taxes on corporations operating within their borders. Corporate organizers and officers should check with their state's tax department or with a local attorney for information and assistance.

12

SUBCHAPTER S
AND OTHER
TAX OPTIONS FOR A
SMALL BUSINESS

Chapter 11 touched on the corporation's basic tax responsibilities. These responsibilities are applicable to corporations of any size. This chapter deals with a few tax problems and planning opportunities of small business corporations. After identifying the problems, the chapter will address Subchapter S corporations, Section 1244 stock, and debt financing.

TAX DRAWBACKS OF INCORPORATION

One of the significant drawbacks of incorporation is the double tax to which corporate income may be exposed. First, corporate income is taxed to the corporation. Next, that part of the corporate income which is distributed to shareholders as dividends is subject to tax again as income of the recipient. This led to the development of a number of methods designed to avoid the double tax. One method was for shareholder-directors not to declare a dividend. Without a distribution, there would be no second tax. Unfortunately, there also would be no dividend income to the shareholders. In many cases, this would be an undesirable characteristic for shareholders.

Congress, in an attempt to crack down on this undistributed corporate income and any accompanying *unneeded* accumulations of cash at the corporate level, passed Section 531 et seq. of the Internal Revenue Code (IRC), which penalizes such accumulations for any corporation "formed or availed of for the purpose of avoiding the income tax with respect to its shareholders . . . by permitting earnings and profits to accumulate instead of being distributed" (IRC Section 532(a)). For an accumulation to be permissible, it must be limited to what is "reasonably" needed for the business. "Need," of course, changes from business to business and from time to time within the same business. The statute also permits an amount of earnings that can be accumulated regardless of need. The formula for determining this amount for any business is found in IRC Section 535(c)(2).

In an effort to avoid this penalty while still avoiding a taxable distribution to shareholders, attempts were made, particularly in closely held corporations where shareholders were also employees or otherwise involved in the business, to distribute its "profits" in the form of nontaxable fringe benefit expenses. For instance, health, life, and disability insurance are obvious ways for the corporation to pick up expenses that are deductible for it but that would be *nondeductible* if paid by the shareholder-employee. Less obvious are meals, automobiles, gasoline, parking, and other similar items paid for (and deducted by) the corporation and received, tax free, by the shareholder. Again, Congress and the Internal Revenue Service (IRS) have made attempts to eliminate or reduce the availability of some of these devices but their success to date has been limited.

A second tax drawback to the corporate form is that the tax benefit of net business losses (the excess of expenses over income) does not, as a rule, pass through directly to the shareholders. While shareholders do not wish their corporations to incur actual losses, if losses are incurred, the shareholders would generally prefer to have those losses passed through to them individually in order to offset their personal incomes from other sources.

Moreover, some "losses" appear only in the accountant's books rather than in the dollars and cents of business operations. A typical form of such losses is known as "depreciation." Depreciation (now also called Accelerated Cost Recovery System—ACRS) is an allowance permitted by IRC Sections 167 and 168 of a reasonable deduction for the loss, due to wear and tear (including obsolescence), of a so-called capital asset. The asset, in order to qualify for depreciation, must be used in a trade or business or be held for the production of income and have a useful life of more than one year. Personal, nonbusiness items, are not eligible for the depreciation deduction.

While there are many ways to calculate the depreciation deduction, a simple example should suffice for the purpose of this book. Suppose Company X bought a machine for $10,000. Assume also the machine was expected to run and be productive for five years before it needed to be replaced. Since the asset, the machine, was to last for an extended period (more than merely the tax year in which it was purchased), the tax law generally requires the taxpayer to deduct the cost of that machine over its productive life rather than all at once in the year of purchase. The *actual* life of the machine, however, is speculative, so various tax conventions have been developed to accommodate the need for some certainty in the tax law. Therefore, if the type of machine typically lasts for five years, the tax code allows the taxpayer to use that term as the useful life of the asset for the purpose of the depreciation deduction.

The actual amount of the depreciation deduction is determined by dividing the asset's basis (normally, its cost less any "salvage value") by its useful life. In our example, you would divide $10,000 (the machine's cost, or basis) by 5 (the machine's useful life). This would give the taxpayer a deduction of $2,000 for each of the five years of the asset's life. The idea is that when the asset finally wears out and needs to be replaced, its cost would have been fully deducted with annual tax savings to the taxpayer to help replace the asset.*

In many cases, however, the asset survives for a much longer period than its prescribed useful life, or the asset's purchase was financed by a borrowing to be paid back over a period longer than the asset's statutory useful life. In some cases, primarily in the area of real property, the asset may actually *appreciate* in value over time. Nevertheless, the depreciation deduction may still be taken under one of the standard formulas permitted in the Internal Revenue Code. Therefore, in any particular year, the deduction for depreciation may not correspond to any actual expenditure or to any real loss in value suffered by the company. These "paper" losses (those found only in the accountant's records) are the type businesspeople desire when they speak of "tax losses." Unfortunately for the typical shareholder, these losses, as others, do not pass through the corporation to benefit the shareholders. Rather, the corporation may take the losses to offset its own income. If the losses exceed the corporate income, the excess loss may be carried over to subsequent years to offset corporate income in those years. The carryover would be added to the losses for

---

* There are many other methods of calculating the amount of depreciation and a wealth of complexities involved. It is important to speak to a trained tax advisor to determine how depreciation affects your business.

the year in question, and if losses still exceeded income the corporation would carry the excess over into the next year, and so on until the carry-overs were used up (i.e., until income in a particular year equals or exceeds losses plus any loss carryover). The shareholders, however, would not get a direct benefit from such losses.

The effect of this process is the logical extension of the concept of a corporation as a separate entity. The corporation is a taxpayer in its own right. As such, *it,* and not its shareholders, uses the tax benefits accorded by depreciation and other write-offs. The only benefit derived by the shareholders would be the reduction or elimination of corporate income which, in turn, reduces or eliminates corporate tax obligations, leaving more after-tax money in the corporate treasury. This money can be used for some combination of corporate expansion, corporate reserves, or distribution as dividends to shareholders.

SUBCHAPTER S CORPORATIONS

There are provisions in the tax law that allow corporate income or losses to pass untaxed through the corporation. Instead, the income or loss is taxed directly to the shareholder on a pro rata basis. That is, if a shareholder owns 50% of the corporation's stock, that shareholder takes 50% of the income or losses on his or her personal tax return.

For example, assume that Corporation X has taxable income of $20,000 this year. This sum would be subject to a 15% tax. Therefore X would pay $3,000. The $17,000 remaining could be distributed as dividends to X's shareholders. If X had only one shareholder, Jane Doe, who earned a salary of $20,000 per year, and X paid her a dividend of the $17,000 remaining after taxes, her total income would be $37,000 and would put her in the 28% tax bracket. Disregarding deductions for this example, Doe would be subject to approximately $7,487 in taxes. Thus the total tax liability in this situation is

$$\$3000 \text{ (Corporation X)} + \$7,487 \text{ (Doe)} = \$10,487.$$

However, if Corporation X elected to be taxed as an S Corporation, there would be no $3,000 corporate tax. X's $20,000 of taxable income would "pass through" to Doe (this would be true regardless of whether the $20,000 was actually paid to her or retained by the corporation). Doe, therefore, would have an income of $40,000 for the year—$20,000 of salary, plus $20,000 "passed through" to her from the corporation. She would be subject to approximately $8,327 in taxes on that $40,000 income.

The total tax in this situation is, therefore, only $8,327, $2,160 less than without the S Corporation election.

As this example indicates, there are some major advantages to obtaining Subchapter S status. The most obvious is the elimination of tax at the corporate level. For the purpose of *federal* income taxation (the relationship to state income tax is discussed later in this section), the S Corporation is treated as if it was a partnership. For the purpose of limited liability, the shareholders of the S Corporation retain their insulation from personal liability for corporate acts. Therefore the S Corporation offers shareholders the best of both worlds; no corporate tax and limited liability.

There are, however, a number of disadvantages to electing Subchapter S status. Some of these are apparent merely by examining the law applicable to S Corporations while others are more subtle and hidden in the financial experiences of the corporation. Therefore, organizers should do a careful analysis of their corporate situation before deciding on whether to seek Subchapter S status.

Advantages of Subchapter S Status

There are advantages to Subchapter S status other than the elimination of the corporate income tax. For instance, there is no *corporate* tax on the profitable sale of corporate assets or upon the liquidation of the corporation. If the corporation were not a Subchapter S Corporation, there would be a corporate tax on such transactions as well as a tax on amounts distributed to shareholders. Another advantage, one that is tied to the absence of the corporate tax, is that corporate losses are passed, subject to certain restrictions, directly to shareholders. This means that shareholders may be able to use corporate losses to offset their income from other sources. In Subchapter C Corporations, losses are not passed on to shareholders but must be carried forward by the corporation and applied to its income in subsequent years.

The pass-through to shareholders available under Subchapter S also has a negative aspect that is often overlooked by organizers. The pass-through applies not only to corporate losses but to corporate income as well. This can have negative consequences when the corporation has income that it retains instead of distributing it to the shareholders. The shareholders will be taxed on their percentage of corporate income regardless of the fact that they did not receive it.

Even if this is the case, however, careful tax planning can minimize the impact of the pass-throughs. For instance, in family-owned businesses, the pass-through of income can be used to benefit the overall family tax situation by giving shares of stock in the S Corporation to children in the family who are likely to be taxed at a lower rate than the adults. If the adult shareholders were going to provide funds for the children anyway (for general support or for college, etc.), this *income-splitting* device has major tax advantages. All that is called for is that the adult give a gift of corporate stock to the children. If the children are over 14 years old, their share of the corporate income will be taxed at their rate (probably the lowest current rate) rather than their parents' which is likely to be higher. For this device to be valid, there must be a real transfer of the shares to the children. IRS often examines these transactions to be sure that they are not shams.

Another advantage of Subchapter S status includes the fact that it also eliminates two other taxes that may be imposed on Subchapter C Corporations (business corporations that do not obtain Subchapter S status). These are the *accumulated earnings tax* and the *personal holding company tax.*

The accumulated earnings tax was developed in part to keep shareholders in a closely held corporation from accumulating earnings in the corporation without distributing them to the shareholders as dividends. This accumulation had the effect of eliminating the double tax since shareholders never received distributions of corporate income on which the second tax would be imposed. Shareholders had incentive to retain corporate earnings until they could be withdrawn in a tax-favored way. To deter this practice, Congress placed a heavy tax on accumulated corporate earnings above $250,000 unless the corporation could show that the excess accumulation was needed for legitimate corporate purposes. Since there is no tax on corporate income in Subchapter S Corporations, there is no prohibition on accumulating corporate earnings. They are taxed regardless of whether they are distributed to shareholders.

The other penalty tax was placed on personal holding companies. Personal holding companies were companies set up by individuals for the purpose of holding their personal, income-producing assets. The individual owners could control the timing and method of distributing this income. To limit this practice, Congress established a penalty tax in addition to the normal income tax imposed on the undistributed income of a personal holding company.

To be classified as a personal holding company, at least 60% of a corporation's income must come from passive sources such as rents, royalties, dividends, or interest. In addition, to be considered a personal holding company, at least 50% (by value) of its stock must have been held by not more than 5 persons at any point during the second half of its tax year. Few active corporations need be concerned about the tax on personal holding companies. In any event, Subchapter S Corporations are totally exempt from the imposition of this tax because shareholders are taxed on all corporate income, distributed or not.

Disadvantages of Subchapter S Status

We have already seen the major disadvantage of Subchapter S status. That is that shareholders are taxed on so-called "phantom income," income received by the corporation but not distributed to the shareholders. There are many ways in which income would be deemed "phantom," the primary one being the re-investment of corporate income into the business. The effect of this scenario would be to tax shareholders on income they never received.

If the corporation had remained a C Corporation, the re-invested profits would be taxed only at the corporate rates. Since this income is not distributed to shareholders, there would be no personal tax on it. In addition, depending on the income level of the corporation, the corporate tax rate might be lower than the personal rate. For instance, the lowest bracket, 15%, covers the first $22,100 of taxable income for single individuals, but goes all the way up to $50,000 of taxable income for corporations. This suggests that if taxable income is to be left in a corporation, it might be appropriate to retain C status for the purpose of accumulating earnings.

An example will help to clarify the problem. Assume a corporation has a single shareholder who is in the 31% tax bracket and who is also the corporation's only employee from which he or she derives his or her entire income. Assume, further, that the corporation has net income *before* deductions for salaries of $100,000. If the corporation was an S Corporation, the tax to the shareholder would be $26,522 regardless of how much of the corporate income was actually distributed. If, however, the corporation was a C Corporation and the shareholder took a $50,000 salary, he or she would owe a tax (disregarding for the purposes of this example all deductions) of $11,127. If the remaining $50,000 was left in the corporation, the corporation would pay $7,500 in tax. Thus, the total tax would be $18,627 or $7,895 less than for the S Corporation shareholder.

There are, however, other tax consequences to the payment or nonpayment of salaries. When salaries are paid, there is for the corporation a payroll tax of 6.2% for Social Security and a 1.45% tax for Medicare. This is in addition to any withholding from the employees' pay and is a tax directly on the corporation. In fact, the corporation is obligated to pay the Medicare tax even after the employee has reached the maximum level of social security wages and is no longer required to contribute. If a C Corporation pays a salary to its shareholder/employee, it will be liable for the 7.65% tax. If the S Corporation pays a salary to its employee, it, too, must pay the payroll tax. But the shareholder/employee of the S Corporation will be able to limit, within reason, the salary he or she takes from the corporation and thereby limit the application of the payroll tax. Nevertheless, the spread between the corporate tax rate and the individual rate in a particular situation may make it appropriate to remain a C Corporation, increase salaries, and pay the extra payroll tax. The net result might still be to reduce the overall tax burden on the corporation and shareholder as a group. You should check with a tax planner to determine the best mix and status for your situation.

There are a number of other disadvantages of S status. Two of these with the most pervasive potential are limitations on deductions and limitations on choosing a fiscal year. The limitation on deductions really involves two different kinds of limitations. One is a limitation on deducting the cost of fringe benefits such as health, accident, and life insurance or meals and hotel costs for shareholder/employees who own 2% or more of the corporation's stock. This means that if the corporation had a health insurance plan that covered employees at a cost of, for example, $300 per month/per employee, the cost of this plan would normally be deducted from corporate income in arriving at taxable income.

If, on the other hand, any of the covered employees owned 2% or more of the corporation's stock, the costs associated with *their* benefits (i.e., $300 per month apiece) would *not* be deductible from the corporation's income. This would mean that full cost of the insurance attributable to the shareholder/employees who hold 2% or more of the corporate stock would be passed through as income to all the shareholders (including non-employee shareholders), pro rata, and subject to taxation as part of their income. If the corporation were a C Corporation, the entire cost of the insurance would be deductible against the corporation's income, regardless of whether there were shareholder employees. If an S Corporation shareholder has insurance or other benefits from a different source, this restriction would be moot. Even if there is no other source of benefits, it is quite possible that the overall tax benefit derived from an S Corporation would make the cost of providing these nondeductible shareholder/employee benefits insignificant. This is an area where careful financial planning and good tax advice are essentials.

A second drawback to Subchapter S is that while C Corporations may choose any fiscal/tax year they wish, S Corporations must generally use the same tax year as their shareholders, which is usually a calendar year, January 1 through December 31. There are exceptions to this rule based upon the S Corporation meeting one of four tests.

1. The first is simply a "grandfather" clause that allows S Corporations that had, before the current restrictions went into effect, received permission from the IRS to use a fiscal year to continue to do so.

2. The S Corporation may "elect" a fiscal year pursuant to IRC Section 444 by filing Form 8716, "Election to Have a Tax Year Other than a Required Tax Year." There are three requirements that must be met for an S Corporation to qualify for a Section 444 election.

- It may *not* be a member of a "tiered structure," that is, it cannot own or be owned by an entity that defers taxes.
- It may not have previously elected a fiscal year.
- It must meet the "deferral period" requirements.

Under a 444 election, the S Corporation must make certain "required payments" to the IRS to compensate the federal government for the "deferral" of taxes paid by the shareholders on corporate income. The deferral period is the period between the end of a requested fiscal year and the end of the calendar year. To qualify, the requested fiscal year cannot result in a deferral period of more than three months.

3. An S Corporation may choose a fiscal year that corresponds to its "natural" year. A corporation's natural year is one in which at least 25% of its gross receipts for the previous twelve-month period were achieved in the last two months of the period and the same was true for the two twelve-month periods prior to the current one. The corporation's fiscal year may then end of the last day of the relevant two-month period.

4. Even if an S Corporation does not elect a fiscal year under Section 444 or have a natural year, it may still use a fiscal year if it can show that there is a "business purpose" for the year. Unfortunately, the IRS has not always accepted the business purposes. Reasons such as hiring and promotion practices, or the use of model years and consistency in internal recordkeeping were not sufficient to permit the use of a fiscal year. On the other hand, the IRS has said that a corporate fiscal year conforming to the tax year of the holders of more than 50% of the corporation's stock is an acceptable business reason. In order to obtain permission to use a fiscal year based on a corporation's natural year or "ownership" year, the corporation must file Form 1128, "Application for Change in Accounting Period."

There are several advantages to choosing a different corporate tax year. Some of them, as already mentioned, deal with the conduct of the business. Others relate to the interplay between corporate cash flow and tax and shareholder cash flow and tax. The flexibility in relation to establishing tax years that was formerly afforded to S Corporations has been significantly reduced. The current rules concerning fiscal year elections by S Corporations make the process difficult and the result less satisfactory.

Other disadvantages for S Corporations are much more limited in scope and apply to specific situations. It is not the function of this book to go into detailed tax analysis of these issues. You should be aware, however, that if a corporation switches from C to S status certain benefits, such as loss carryovers or excess investment credits, may be lost. Similarly, there may be negative tax consequences if the S Corporation had obtained benefits by using certain methods of inventory valuation while still a C Corporation. You should check with a tax advisor as to how the corporation will be affected if you are contemplating a switch from C to S status.

State Tax Treatment of Subchapter S Corporations

While Subchapter S eliminates, for the most part, *federal* income taxation of corporate income, the same is not necessarily true of state income taxation. Many states do recognize the status and do not tax the income of S Corporations. Other states require the corporation to apply separately. Even in those states that recognize Subchapter S status, many of them impose a corporate tax on that percentage of the corporation's income that corresponds to that percentage of the corporation's stock held by nonresidents of the state. Other states that recognize the corporate status, nevertheless tax nonstate resident shareholders on their share of income from the S Corporation. Finally, some states do not recognize the status at all and tax the corporation on its income as if it were a C Corporation.

ELIGIBILITY REQUIREMENTS FOR SUBCHAPTER S STATUS

Subchapter S is comprised of IRC Sections 1361–1379. These sections allow certain types of corporations, denominated as "small business corporations," to be taxed similarly to (but not exactly like) partnerships. Thus, for the most part, there is no corporate tax to pay. The shareholders retain the liability protection offered by corporate existence, yet largely avoid two of the major drawbacks of the corporate form: double taxation and no pass-through of corporate losses.

There are several statutory requirements which do limit the number of corporations eligible for Subchapter S treatment. These requirements are found in IRC Section 1371 and include:

1. The corporation must be a domestic (U.S.) corporation.
2. It may not have more than 35 shareholders.
3. The shareholders must be (with certain limited exceptions) individuals.
4. There may not be a nonresident alien among the shareholders.
5. There may be only one class of stock.

These requirements are more complex than might initially appear. For instance, for the purposes of Subchapter S, what is an "individual" or "one class of stock"? The law has adopted special meanings for the words. The following sections will address each of the requirements and identify and discuss any problems they raise.

The Corporation Must Be Domestic

This requirement is actually rather straightforward. It merely indicates that in order to be eligible for Subchapter S status, the corporation must have been incorporated in the United States. This requirement works in conjunction with the requirements that the shareholders of the corporation be individuals who are not nonresident aliens.

The Shareholders Must Be Individuals

This requirement is somewhat misleading. While it is clear that neither corporations nor partnerships may be shareholders of a Subchapter S Corporation, certain "trusts" may hold shares in an S Corporation. A trust is an entity that holds property, under the direction of a trustee, for the benefit of another person, known as a beneficiary. A "qualified Subchapter S trust," one that may hold shares in an S Corporation, must meet certain requirements. It may have only one beneficiary who must be a U.S. citizen or legal resident. It must distribute all of its income to the beneficiary and, if the shares held by the trust are distributed, either during the life of the trust or upon its termination, they may be distributed only to the beneficiary. Finally, the interest of the income beneficiary must end at the earliest of the termination of the trust or upon his or her death. If a shareholder is not an individual or a qualified Subchapter S trust, the corporation will not be able to obtain S Corporation status.

If these rules seem somewhat complicated, the typical organizer of a Subchapter S Corporation can find some relief in the fact that this issue does not arise too often. It is relevant only to certain specialized situations and in such situations the advice of an attorney or accountant should be sought. What is clear, however, is that a corporation and a partnership *cannot* be shareholders in an S Corporation.

The Shareholders May Not Include a Nonresident Alien

This requirement goes along with the prohibition on foreign corporations qualifying for Subchapter S status. This rule prohibits nonresident foreign nationals from setting up a domestic corporation and qualifying it as an S Corporation. In order to be an eligible shareholder, an individual must be a citizen or legal permanent resident of the United States. If any shareholder fails to meet this requirement, the corporation will not qualify for S status.

There May Be No More Than 35 Shareholders

Since only individuals and qualified trusts may be shareholders of an S Corporation, this requirement appears to be easily understood. The goal of the Subchapter S was, for the purpose of income tax, to treat small business corporations like partnerships. A rule developed that 35 or fewer shareholders was the appropriate limit for such small corporations. However, the law permits a husband and wife owning shares together to be treated, for Subchapter S qualification, as if they were only one person. Be that as it may, if there are ever 36 or more shareholders, the Subchapter S status will be denied or withdrawn.

There May Be Only One Class of Stock

Because Subchapter S was intended to assist corporations with structures closely related to general partnerships, the idea that each shareholder should have essentially equal rights in relation to each other shareholder (as partners do in a partnership) was translated into a requirement that there be only one class of shares. Even this apparently simple directive, however, has been modified by caselaw and IRS rulings.

For instance, for the purposes of Subchapter S, only "issued" and "outstanding" stock is considered. If there is "authorized" but unissued stock of a different class, it will not disqualify the corporation from S Corporation status. Stock is considered to be of different "classes" for S Corporation purposes if the shares are not identical with respect to the rights and interest that they convey in the control, profits, and assets of the corporation. Nevertheless, shares of stock which are identical in all respects except that they have different voting rights have been held to be only one class of shares. Any distinctions in dividend payments, liquidation rights, or any other modifications of voting power, however, disqualify the corporation from S Corporation status.

In addition, the IRS has made clear that "a straight debt instrument" will not be treated as a second class of stock so long as it meets certain requirements.

- The instrument must be in writing and make an unconditional promise to pay a definite sum either on demand or by a fixed date;

- The instrument must also set an interest rate and specify the dates for the payment of interest. The payment dates cannot be left to the corporation's board or be based upon the profitability of the company;
- The debt instrument cannot be convertible into shares of stock; and
- The lender must be eligible to hold stock in an S Corporation.

If any of these requirements is not met, however, the IRS may examine any purported debt instrument to assure itself it is not a form of disguised stock.

ELECTING SUBCHAPTER S STATUS

If the corporation qualifies as a "small business corporation," it may become an "electing small business corporation" (electing to be taxed as an S Corporation) by filing Form 2553, "Election by a Small Business Corporation." This election requires the consent of *all* the corporation's shareholders, and must be made prior to the taxable year for which it is to be effective, or by the fifteenth day of the third month of that taxable year. The election is then effective for that year and all succeeding years, unless it is terminated in one of the following ways:

1. The corporation ceases to meet any of the various eligibility requirements for S Corporation status.
2. The corporation terminates its own election by filing a revocation with the IRS. Though the revocation is formally filed in the name of the corporation, it requires the signatures of all the shareholders.
3. A corporation converted to S status from standard (Subchapter C) status has excess passive income for three successive years and has at the end of each of those years accumulated earnings and profits dating from before the conversion.

This last basis for terminating an election is applicable only to corporations that began their existence as C Corporations (which are subject to the standard corporate tax) and later converted to S Corporation status. At the time of the conversion the C Corporation might have "retained earnings," that is, earnings from various years that were not distributed to shareholders. While these earnings would have been taxed at the corporate level, they would not have been taxed to the shareholders because they were not distributed. If this is the case (i.e., C Corporation's earnings and profits remain undistributed) for three successive years *and* for each of those years the S Corporation has excess net passive income* (i.e., net passive investment income in excess of 25% of the company's gross receipts) the S Corporation status will be terminated. Remember, however, that the terminating factor applies only to corporations that converted from C to S Corporations and then only in particular and controllable financial circumstances.

On the other hand, an S Corporation that is subject to this termination, in that it converted from a C Corporation and has accumulated earnings and profits at the end of each year but has excess net passive income for only two (rather than the prohibited three) successive years, does not get off with no repercussion at all. Instead, in each year where it exists, the excess net passive income (or the corporation's taxable income if less than the excess passive income) will be taxed to the corporation at the maximum rate applicable to corporations. This, of course, is an exception to the general rule that Subchapter S Corporations pay no tax themselves.

The Tax Reform Act creates another exception to this general rule. This exception also involves a corporation which converted to S status from C status. If, at the time of the conversion, the C Corporation owned assets that had appreciated in value, there existed what is known as "built-in gain." If, within 10 years of the conversion from C to S status, the corporation disposes of any assets with built-in gain, the gain will be recognized and taxed to the corporation at the highest rate applicable to corporations for that year. The rate will be applied to the lesser of the recognized built-in gain or the taxable income of the corporation as if it were a C rather than an S Corporation. The total amount of gain that can be taxed to the corporation is limited to the amount of built-in gain on the date of the conversion to S Corporation status. Thus if assets continue to appreciate in value after conversion this rule does not apply. However, all gains of preexisting assets recognized within the 10-year period are presumed to be built-in gains. It is up to the corporation to prove that the appreciation arose after conversion.

Taxation of the Subchapter S Shareholder

While its S Corporation election is in effect, a corporation generally is not subject to corporate income taxes. Instead, each shareholder (determined as of the last day of the corporation's tax year) includes in his or her income the amount he or she *would* have received as a dividend if the corporation had distributed all its taxable income for each tax year, pro rata,

---

* This generally involves such items as rents, royalties, and income from securities and investments.

to its shareholders. Often, however, the corporation's earnings are not distributed to shareholders but are retained by the corporation.

If these "constructive dividends" actually are paid out at a later date, they will not subject the shareholder to a second tax. Each shareholder computes the total amount of constructive dividends previously treated as received, then subtracts from that amount the total amount of any of the corporation's *losses* that have been passed through to him or her. The result is the shareholder's "net share of the corporation's undistributed taxable income." If the corporation then distributes dividends, the shareholder will not be taxed, *up to* the amount of the shareholder's "net share of the corporation's undistributed taxable income." Any dividends in excess of the amount of the shareholder's "net share" are fully taxable.

Just as the corporation's taxable income is "passed through" to its shareholders, so are its losses—but to a more limited extent. In fact, one of the purposes of an S Corporation is to permit small business corporations realizing losses in their initial stages of operation to pass through these losses to their shareholders to offset income the shareholders may receive from other sources. Thus, with an S Corporation, each shareholder may use subject to the limitations of TRA his or her share of the corporation's losses to reduce his or her income.

The "pass-through" of tax losses is not unlimited, however. A shareholder may not deduct a share of the corporation's tax loss that exceeds that shareholder's "investment" in the corporation. At a given time, a shareholder's "investment" equals the "basis" of his stock plus any debt the corporation owes the shareholder; that is, (the cost of the stock to the shareholder plus the amount of "constructive dividends" the shareholder is considered to have received minus the amount of dividends actually paid which have been previously taxed as "constructive dividends" minus losses previously "passed through" to the shareholder) plus the amount of any loan by the shareholder to the corporation.

For instance, in the case of shareholder A:

Stock purchase price	$100
Corporation's debt to A	100
"Constructive dividends"	
attributed to A in the past	100
A's investment	$300

If A owns 50% of Corporation X's stock and X has a tax loss of $500 in 1991, A's share of the loss is $250 (50% of $500). Subject to the "Passive Loss Restrictions" of the Tax Reform Act of 1986, A may use the entire $250 loss to offset other income because his or her "investment"

($300) is greater than $250. However, the utilization of the $250 loss reduces A's investment to $50 ($300 − $250 = $50). Therefore, in 1992, if the corporation loses $200, A's share of the loss would be $100 (50% of $200); however, unless A has made additional "investments" in the corporation, A may use only $50 of that loss to offset income from other sources.

TAXATION OF THE S CORPORATION AND ITS SHAREHOLDERS

We have already discussed the effect on the corporation of electing Subchapter S status and have alluded to the benefits to be obtained by the shareholders of S Corporations. In this section we will discuss the taxes assessed directly against the corporation and their impact on shareholders as well as those that pass through the corporation directly to the shareholders. We will also examine the process by which these shareholders compute their federal tax obligations due to their ownership of S Corporation stock.

Corporate Taxes

There are several situations in which an S Corporation itself, and not its shareholders, is liable for income taxes. These all involve a situation where a C Corporation has taken a corporate tax benefit or avoided a tax liability and then shifts to S status. These situations are:

- Tax on excess passive investment income where the S Corporation has accumulated "earnings and profits" from its C Corporation days.
- Tax on capital gains of C Corporation that elects S status.
- Recapture of prior year investment tax credit taken by a C Corporation that converts to S status.
- Recapture of LIFO tax.

Accumulated C Corporation Earnings and Profits

Assume that a C Corporation had earnings and profits (E&P) in a particular year that have not been distributed to shareholders. Since a C Corporation is a taxable entity, its shareholders would pay no individual tax on the nondistributed corporate E&P. If the C Corporation converts to S status in a subsequent year with the E&P still undistributed, there still would be no tax to the shareholders on this undistributed amount. When E&P are distributed to the shareholders, they are taxed as a dividend to them. In addition, the Internal Revenue Code imposes a tax at the highest corporate rate directly on the S Corporation if in any year in which it has C Corporation E&P it has passive investment income in excess of 25% of its gross receipts. The tax is applied against the "excess net passive income." If there is excess net passive income for three consecutive years, the S status of the corporation would be revoked.

Capital Gains

If a C Corporation has property that has appreciated in value and that it wishes to sell, it cannot switch to S status, sell the property, and thereby avoid a corporate tax on the "built in" gain. The IRC Section 1374 imposes a tax on the net recognized built-in gain less certain loss carryforwards permitted to be subtracted from the built-in gain. The tax imposed is directly on the corporation and at the highest corporate rate.

Recapture of Investment Tax Credit

If a C Corporation took an investment tax credit and then elected to be taxed under Subchapter S, the election, itself, would not trigger the recapture of the credit. However, if the S Corporation disposes of the assets upon which the investment tax credit was based prior to the end of the useful life of those assets, the credit will be recaptured. The S Corporation, not its shareholders, will be responsible for paying the tax.

Recapture of LIFO Benefits

If a C Corporation has valued inventory on a "last in first out" (LIFO) basis and then converts to S status, the S Corporation will be subject to a recapture of LIFO benefits. The LIFO method of inventory valuation essentially treats the cost of goods sold by taking the cost of the most recent inventory addition as the basis of each piece of inventory sold. This means that for tax purposes, the sale of an item from inventory is treated as being from the last lot of inventory purchased. Since this lot normally would have been purchased at a higher price than earlier inventory purchases, the spread between the sales price of the item and its cost would be the smallest and the corporate tax the lowest. If there was then a conversion to S status, the new corporation would not be taxed on the spread of the sale of the earliest, presumably cheapest, inventory. The recapture taxes the S Corporation, itself, in its first year on the excess of the inventory's value using the "first in first out" (FIFO) method. This LIFO recapture amount would be added to the S Corporation's income and the tax owed would be paid over a four-year period.

Taxation of the Shareholder

Despite the fact that some taxes are imposed directly on the S Corporation, generally speaking, the tax obligation of Subchapter S shareholders is determined in much the same way as that of partners in a partnership. Subchapter S Corporations report their annual financial data on IRS form 1120S (see Appendix 28). There are places on that form for the corporation to enter its income from each of various sources as well as the amounts for specific deductions. There are also places to enter the few taxes for which the S Corporation, itself, is liable.

There are several schedules to form 1120S that break down elements of the income or loss of the S Corporation. Schedule K, for instance, states the corporate income or loss that is passed through directly to the shareholders. Schedule K-1 is used to apportion the income and loss to each shareholder on a pro rata basis. Each shareholder will then transfer the items from his or her K-1 to his or her personal income tax return in accordance with TRA's rules.

Determining the pro rata share of any shareholder is, as are many aspects of Subchapter S, more complex than might at first appear. The first issue is to determine which items of corporate income and expense are to be reported on the corporation's 1120S form. These items are known as "nonseparately stated items" and are set out specifically. Not all items of income or expense, however, are reported on the corporation's return. Some of them are reported only on Schedules K and K-1 and are passed directly through to the shareholder to be reported on his or her return. These pass-through items are known, not surprisingly, as "separately stated items." The rule to determine whether an item is to be separately stated is found in IRC Section 1366 and depends on whether an individual item treated separately can affect the tax liability of a shareholder. Although the Code does not provide a listing of separately stated items, they include, for instance, such things as charitable contributions, portfolio interest expense, tax exempt income, capital gains and losses, foreign income and loss, and so on.

Once the determination is made as to which items are to be separately stated and which to be aggregated on the 1120S form, there remains the determination of each shareholder's pro rata share of corporate income and loss. If shareholder interests in the corporation have not changed at all during the tax year, this process is very simple. A 10% shareholder, for instance, would take 10% of each item of income or loss reported on Schedule K or on Form 1120S. If, however, the percentage interests changed during the year, the tax code requires an analysis of these interests on a *daily* basis. This means that each element of income or loss reported by the S Corporation would have to be divided by 365 to obtain a daily figure and the shareholder's percentage would have to be applied for each day. Thus if a shareholder held 25% of the corporation's stock for 150 days and 50% of the stock for 215 days two calculations would have to be made for each element of income or loss. First, you would multiply the daily income or loss figure by 150 and multiply that figure by 25%. Next you would multiply the same number by 215 and multiply the result by 50%.

As an example, suppose in the hypothetical given above, a particular item of income was $3,650. To get the daily figure, you would divide this number by 365 and get a quotient of $10. Since the shareholder owned 25% of the corporation's stock for 150 days, you would multiply $10 (the daily income figure) by 150 days for a total of $1,500. This would be multiplied by 25% to get the first part of the shareholder's pro rata share of this item of income. The result is $375. The same process would be applied to the 50% ownership period; $10 × 215 (days) = $2,150 × 50% = $1,075. The two figures would be added together and this shareholder would report $1,450 as his or her share of this item of corporate income.

After examining the advantages and disadvantages of Subchapter S status in relation to the circumstances of your corporation, you will be in a better position to decide whether to make the election. It is important that you seek professional assistance in deciding which way to go. Keep in mind, however, that the decision to go either way is not final. A C Corporation can elect S status during the first two and one half months of any of its tax years. Similarly, an S Corporation can choose to be a C Corporation or may become disqualified for its S status at any time. The only restriction on eligible corporations is that an S Corporation that has reverted to C status cannot become an S Corporation again for a period of five years.

SECTION 1244 STOCK

In most instances, when a small corporation's stock is sold or exchanged by a shareholder at a loss, or becomes worthless, the loss is considered a capital loss. This means that the holder of the stock must offset the amount of this capital loss against any capital gains he or she may have enjoyed during the year. If the individual has no capital gains to set against the capital loss, then the loss may be used to offset "ordinary income" but only to a limited extent.

However, it is possible for a small corporation to issue what is known as Section 1244 stock. This allows losses on eligible stock to be given a different tax treatment. If the stock is sold, exchanged, or becomes worthless, the shareholders of Section 1244 stock may deduct their loss on this stock from their personal income from other sources up to $100,000 for a husband and wife filing a joint return, or $50,000 for other taxpayers, in the year in which the stock is sold, exchanged, or becomes worthless.

A corporation may be eligible to issue and shareholders eligible to enjoy Section 1244 stock if they meet the following tests:

1. The corporation must be a "small business corporation," that is, the aggregate amount of money and other property received by the corporation for stock, as a contribution to capital, and as paid-in (capital) surplus, does not exceed $1 million.

2. Section 1244 benefits are available only to individuals or partnerships, not to corporations, trusts, and so forth, and a shareholder claiming a loss on 1244 stock must be the holder of an original issue of the stock, that is, an original purchaser from the corporation.

3. The stock may be either common or preferred.

4. The stock must be paid for with money or property, not services to the corporation, securities, or other stock.

5. For the five years preceding the year in which the Section 1244 stock becomes worthless (or since the corporation's inception if it has not been in existence for five years), the corporation must derive more than 50% of its total gross receipts from sources other than rents, royalties, dividends, interest, proceeds from sales or exchanges of securities, or annuities.

The advantages of Section 1244 are important when a small corporation does badly or goes out of business after having done poorly. The loss on the stock for qualifying shareholders can be used to offset ordinary income rather than being treated as a capital loss.

DEBT FINANCING

"Thin incorporation" is a term used to describe a corporation that has incurred a large amount of debt in proportion to the money it has received from the issuance of its stock. A corporation would want such a financial structure so it may take a tax deduction for interest payments on the debt, particularly when the debt is owed to the shareholders, because no deduction is allowed when the corporation distributes dividends to its shareholders.

For instance, if the corporation needed to raise $10,000, it could do so in two ways: It could sell its stock for $10,000, or it could borrow some or all of the $10,000.

1. If it sells stock and the corporation made profits it could distribute those profits as dividends to its shareholders. The distribution, however, would not be deductible from its gross income so as to reduce the amount of its taxes.

2. On the other hand, when the corporation borrows and pays interest on its debts, it may deduct the amount of these interest payments from its gross income and thereby have a smaller taxable income. Of course, if the corporation is failing and not making money, the requirement to make interest payments on debt can be troublesome. Many marginal corporations go under because of burdensome debt service.

Thus, if Corporation X made a before-tax profit of $10,000 in 1995 and distributed all of it to its shareholders as dividends, X would still be subject to corporate taxes on that $10,000. If X paid $10,000 in interest on debts, however, it could deduct the $10,000 from its income, leaving it with no taxable income. It should be noted, however, that this will also eliminate profit. If the debt is owed to shareholders, this is relatively unimportant. If, however, the debt is owed to outsiders, the loss of profits due to interest payments is a serious problem to the owners.

These results may tempt organizers to create a creditor relationship with their corporation. It is possible to do this; shareholders may be creditors of their corporation. When the proportion of debt to equity exceeds 4:1, however, the IRS tends to become suspicious that the "debt" is really a disguised form of equity. In this situation, corporation/shareholder debt instruments have been known to be reclassified for tax purposes as a form of preferred stock. The IRS will look to the ratio of debt to equity, the amount of equity itself (to determine if it is adequate under the circumstances), and also whether the shareholders are "creditors" of the corporation in the same proportions as they are shareholders. While none of these factors are determinative, they contribute to an overall impression that the "debt" is really an equity investment. If the IRS comes to that conclusion, it will disallow the corporation's deductions for "interest" paid and reclassify the distribution as a dividend. Since dividends are not deductible, the amount of the distribution will be added to reported income for the year in question and taxed. This means the corporation will be subject to an increase in tax for the year in question together with interest and, perhaps, penalties for the original underpayment.

THE TAX REFORM ACT OF 1986

The Tax Reform Act of 1986 made several major changes in the tax laws that will affect shareholders both as principals in their corporations and as investors. Among the most basic changes affecting shareholders as investors are the repeal of the dividend exclusion and the elimination of the favorable treatment accorded to long-term capital gains.

Dividends and Capital Gains

Under prior law, shareholders could exclude from their ordinary income the first $100 of qualified dividends received from corporations ($200 for a married couple filing a joint return). This limited to a small degree the impact of the double tax imposed on shareholders. The repeal of this exclusion, therefore, had a negative impact on shareholders. Of even greater financial significance was the repeal of the long-term capital gains treatment.

Previously, a noncorporate taxpayer who held a capital asset (including corporate stock) for more than six months, and then disposed of it for a gain, could exclude 60% of that gain and include only the remaining 40% in his or her gross income. If several assets were disposed of, long-term gains and losses would be netted out as would short-term gains and losses. The long- and short-term results would also be netted, and net long-term gain received the special treatment. The effect of this was to tax long-term gain at only 40% of the rate applied to one's ordinary income. Under the new law, this special treatment has been eliminated and net long-term gain will be fully taxed at ordinary income rates with a cap of 28% for tax years after 1990.

One benefit to help counteract these changes has been the allowance of long-term capital *losses* to offset ordinary income on a dollar-for-dollar basis (up to a $3,000 per year limit) rather than the two dollars of long-term loss needed to offset each dollar of income under prior law. Net losses in excess of $3,000 may be carried forward to subsequent years.

Depreciation

There have also been several changes in the depreciation (or ACRS) rules. These changes will affect, often negatively, corporations and shareholders in S Corporations. In particular, the useful life (known as the "recovery period") of many capital assets has been lengthened, thereby making depreciation slower and the annual write-offs for depreciation smaller. Among the items given longer useful lives are cars and light trucks (up from 3 years under old law to 5 years under the Tax Reform Act of 1986), office equipment (up from 5 to 7 years) and housing (up from 19 to 27½ or 31½ years). Moreover, the investment tax credit was repealed retroactive to January 1986.

On the other hand, the rate at which certain items may be depreciated was increased and the allowable expensing (i.e., deducting the cost of capital assets all in one year rather than depreciating the cost over the useful life) of an asset was increased from $5,000 to $10,000.

Passive Losses

Among the other major changes affecting corporations and shareholders is the limitation on the use of "passive" losses to offset income from other sources. Passive activity is one of three new income categories included in the Act. The others are active income and portfolio income. Losses from a passive activity cannot, generally be used to offset income from either of the other categories, but are limited to offsetting income from passive activities.

Passive activities may be defined by reference either to the taxpayer or to the activity. For instance, any trade or business may be deemed "passive" as to a taxpayer if that taxpayer does not "materially participate" in it. "Material participation" requires involvement in the trade or business in a regular and substantial way. The Internal Revenue Service (IRS) has adopted temporary rules (found at Section 1.469-5T(a) of the IRS regulations) to determine whether a taxpayer "materially participates" in a trade or business. The regulations establish seven tests to determine material participation. If an S shareholder meets any one of them, he or she will be deemed to have materially participated. The first four tests apply to the amount of time the shareholder participated in the business in the current tax year. The next two apply to his or her participation in any of the three previous tax years. The final test is a general "facts and circumstances" examination of the shareholder's activities in the business. It should be noted here that a limited partner generally cannot materially participate in the affairs of partnership. Thus losses from a limited partnership may not be used to offset the limited partner's income from another income category (i.e., active or portfolio). However, the test for material participation is applied to proprietors, general partners, and shareholders in an S corporation. For a C corporation, the test is whether one or more shareholders who, between them, own a majority of the corporate stock, materially participate. If so, the *corporation* will not be deemed to be engaged in passive activities.

The alternative referent for passive income (or loss) is the activity itself. The Tax Reform Act of 1986, for instance, deems any rental activity as passive. Thus, rental of real estate, cars, equipment, and so forth are presumed to be passive activities.

The effect of defining an activity as passive is that any losses (including depreciation) generated by the activity cannot, in general, be used to offset income from other categories (although such losses *can* be used to offset income from *other* passive activities). This, in essence, severely restricts the tax sheltering of income through the use of paper losses generated by certain types of activities (rental) or for inactive investors.

Rental Real Estate Activities

The law did allow a small window of relief from the passive loss rules in relation to rental real estate activities. In such cases, a person who "*actively* participates" in the rental activity may use up to $25,000 of passive losses to offset income from nonpassive sources. The benefit of this exception diminishes as the taxpayer's adjusted gross income exceeds $100,000. At that point, one dollar of the allowable deduction is lost for every two dollars of adjusted gross income. Thus the entire allowable $25,000 deduction is eliminated when the taxpayer's adjusted gross income hits $150,000.

The "active participant" requirement for allowable passive losses in real estate situations is *not* the equivalent of "material participation" for determining whether other types of activities are passive. All that is required for "active participation" is that the taxpayer does participate in some meaningful way. This does not require day-to-day involvement but does require the taxpayer to be involved in the general direction of the activity. As a bare minimum, the taxpayer must hold at least a 10% interest in the activity. One who holds a smaller interest or a limited partner—regardless of the size of the interest held—is precluded from being an "active participant" and taking the benefit of this exception.

To the extent actual passive losses cannot be taken by the taxpayer in any particular year, they are not lost but may be carried forward and used to offset the taxpayer's passive income in subsequent years. If the activity giving rise to the passive losses is disposed of prior to all accumulated losses having been taken, those losses may be used to reduce any gain otherwise to be recognized through such disposition.

In addition, there are a variety of other changes wrought by TRA, running from tightening the standards and limiting the deductibility of business meals, to imposing a new alternative minimum tax on corporations, to extending the "at-risk" rules concerning the deductibility of losses to real property investments. While these will all affect taxpayers significantly, they are beyond the scope of this book. Tax planning and accounting should, therefore remain a major concern to corporations and their shareholders, who should seek professional advice in this area.

13

LIMITED LIABILITY COMPANIES

Historically, there has been a gap in the organizational choices available to entrepreneurs who engage in business activities. Several forms of business provided limited liability for its owners, but there were often negative tax consequences, such as double taxation, as the price for such protection. Alternatively, there were forms, such as sole proprietorships and general partnerships, in which there was no income tax on the business organization, but the owners were fully liable for its obligations. The law attempted to fill this gap, through the creation and use of limited partnerships and subchapter S corporations, but these attempts were only partially successful.

Limited partnerships were not subject to income tax and the *limited* partners were protected from individual liability. The form, however, required at least one general partner and the general partner was personally liable for the obligations of the limited partnership. Organizers attempted to get around this problem by setting up a corporation owned by the limited partners to serve as the sole general partner. The concept was that the corporation would be lightly capitalized and there would thus be no partner with substantial assets who would have personal liability for the debts of the partnership. The IRS, however, could refuse to treat such an organization as an association taxed as a partnership and treat it instead, for tax purposes, as if it were a corporation. Moreover, regardless of the tax status of the limited partnership, there were two organizations, the corporation and the limited partnership, that had to keep books and records and file annual reports and tax returns (although it was only an information return in the case of the limited partnership).

While a subchapter S corporation involved only one entity, limited liability, and a pass-through tax structure, it, too, had significant drawbacks. For instance, there may be no more than 35 shareholders in a subchapter S corporation and they have to be, with minor exceptions, real persons who are not nonresident aliens. Therefore, there cannot be a corporate shareholder nor can there be foreign investors. In addition, there may be only one class of corporate stock so that the ability to allocate income among the shareholders may be less flexible than desired.

Because of the drawbacks of the more traditional forms, entrepreneurs and the business community sought the creation of a new type of entity to fill the perceived gap in existing structures. That entity was the Limited Liability Company (LLC). The form has been in existence in other parts of the world, particularly Europe and Latin America, for some time. The first modern LLC statute in the United States was passed in Wyoming in 1977. Since then, the great majority of states and the District of Columbia have passed statutes that permit LLCs to be organized within their jurisdiction. This chapter will discuss the attributes and advantages of the LLC, the process of organization and the ongoing, as yet unanswered, questions concerning their existence and future.

CREATION OF LIMITED LIABILITY COMPANIES

As with corporations, LLCs are artificial entities permitted by state statutes, which set out the legal requirements to establish an LLC. Usually, this involves the preparation and filing of a document, often called a *Certificate of Formation* or *Articles of Organization,* that must be filed with a state official. In addition to the Articles of Organization, most state statutes also permit LLCs to have an Operating Agreement between its members that provides for its internal operation and establishes the relationships between them. While an Operating Agreement is not required by the statute, it is both prudent and useful for the organizers to establish one. It functions like a partnership agreement in a general partnership or, to some extent, like a shareholder's agreement in a closely held corporation.

Articles of Organization

The Articles of Organization is the document that establishes the LLC. The state statute sets out the required contents of the Articles, which typically are quite basic. As with Articles of Incorporation, Articles of Organization include certain identifying information about the LLC and its members, together with certain technical provisions. The document generally does not contain great detail about the operation of the LLC.

Heading

The heading of the Articles sets out the name of the LLC and often includes a certification by the member, manager, or other organizer as to the truth of the contents of the Certificate. For example, the heading might read

ARTICLES OF ORGANIZATION
For
XYZ, A Limited Liability Company

The undersigned, who is authorized to sign and file this document, certify(ies) as follows:

Name

The Articles must include the name of the LLC. Most states require the words *Limited Liability Company* (or an abbreviation such as LLC) to accompany the name. In a few states, alternative designations are permitted but in each case, the limited nature of the principals' liability must be indicated. As with the names of corporations, an LLC may not choose a name that causes confusion or is "deceptively similar" to the name of an existing organization. Again, as with corporations, most states permit the organizers of an LLC to reserve a name for a period of time before filing the Articles.

Registered Office and Agent

All states require LLCs to have a registered agent and a registered office. The agent, whose job it is to receive official notices and the service of process for the LLC, must be a natural person who actually resides within the state or a corporation licensed to do business there. Often, the LLC will name one of its members or its attorney as the registered agent. There are also a number of corporations who are in the business of serving as the registered agent of other corporations and LLCs. It is important for the LLC to name as its registered agent a person or corporation in whom it has complete confidence. The failure of the agent to transmit notices or legal process it receives could have a very negative impact on the LLC.

The registered office must be within the jurisdiction and must be where the registered agent is located. It need not be the business office of the LLC or even connected with it other than as the registered office.

Some jurisdictions also require that the LLC state in the Articles the address of its principal office, which could be the same as the registered office.

Number of Members

While a few states permit one member LLCs, these are a distinct minority. Most states require a minimum of two members to establish and maintain an LLC. No state has set a maximum number of members the LLC may have. Many jurisdictions require a statement in the Articles that there are at least the statutorily required minimum number of members at the outset of the LLC. On occasion, the initial members must be named in the Articles. Often, when the LLC is to be managed by only some of the members or by outside managers, the managers must be named even though members need not.

Duration

While some states permit LLCs to have perpetual duration, most do not. Even if your state permits an LLC to have perpetual existence, there are important tax reasons, which will be discussed later in this chapter, why you might choose not to avail yourself of this option. Where perpetual existence is not an option, the statutes usually establish several events any of which would terminate the LLC. These include:

- The time or an event stated in the Articles.
- The consent of all members.
- A specified date from the formation of the LLC.
- The death, resignation, expulsion, or bankruptcy of a member (although most statutes permit the Operating Agreement to provide for or the remaining members to agree to continue the business).
- Judicial dissolution.

Purposes

An LLC may generally conduct any lawful business although there are a few jurisdictions that impose some restrictions on the activities of an LLC. Some states do not even require a statement of purpose in the Articles. Often, the statement that the LLC is authorized to engage in "any lawful purpose" is sufficient. In the typical case, the broadest possible statement is desirable. There are, however, occasions where the organizers (or some of them) would want more restrictive language in the Articles. In such situations, the organizers should set out a more precise statement of what the LLC is authorized to do. Even in these situations, though, it is often useful to insert an inclusive provision allowing the LLC to engage in all activities reasonably necessary or proper for it to attain its main purpose. Organizers should also keep in mind that many state statutes grant very broad powers to LLCs as a matter of course. These powers need not be repeated in the Articles in order for them to be operative. However, any powers that are not desired should be specifically eliminated in the Articles.

Other Provisions

Many states permit the Articles to include other provisions that the principals believe are important enough to be stated in the chartering document. These provisions may also be included in the Operating Agreement. They include issues such as the admission of new members, certain financial matters, transfer restrictions and rules of internal organization. In many cases, the statute will set out the applicable provisions and these provisions will be in effect unless the Articles or the Operating Agreement provide to the contrary.

The Operating Agreement

The Operating Agreement may be the single most important document in the formation and operation of an LLC. It is very much like a partnership agreement in that it is a contract between the members in relation to their rights and responsibilities in the operation of the LLC. It is also very much like the bylaws of a corporation in relation to the operating procedures of the LLC. Many of the provisions we will discuss here will be reminiscent of provisions in the sample bylaws discussed in Chapter 9.

Like the Uniform Partnership Act that is in force, in whole or in part, in most states, most LLC statutes set out some specific, mandatory provisions for the creation and operation of the LLC. They may also set out some provisions that will apply *unless* they are modified by the organizers. Finally, the statutes may not address certain issues, leaving it instead to the will of the organizers to create a structure to suit their needs.

Most state statutes offer considerable leeway for organizers to create a customized organization. This is accomplished through the Operating Agreement, the vehicle through which the will of the organizers is stated and the personality of the LLC is created. It is important that the organizers and their advisors take advantage of the flexibility that is built in to most LLC statutes by drafting an Operating Agreement that meets their structural needs and resolves anticipated questions. The remainder of this section will discuss the issues that should be addressed in the Operating Agreement and the factors that members should consider in making decisions about the LLC.

Membership

Members are the owners of the LLC and usually achieve their status by making contributions to it. There are several options concerning membership and the needs of the LLC as well as the desires of the organizers that will dictate the choices made.

Number of Members

As mentioned earlier, there is no upper limit to the number of members an LLC may have, although there is generally a minimum number. If the organizers wish to limit the size of the LLC, they may do so in the Operating Agreement. The Operating Agreement may also set out the procedure for admitting new members regardless of whether there is a limit on the size of the organization. If the number of members in an LLC is large, there is the possibility that the LLC will have to comply with state and federal securities laws. Therefore, it will be prudent for the organizers to determine early in the process whether they wish to limit the size and qualify for an exemption from such laws or whether they are willing to risk being subject to such laws (with the commensurate expenditure of time, energy, and money) in order to attract a large number of members and a large capital contribution.

Classes of Members

Members of an LLC may be divided into as many classes as the organizers believe will suit their needs. This is quite important in the flexibility of the organization because each class can have different voting rights, different shares of profits and losses, and different distribution rights. These rights may be determined independently of the capital contribution of the members and should be spelled out in the Operating Agreement. If there are to be classes of membership, the various classes should be clearly defined in the Operating Agreement and the powers and duties of each class should be set out. In addition, a statement of the qualifications for membership in each class should be provided.

Thus, for the purpose of example, the organizers who had the original business idea and contacts to begin the business may be Class A members who, between them, have 60% of the voting rights and 35% of the right to profit, gain, or loss. Class B members may have contributed 90% of the cash to the LLC but are given only 30% of the voting rights and 50% of the profit, gain or loss. Finally, Class C members may contribute the labor to run the business. They may be entitled to a salary for their labors and 10% of the voting rights and 15% of the right to profit, gain, or loss.

Types of Members

Normally, any person or entity may be a member of an LLC. Thus, corporations, partnerships, and trusts, among others, can be members of an

LLC. The only factors limiting this eligibility are state law and the Operating Agreement. Similarly, an LLC may own stock in a corporation or be a partner in a partnership. The Operating Agreement should state any restrictions the organizers wish to impose concerning these provisions.

Contributions of Members

Contributions to an LLC may generally be made in cash, promissory note, property, or services. The Operating Agreement should set out the contributions that are permissible and those that are to be made by each original member. If these contributions include labor, the Operating Agreement should explicitly lay out this fact and set up a method to value the services and to determine if the agreed upon services have actually been provided in an acceptable manner.

Voting Rights of Members

Traditionally, corporate shareholders and partners in a partnership vote in proportion to their ownership interests in their corporation or partnership, respectively. LLCs are different. While most state LLC statutes provide that if no alternative plan is included in the Articles or Operating Agreement, members will vote on a proportionate basis, it is clear that LLCs *can* apportion voting rights among its members in any way it pleases.

The Operating Agreement should set out the voting rights of different members or of different classes of members. The Operating Agreement should also establish the percentage of votes needed to carry a proposition. In many cases, that will be a majority of interests voting. In some cases, the members may desire a greater than majority or even a unanimous vote for particular types of decisions. For certain matters, for example, for the election of managers, the Agreement might set out how the members had previously agreed to vote. The Operating Agreement should set out the areas where a greater than majority vote is needed and should set out the required percentage or the desired result for each such issue.

Finally, the method of electing managers, if any, should be spelled out in the Operating Agreement. As will be described on p. 128, managers are often chosen to run the LLC for the members. Therefore, the process for electing and removing managers should be decided on by the organizers and included in the Agreement.

Meetings of Members

Most state statutes do not require the meeting of members. To the extent that members will be actively engaged in LLC decision making, however, it will be necessary for them to meet. The Operating Agreement should spell out the schedule and location of regular meetings. It should also spell out how special meetings of members may be called. In either case, there should be a provision for how to give notice to members of the time, place, and purpose of the meeting. Finally, there should be a provision about how membership decisions can be made without a meeting, for instance through the use of a conference call, an on-line computer program, or a written consent to the action by some number, up to 100 percent, of the members.

Managers

Like partnerships, it is assumed that all members have a right to participate in the management of the LLC. If the Articles or the Operating Agreement do not provide to the contrary, members will have management rights in proportion to their ownership of the LLC with a majority of interests controlling the decision making. The Articles and Operating Agreement, however, may modify this general rule. Management of an LLC may be placed with only some of the members or with a manager or managers who are not members of the LLC at all. The manager(s) may be individuals or other business organizations.

Powers of Managers

Managers are, in many ways, analogous to officers of a corporation in that they carry out the day-to-day activities of the LLC. As managers, they are fiduciaries to the LLC and must act in its best interests. This is quite important because in many jurisdictions, the act of a member or manager, if within the normal scope of the LLC's business, may bind the entire LLC. This may be so even if that member or manager did not have authority from the LLC to so act. Therefore, it is important that the Articles, Operating Agreement, and other public documents make clear who is authorized to act for the LLC in its general affairs. While such notice may not absolutely protect the LLC from the unauthorized actions of members or managers, it may reduce the breadth of the LLC's exposure. It is a basic legal principle that anyone who knew or should have known that a member or manager did not have authority to bind the LLC cannot do so by dealing with that person. Thus, the more broadly disseminated the restrictions, the less likely anyone dealing with the LLC will be able to show they neither knew nor should they have known of the restrictions.

Voting by Managers

Managers, unlike members, typically vote on a one-person, one-vote basis. It is possible, however, to arrange the management structure so that certain managers will have more power than others. This may be done through classifying managers or by permitting some managers to vote for only some issues. The organizers need to consider carefully how much power they want managers to have and whether there is any class or group of managers that they want to have more power than the others. For instance, there may be a group of nonmember managers who are to run the day-to-day operations of the business. There may also be a group of member managers who stay out of routine affairs, but who wish to retain power over certain types of decisions. This could be accomplished by permitting the nonmember managers to vote on routine matters, but not on specified extraordinary ones. Alternatively, the member managers could be given veto power over the vote of nonmember managers on certain issues. Any such provisions need to be spelled out in the Agreement.

Liability of Managers

Managers are fiduciaries of the LLC. As such they owe duties of care and loyalty to the organization. If they breach either of these duties, they will be liable to the LLC for any injury they cause. This does not mean they are liable to third parties. The limited liability accorded to LLCs generally protects their members, employees, and managers from liability to outsiders. Managers, however, may be liable to the LLC itself. These liabilities are enforced through the device of a derivative lawsuit by which a member brings a suit in the name of the LLC and against the manager in which he or she claims an injury to the LLC. If the suit is successful, it is the LLC rather than the member or members who brought the suit who receives the benefit of the judgment.

Rights of Managers

Managers are entitled at least to have complete and accurate information about things such as the financial, business, and personnel matters of the LLC. This follows from their exposure to liability to the LLC for any negligent acts they commit. If the manager is to have greater rights or if their rights (and, presumably, their liability) is to be limited, these issues should be spelled out in the Operating Agreement.

Managers are also permitted to deal directly with the LLC. This means they can sell to, lend to, buy or borrow from, or engage in other business transactions with their LLCs. In doing so, however, they remain fiduciaries and are bound by fiduciary duties to the LLC. If the organizers wish to limit the right of managers to do business with the LLC, they should so state in the Operating Agreement.

Removal and Resignation of Managers

Generally, managers may resign and the Operating Agreement should describe the process by which a resignation can be made. A more difficult decision concerns the removal of a manager. As with the removal of directors, managers generally may be removed by members with or without cause. Restrictions on this power of members should be included in the Agreement and the procedure for removal should be provided as well.

Distributions

Unlike corporations, distributions in an LLC need not be geared to the contributions of the member. In fact, most state laws permit the LLC to establish any distribution pattern it chooses. When we speak of distributions here, we mean distribution of profits and losses, distribution of gains from the sale of assets and final distributions on the dissolution of the LLC. The distribution percentages need not be the same for each element to be distributed.

The IRS also has some concerns about distribution patterns. It seeks to make certain that the pattern has real economic validity and is not just a scheme to evade taxation. Moreover, the IRS has the power to disregard, for the purpose of taxation, an otherwise valid state law distribution system. Therefore, IRS concerns must be a consideration in forming any distribution pattern. When the pattern is finally arrived at, it should be spelled out in detail in the Operating Agreement.

In a related manner, the Agreement should set out whether and for what services members will be compensated by the LLC and in what amounts. Compensation is often provided for working as an employee of the LLC or for providing professional services to it. If compensation is likely to be modified over time, the method for deciding on the modifications, including any formula or guidelines, might be included.

Dispute Resolution

Organizations are generally well advised to develop a dispute resolution mechanism early in their existence. This serves several useful purposes. First, it creates a rational, legally enforceable mechanism to resolve disputes before any disputes have actually arisen. At that stage, there is a spirit of cooperation between the parties and a desire to make things work. When a dispute does arise, that basic cooperation may have long since vanished and each party is more likely to have only victory in mind. He or she is then less inclined to compromise to resolve the dispute or to create a mechanism to do so that might weaken his or her position.

The second purpose is that it promotes efforts by parties to resolve disputes at earlier stages. When the parties know there is a mechanism in place that they can be legally required to undertake, they may be more apt to attempt to avoid disputes or to compromise them before the mechanism is invoked. Finally, the mechanism allows the business of the LLC to progress while the dispute is being resolved rather than allowing it to paralyze the organization and further damage its business.

Transfer of Interests

The question of whether to permit and, if so, the method for transferring interests in an LLC has significance both for the internal operation of the organization and, as we will see later in this chapter, for its tax treatment by the IRS. The question arises in several forms, such as:

- The admission of new members by the LLC.
- The resignation of existing members.
- The transfer of an interest from an existing member to a third party.
- The obligation of a member to buy or to sell his or her interest to another member or to the LLC on the occurrence of a particular event.

Admission of New Members

Most state laws do not include procedures for the admission of new members by an LLC. Nevertheless, the Articles or the Operating Agreement should contain the LLC's thinking on this important subject. For instance, is the issue of admitting a new member so important to the existing membership that it ought to be accomplished only with the unanimous consent of existing members? Even if unanimous consent is not a requirement, should any member or class of members have veto power over an admission? In addition to the question of whether to admit new members and the procedure for doing so, there is the question of what contribution should be required and what share of the LLC should be given to such a member.

Termination of Membership

Memberships may terminate based on any of several events. Many state laws set rules concerning termination that will be in effect unless the Operating Agreement provides to the contrary. Among the most common statutory events of termination are

- The assignment of a member's entire interest in the LLC.
- The filing by a member of a voluntary petition in bankruptcy.
- A member being adjudicated a bankrupt in an involuntary proceeding.
- The death of a member.
- The resignation of a member.

Since, in many states, the Operating Agreement can create alternate provisions, it would be wise for the organizers to consider when a membership ought to terminate and to so provide in the Agreement. For instance, bankruptcy, whether voluntary or involuntary, may transfer the bankrupt's LLC interest to the bankruptcy estate and make it available to the member's creditors. To avoid having the creditors involved, even only in a financial way, with the LLC, the organizers might choose to terminate the membership upon the occurrence of the bankruptcy. Similarly, the remaining members might not want a person continuing as a member if that person has transferred his or her interest to another or one who is no longer interested in the LLC and wishes to resign. Having such a person remaining as a member of the LLC could be disruptive or even more harmful to the organization. Thus, provisions setting out the fact and method of termination would be appropriate.

Transfer Restrictions

We have pointed out that the ability to transfer interests in the LLC has tax and operational consequences. Some of the same considerations are at play here as in the admission of new members generally, but there are also important differences. A distinction must be made between transferring one's membership in the LLC and merely assigning one's economic rights in the organization. The former transaction brings a new member into the LLC with all the power and rights of membership. The latter transaction merely gives the assignee the rights to distributions and calls on the LLC's assets that the assigning member has and no right of membership is conveyed. In both a transfer of membership or an assignment of rights, a member is usually attempting to transfer his or her interest for a price or for the discharge of a pre-existing obligation. His or her interest is purely economic.

The LLC's interest, on the other hand, is much broader although it is usually limited to complete transfers. These situations raise questions about the internal compatibility and efficiency of the LLC, its tax status and, in some cases, its exemption from registration under the federal and state securities laws. To protect the interests of both the member and the LLC, the Operating Agreement should set out the terms of permissible transfers and assignments.

Subject to the IRS rules concerning tax status, these terms could include a requirement that the selling member first offer the membership to the LLC to buy back and retire. If the LLC cannot or will not buy the membership, the membership interest might be offered, pro rata, to the remaining members. In each case, there should be a time limit within which the LLC or the members would have to respond. In addition, there might be a provision to the effect that if a member receives an offer to buy his or her shares, and the member is prepared to sell, the member must give the LLC and its members, pro rata, the opportunity to match the offer. In this way, the LLC can maintain control of who may become a member.

Another way to restrict the transfer of a membership interest is to require that any new member be approved by the existing members or by the manager(s). This could be by a unanimous vote or by a super majority. In either case, restricting transferability is very important. One of the factors that the IRS looks at to determine whether an LLC will be taxed as a partnership or as a corporation is how freely interests in the entity are transferrable. The greater the restriction on transferability, the more likely the IRS will decide this issue in favor of taxing the LLC as a partnership.

Buy/Sell Agreements

Buy/sell agreements are arrangements worked out between members of the LLC that, upon the occurrence of a described event, require one member to sell his or her LLC interest to the other(s) and require the other(s) to buy it. Usually the event that triggers a buy/sell agreement is the death or the incapacity of one of the members. The purpose of the agreement is to prevent persons who were not members of the LLC from becoming members through inheriting a deceased member's interest or through someone acting on behalf of an incapacitated member. A buy/sell agreement usually sets out the terms of the transaction including the price, the method of payment, and any provisions concerning the resignation of managers who hold their position by virtue of the selling member's ownership.

Amendment of an Operating Agreement

An Operating Agreement is a contract between all of the members of an LLC. As such, it must be consented to by each original member and any member that is subsequently admitted to the organization. However, the original Agreement may, over time, prove to have defects or omissions that need to be corrected for the smooth and efficient operation of the LLC. Therefore the Agreement needs to be susceptible to amendments. Since the Agreement is a contract, the normal rule would be that any amendments have to be agreed to by each of the parties to the contract, that is, the members. Thus, if the group wants to leave the original Agreement intact unless all of the members agree on an amendment, it would opt for unanimous consent to any changes. On the other hand, if the group wishes to ease the process of amending the original Agreement, it may provide in the Agreement that a smaller number of members, perhaps a simple majority, would be sufficient to amend it and thereby bind all of the members.

TAX ASPECTS OF LLCS

Corporations and their shareholders are generally subject to "double taxation." The first tax is on the corporate level on its taxable income. The second tax is on the shareholder level on that portion of the corporation's taxable income that is distributed to its shareholders as dividends. Investors and businesspeople have long sought ways of avoiding this double tax without losing protection from individual liability or losing business and management flexibility. They have found one in the LLC to the extent that the IRS treats an LLC as an association taxed as a partnership. Whether it will be taxed as a partnership depends on how it measures up under the various criteria set up by IRS to determine the tax status of an organization.

IRS Criteria to Classify Organizations

The IRS has developed a test utilizing several corporate characteristics to determine whether an organization should be taxed as a corporation or as a partnership. The test is whether the organization exhibits more characteristics of a corporation than of a partnership among the four corporate characteristics identified by IRS. The four are:

- Limited liability.
- Centralized management.
- Free transferability of interests.
- Continuity of life.

Keep in mind that the test requires that an organization exhibit *more* corporate characteristics than noncorporate characteristics to be classified as a corporation for tax purposes. This means that an organization must have at least three of the four listed characteristics to be taxed as a corporation. Merely having two will not subject an organization to corporate tax.

Limited Liability
The IRS considers an organization to have limited liability when under the law of its state of organization no member has personal liability for the obligations of, or the claims against, the organization. LLCs were specifically designed to provide their members with limited liability. This corporate characteristic is, therefore, always present in an LLC and is largely outside the control of the members. Therefore, an LLC will always have at least one corporate characteristic.

Centralized Management

This corporate characteristic is surprisingly difficult to define. Its name suggests that when one person or group of persons manage the organization for all of its members, there is centrality of management. In fact, this is essentially the IRS definition. IRS regulation 301.7701-2(c)(1) says an organization exhibits centralized management when

> any person (or any group of persons which does not include all the members) has continuing, exclusive authority to make the decisions necessary to the conduct of the business for which the organization was formed.

Unfortunately, the regulation goes on to create some confusion. It does so by stating that a limited partnership organized under a state statute like the Uniform Limited Partnership Act or the Revised Uniform Limited Partnership Act (one or the other of which has been adopted, in whole or in part, in many jurisdictions) will *not* be treated as having centralized management. You will recall that the essence of a limited partnership is that there are one or more limited partners who have only limited liability for the organization's debts but in exchange for this benefit give up almost all right to manage the partnership. Instead, the general partner(s) have management responsibility and personal liability.

On the other hand, IRS has ruled that where members of an LLC select managers to run the business for them, there *is* centrality of management. The IRS has gone so far as to rule that a Colorado LLC with 5 members who, pursuant to the state law that *requires* managers, elected themselves as the managers of the organization, *had* centralized management. Whether this means that having managers always will equate with this corporate characteristic is uncertain. However, the risk is clearly present that an LLC with managers might be deemed to have this characteristic as well as limited liability. The message, then, is that if all members are to manage the LLC, they should do so as members and not as managers. In addition, if the LLC does have managers, the Operating Agreement should provide the members with as much oversight and control over the managers as possible.

Free Transferability of Interests

It is a characteristic of corporations that a shareholder may transfer his or her shares to another person. This means that if an LLC member is able to transfer to a nonmember *all* of his or her membership interest without the consent of the remaining members, the corporate characteristic of free transferability of interest will exist. "All of his or her interest" means all of the incidents of membership, not merely the member's interest in the profits or capital gains of the LLC. Thus, if the members wish to avoid implicating this corporate characteristic, they should include transfer restrictions in the Articles or Operating Agreement. A point to consider, however, is that if the LLC is seeking investors who will not be intimately involved with the organization, restrictions on their ability to transfer their shares may inhibit the LLC's ability to attract such investors.

The nature of the restrictions on transferability is also very important. For instance, the IRS has held that merely giving a right of first refusal to the LLC or its members does not completely protect the LLC from the imposition of this corporate characteristic. The safer course where restrictions are desired is for the Agreement to require consent to the transfer by the independent managers of the LLC or by a majority in interest of the membership. Even the issue of majority, as opposed to unanimous, membership consent is not clearly established as a sufficient restriction although it appears that that is the way the IRS is moving.

Continuity of Life

This corporate characteristic is also deceptively simple. Continuity of life, however, does not relate solely to the perpetual duration of the entity. Certainly, if an organization is legally permitted to have perpetual duration and chooses to do so, there will be continuity of life. On the other hand, there are several instances where an organization has limited its existence to a fixed number of years or until the completion of a finite task, but the IRS has ruled that it had continuity of life. The real issue for IRS is whether the addition or removal of a member will terminate the legal existence of the organization. With a corporation, a separate legal entity whose existence is not tied to the identity of its shareholders, the coming or going of shareholders does not effect its continuity. Partnerships, however, are merely aggregates of individuals. When any part of that aggregate changes, theoretically, at least, the partnership changes.

In deciding whether an LLC is more like a corporation or a partnership in this regard, we are once again confronted with a series of contradictions. Since an LLC is liable for its own obligations, it appears to be a separate entity, like a corporation. On the other hand, all members are entitled to share in management, which makes it look like a partnership. In addition, most state laws require that the Articles of Organization set a date for the termination of the LLC's existence. These same laws, however, generally allow the Articles or the Operating Agreement to provide for the termination and/or continuity of the LLC and therein lies the manner of avoiding this corporate characteristic.

The Agreement might provide that the death, resignation, removal, insanity, or bankruptcy of any member or the transfer of his or her interest, terminates (or, to use the legal phrase, dissolves) the LLC. The Agreement could also provide that the unanimous consent of the members would, nevertheless, permit the LLC to continue. The IRS has agreed that such a provision does not give the LLC continuity of life. There is some doubt about whether permitting less than the unanimous agreement of members to continue the LLC would be enough to negate the continuity of life characteristic.

Strategic Decisions

Given the uncertainties about the implementation of the IRS criteria in reference to LLCs, there are many strategic decisions that the organizers have to make concerning its organization and operation. The first such decision is whether the organizers care about the tax status of the LLC. Generally this is a foregone conclusion because there are other forms of business they could have chosen that would have accommodated their limited liability and flexibility concerns. Therefore, assuming the tax status of the LLC is an important issue, the organizers must make sure that they create an entity with the greatest possibility of being treated for tax purposes as a partnership. Remember, an LLC may exhibit two of the corporate characteristics and still be treated as a partnership. One of those characteristics, limited liability, is a fundamental element of the LLC's identity. Therefore, the LLC may have only one of the remaining three characteristics if it wishes to qualify as a partnership for tax purposes.

The organizers must then weigh the advantages and disadvantages of several competing possibilities. For instance, is it worthwhile to limit the free transferability of interests, which might discourage investors, in order to obtain a favorable tax status? Of course, the absence of the favorable tax status might also discourage investors. Similarly, is the efficiency of a centralized management so important that it is worth jeopardizing the "partnership" status? Finally, does there need to be continuity of existence, which will simplify the bookkeeping and financial administration of the LLC, or can accommodations concerning existence be made so that there will be no taxation of the LLC?

Each of these items may be addressed in the Articles or the Operating Agreement. The organizers should examine each of the characteristics and decide which can be brought within the IRS guidelines without sacrificing other organizational values. Where none are susceptible to such accommodation, the organizers must make hard choices about sacrifice. Generally, however, these characteristics can be adapted to meet the IRS test and the LLC can provide its owners with the combination of limited liability, managerial flexibility, and favorable tax treatment the LLC was designed to promote.

COMPARISON WITH OTHER BUSINESS FORMS

The emergence of LLCs has had a powerful impact on the business landscape. While there is still much to be learned about how to operate LLCs and about how the law, particularly the tax law, will treat them, if it is established that, as a matter of course, LLCs will be taxed as if they were partnerships, several forms of business could become obsolete.

Sole Proprietorships

In those states where one-person LLCs are permitted, the sole proprietorship would become an unnecessary business form. Businesspeople could enjoy the protection from personal liability, the single taxation of sole proprietors and only insignificantly greater administrative burdens. The difficulty would arise in those states that did not permit one-person LLCs. Even in those jurisdictions, the problem could be addressed in at least two ways. The first is to bring into the LLC a second person, a family member or another person who is trusted by the proprietor, and give that person a very small ownership interest. The proprietor would then develop an Operating Agreement that would vest substantially all management responsibility in him or herself. The second method of avoiding this problem would be to organize your LLC in a state that permits one-person LLCs and seek to operate in your own jurisdiction as a foreign LLC. It is not yet completely clear as to what restrictions states will place on foreign LLCs and, therefore, this method involves some risks. These questions should be more clear, however, in the not too distant future.

Partnerships

Limited partnerships were developed to provide a vehicle giving investors limited liability with partnership tax treatment. The trade off for these benefits was that the general partner(s) had unlimited personal liability. In addition, the limited partners gave up essentially all rights to manage the partnership's affairs. An LLC, on the other hand, would permit each member to have limited liability *and* the right to participate in management. Moreover, the management could be structured much more flexibly than with a limited partnership.

General partnerships would also be affected. They permit flexible management opportunities, but expose all partners to unlimited personal liability. Thus, except to the extent that state laws required certain types of businesses to be conducted in the partnership form, the prevalence of this form of business would also diminish.

Corporations

Even corporations might be affected by the arrival of the LLC. Clearly, certain tax advantages could be a motivating factor in choosing the LLC form. The greater flexibility in permissible contributions and method of distributing profits, gains and losses is another possible advantage of the LLC. Finally, voting rights are more easily tailored in the LLC. With corporations, voting is usually based on capital contributions and while corporations may create different classes of shares to limit or to eliminate voting rights, this may limit the possibilities of the corporation to tailor its tax situation.

Corporations may do this through the use of subchapter S of the Internal Revenue Code, which permits certain types of corporations to be taxed as if they were partnerships. Among the qualifying characteristics for subchapter S status are

- One class of shares.
- Not more than 35 shareholders.
- Shareholders generally must be natural persons.
- Shareholders may not be nonresident aliens.

The LLC, on the other hand, has none of these restrictions. There may be unlimited members of any type. Membership may be divided into classes and nonresidents may hold memberships.

Tax Disadvantages of LLCs

There are several tax disadvantages of LLCs that might suggest choosing a standard subchapter C corporation as the form for conducting your business. These include the fact that the top corporate tax rate is lower than the top individual rate. Therefore, rather than have LLC income pass through to high-bracket members, it might be advantageous to create a corporation and to allow the income to be taxed at corporate rates and retained by the corporation. It might then be distributed at a later time in a manner that is deductible to the corporation and not taxable to the shareholder. Alternatively, retained earnings by the corporation enhance its net worth. Thus the shares of the corporation would, presumably, be worth more. If they are sold by a shareholder, the gain on the shares would normally be taxed at a capital gains rate which is lower than the top rates on income.

Finally, there are several deductions from income that are not permitted to subchapter S corporations or to partnerships that are permitted to subchapter C corporations. This includes many of the benefits that employees, including shareholders or members, might receive from the business. For instance, health insurance is a deductible expense in C corporations, even if the shareholders, as employees, are covered by the insurance. In partnerships and S corporations, these expenses are not deductible to any partner or to any shareholder who holds more than 2% of the S corporation's stock. Therefore, there are several reasons why the C corporation will survive, but the long-term future for the S corporation is in doubt.

CONCLUSION

This overview of an important new form of business is merely intended as a brief introduction. State laws vary on what is permissible concerning LLCs and you need to consult a local practitioner for detailed advice on how an LLC works in your jurisdiction. In addition, the rules of how foreign LLCs will be treated are still in a process of development. Finally, while it appears that LLCs can be treated as partnerships for tax purposes, the rules here, too, are in flux. Thus, you should consider an LLC as the form for your business but only after consultation with a local expert and careful examination of the risks and rewards.

14

TAKING FUNDS FROM THE CORPORATION

We have previously examined some tax consequences of incorporating and looked at a few methods by which some of the more common negative aspects can be avoided or, at least, minimized. As Chapter 12 pointed out, Subchapter S can play a major role in reducing negative tax consequences by eliminating the double tax to which corporations are normally subjected. On the other hand, there are drawbacks to the use of Subchapter S that make its use undesirable to some corporations. Depending on the circumstances of a particular corporation, careful tax planning may provide to a Subchapter C corporation much of the benefit of S corporations without the drawbacks and limitations imposed by Subchapter S. This chapter will examine some methods by which shareholders can withdraw corporate cash and benefits in ways that are deductible for the corporation, thus reducing corporate income. Many of these benefits have the added attraction of not being taxable as income to the recipient. In this way, corporate taxes may be reduced or eliminated while the shareholders still receive the benefits of corporate income.

Some of these methods, such as income splitting, have been addressed in prior chapters, while the forms and tax consequences of executive compensation will be examined in the next one. Here, we will discuss:

- The benefits of shareholders capitalizing their corporation with a combination of debt and equity
- Leasing by the shareholders to the corporation of space and equipment needed in the corporation's business
- Purchase or lease by the corporation of goods and services that may be used by shareholder/employees.

Keep in mind that since each corporation has different circumstances and needs, there is no single set of tax-saving activities that can be universally applied. Moreover, the Internal Revenue Service (IRS) has the right to disallow certain claimed deductions if they are fraudulent. The IRS may also disallow them even if they are not fraudulent but are unreasonable under the circumstances. In the aftermath of such a disallowance, the taxpayer may be faced with increased taxes, interest charges on the overdue balance and, in some cases, penalties. If the taxpayer wishes to challenge the disallowance, there are appeal rights within the IRS and, if those fail, access to the federal district court or the Tax Court. Each of these avenues offers the opportunity to redress a wrongful disallowance, but each also involves the expenditure of a significant amount of time, energy, and money. It would, therefore, be much wiser to plan your expenditures carefully and to document them with complete and accurate records.

CORPORATE CAPITALIZATION WITH DEBT

Earlier, in a discussion of the capitalization of a corporation, the distinction was made between debt instruments and stock. It was pointed out that stock meant ownership in the corporation and offered the shareholder a chance to increase his or her wealth through the increase in the value of the corporation. It was also pointed out that if the corporation performed poorly and was liquidated, the shareholders would be the last to be paid off and that the common shareholders are the last of the shareholders to be paid. Debt holders, on the other hand, are in a much more secure position as far as the return of their investment is concerned. While an investment in a debt instrument is one that offers little or no opportunity for growth, the debt holder will be paid his or her interest before shareholders receive a dividend on their stock. In the event of a liquidation, debt holders will be repaid the amount owed before the shareholders can receive from the corporation a return of their capital. If there is not enough money to pay the debts or if the debts are paid but there is not enough to pay the shareholders, the unpaid (or partially unpaid) shareholders have no recourse (unless they allege mismanagement by the corporate directors or officers) and will lose their investment. Keep in mind that in such a situation, Section 1244 stock may be a significant benefit to these shareholders. The debt holder, however, will not participate in the growth of a successful corporation. If the corporation does particularly well, the value of the note held by a lender does not increase nor, in the typical case, does the rate of interest payable on that note.

In many closely held corporations, the shareholders also lend money to it. When this occurs, many of the negatives associated with holding debt instruments do not apply. For instance, the shareholders will participate in the growth of the corporation through their stock ownership. They will receive regular payments from the corporation, whether denominated as interest or as dividends, through their holding of debt and equity. Moreover, as creditors, they may be protected from some of the risks of their investment because they will be eligible to receive a distribution on liquidation of the corporation, along with the other creditors, before the shareholders are repaid. If there is not enough money to pay even the creditors, the advantage to being in the shareholder/lender's position is clear. In the status of lender, a shareholder will receive funds as a creditor that he or she would not have received as a shareholder. Therefore, part of their contribution to the corporation may be returned to them by investing it as debt. In order to put such a contribution in the best possible light, all of the formalities of a loan should be observed. There should be a board resolution authorizing the corporation to borrow and a promissory note evidencing the debt. Interest should be charged, and the terms of the note should be observed. Finally, the ratio of shareholder-held debt to equity must be reasonable so that the IRS will be less likely to call the interest a constructive dividend.

Another major advantage of having the principals contribute capital partly as equity and partly as debt is associated with the tax consequences for the corporation of this structure. As you may recall from the discussion of capitalization, dividends that are distributed to the shareholders are not deductible expenses for the corporation, but payment of interest to debt holders is. This is true, with some limitations, even if the debt holders are also the shareholders in the corporation. The benefits of this consideration can best be illustrated by an example.

Suppose a Subchapter C corporation had been capitalized with $400,000 of equity. Suppose also that in the current year, the corporation has gross income of $100,000 and deductible expenses of $70,000. The $30,000 excess is, of course, taxable to the corporation. If it distributes all (or any part) of the after-tax excess to the shareholders, they will be taxed on their portion of the distribution. If, instead of capitalization of

$400,000 of equity, the shareholders contributed $150,000 of equity and the balance of $250,000 through a loan to the corporation bearing interest at the rate of 10% per year, the tax situation of the corporation would change dramatically. There would still be gross income of $100,000 but the deductible expenses would be increased because of the interest paid to the shareholders on their loans.

The interest paid to the creditor/shareholders would be $25,000 (a loan of $250,000 × 10% interest). The corporation's deductions increase by $25,000, and its taxable income decreases by a like amount. Therefore, the corporation would have $100,000 income and $95,000 in deductible expenses, leaving a taxable income of only $5,000. The shareholders would receive from the corporation the same amount (and, perhaps, even more) as they would have received from the dividend distribution. They will, of course, be taxed on what they receive, regardless of whether it is interest income or a dividend. There will not, however, be a corporate tax on the amount distributed as interest. The effect of this is to save a significant amount of money for the corporation and its shareholders. The corporation that was fully capitalized with equity would pay a tax of $4,500 on its $30,000 taxable income ($30,000 × 15%). If the balance of $25,500 were distributed to shareholders who were each in the 28% tax bracket, they would pay a total of $7,140 in tax on the dividend. Thus, the total tax on the $30,000 corporate profit would be $11,640.

If the corporation had been capitalized with the combination of debt and equity just described, the tax picture would be quite different. The corporation would already have paid out $25,000 in interest to the shareholders, which would leave taxable income of only $5,000. The corporation would pay a tax of $750 ($5,000 × 15%), leaving an after-tax profit of $4,250 to distribute ($5,000 − $750). When added to the $25,000 interest payment, the shareholders will have received $29,250 of the corporation's gross income. They will be taxed at the rate of 28% on this income, which will result in a tax obligation of $8,190 ($29,250 × 28%). They will, therefore, have paid a total tax on income derived from the corporation of $8,940. This amount is a savings of $2,700 over the tax on corporate income and distributions based on a capitalization of 100% equity.

The process of combining debt and equity in a corporate capitalization is known as *thin incorporation.* It involves capitalizing a corporation with the highest ratio of debt to equity that would be reasonable under the particular circumstances of the corporation. If the debt is held by the shareholders of the corporation, the IRS will be concerned that the debt is just another form of equity and the interest payments nothing more than camouflage for nondeductible dividends. The tax code gives the IRS the power to examine such situations and to disallow as a *constructive dividend* some or all of the deductions associated with the debt. The Code sets out several factors to be considered in determining whether there truly was a loan by a shareholder to the corporation, including:

- Whether there is a written instrument containing the corporation's unconditional promise to pay a certain sum by a particular date or on demand
- Whether the debt is subordinated to or has a preference over other indebtedness of the corporation
- The overall ratio of corporate debt to equity
- Whether the debt is convertible into stock.

These factors should, once again, underline for the principals of a corporation the importance of observing corporate formalities when lending to the corporation. They also should serve as a reminder not to overstep reasonable bounds of sound financial planning.

An additional advantage to the organizers of using debt to capitalize the corporation occurs if and when the corporation becomes very successful. At that point the corporation can start returning capital to its investors. One advantage of the repayment of debt is that it is a tax-free event, whereas the redemption of stock (which is another way of returning capital to shareholders) may involve undesirable tax consequences. For example, assume a C corporation earns significant profits that the shareholders wish to take out of the corporation. The obvious methods to achieve this end is for them to declare a dividend or to increase their salaries and/or fringe benefits. When their salaries and fringes are already near the limit of what the IRS will accept as "reasonable," this avenue is fraught with risk. If the IRS were to disallow the deduction for increased compensation, the corporation could be subject not only to additional taxation but also to penalties for its invalid deduction and interest on its underpayment of taxes. Declaring a dividend would not give the corporation a deduction and would result in the double tax that most corporations and shareholders try hard to avoid.

A method that would satisfy both the shareholders' need for cash as well as their desire to avoid taxation on the distribution is the repayment of debt by the corporation. The corporation's interests are not injured since we are assuming it is in a financial position to make some form of distribution anyway. The shareholders' interests are also protected. They can receive the repayment without it affecting their ownership interest in the corporation because no stock is involved in the transaction. Furthermore, since they are merely receiving what they had previously loaned to the corporation, there is no income involved and, therefore, no tax. There is, of course, a long-term effect in that the corporation, by repaying debt, is reducing for subsequent years the amount it will pay out in interest, thereby reducing its deductions and, all other things being equal, increasing its taxable income.

SHAREHOLDER LEASES TO THE CORPORATION

Generally speaking, rent paid by the corporation for items used in its business activities is deductible. This is true even if the rent is paid to a shareholder of the corporation. The issue for the allowance of this deduction (when the claimed payment was made to a shareholder) is whether the rent being paid is reasonable. This is essentially asking the question, "Would a corporation dealing at arm's length with a lessor expect to pay the rent being charged?" If the answer is yes, the deduction will be allowed. If the answer is that a corporation dealing at arm's length would pay less, the excess rent will be disallowed as a deduction. Similarly, if the rent for a particular item is reasonable in amount but the item is one not really used by the corporation, the deduction will be disallowed. The effect of a disallowance is that the tax owed by the corporation will be increased, and interest and penalties will be added to the bill.

Nevertheless, if the shareholder owns property that the corporation needs for its business, the shareholder should consider leasing it to the corporation rather than contributing it in exchange for shares of stock. If the corporation has enough working capital to conduct its business and enough income to pay the rental fees, the use of a lease gives the shareholder added protection against loss. It also gives the corporation a tax deduction for the expenditure. The deduction has the effect, as does the deduction for the payment of interest on a debt, of reducing the corporation's income. This reduces its tax liability while allowing it to make a distribution of its revenue to its shareholders. There is an added advantage in that the shareholder may be entitled to deductions on his or her tax return for the depreciation and/or maintenance costs associated with the property leased to the corporation. This would shelter some or all of the income derived by the shareholder from the lease. In some cases, it might even shelter other income of the shareholder, thus making the alternative of leasing property to the corporation one clearly worth exploring.

Assume you own items that are needed by your corporation and you are willing to make them available to it through a lease. Aside from the tax advantages to the corporation and, through it, to the shareholders, there may also be advantages to the lessor of the property. The main benefit to the lessor is the possibility of taking a deduction for the depreciation of that property. As we know, the IRC permits a deduction for loss due to the ordinary wear and tear and obsolescence of a capital asset used in a trade or business or held for the production of income. Property that is leased to the corporation may be considered held by the lessor for the production of income even if the leased property is not normally used in the lessor's trade or business. The amount of the deduction in any year and the number of years during which the lessor may depreciate the property depend on the nature and value of the property and the date when it is first put into service. In addition, the passive loss limitations added to the code in the Tax Reform Act of 1986 might affect the immediate usefulness to the lessor of the depreciation deduction.

Despite the technicalities of the tax law, the benefits of leasing can be significant. For instance, if a shareholder has an extra room in his or her home, the room could be leased to the corporation as its office. The corporation would pay the shareholder a fair market rent for the space (which would be deducted from the corporation's income). This would, as has already been observed, result in a distribution to the shareholder without the intervention of the corporate tax. Furthermore, since the building (or the part of the building) where the office space is located is a capital asset, it may be depreciated. The shareholder/lessor may deduct from his or her personal income an amount permitted by the IRC. This deduction may be large enough to shelter all or part of the rental payment made for the space by the corporation.

For example, if the rental payment were $300 per month ($3,600 per year), the shareholder would have an additional $3,600 per year in income, which would be subject to personal income taxation. If, however, he or she were able to claim in that same year a deduction for the use of the space, of, hypothetically, $3,000, the increased income *subject to tax* would be only $600. The shareholder would still have received the full $3,600, but the deduction for depreciation would have wiped out, on paper, most of the rental income. I use the phrase *on paper* because in most cases involving the depreciation of real property (buildings), there is no actual loss in value because of wear and tear. In fact, generally speaking, real property continues to *increase* in value over time.

The depreciation deductions taken previously will ultimately be *recaptured* upon the sale of the property. This is accomplished by reducing the lessor's basis in the property by the amount of depreciation claimed and taxing the gain, represented by the difference between the adjusted basis of the property and its sale price. Recapture will not occur until the sale of the property, which may be years down the road, and, as we know, tax deferral is a major element of tax planning. If the lessor provides the corporation with a capital asset other than real property (a delivery truck, for instance), the depreciation deduction will still be available. In this case, though, there probably will be an actual loss in the value of the asset due to its wearing down. If that is so, there may be no problem concerning the recapture of the deductions since the asset will most likely be scrapped or sold for less than its adjusted basis.

It is also possible that the deduction for depreciation will exceed the income derived from the leasing of the asset. In such a case, the lessor may be entitled to use the excess deduction to offset income from completely separate sources. This is what is known as a *tax shelter*, although the availability of such devices has been severely curtailed by the Tax Reform Act of 1986. This Act was the culmination of a long effort by the IRS and Congress to close various loopholes in the law that had allowed certain taxpayers to avoid paying what was considered their fair share of taxes. Nevertheless, the Act still permits the sheltering effect of depreciation deductions in several instances, and shareholders would be wise to determine if they are able to take advantage of those instances.

There is also a nontax advantage for a shareholder who leases property to his or her corporation. As you recall, the limited liability offered to shareholders protects them from personal liability for the acts of the corporation. They can only lose their investment in the corporation. If the corporation's assets are not sufficient to pay its liabilities, the creditor cannot seek additional compensation from the personal assets of the shareholders. If a shareholder has contributed property to the corporation *in exchange for shares*, that property belongs to the corporation and is available to be used in meeting the corporation's obligations. If, however, that property was only leased to the corporation, it remains the property of the shareholder and cannot be taken by a creditor. Thus the shareholder insulates himself or herself even further from the liabilities of the corporation.

ACQUISITION BY THE CORPORATION OF GOODS AND SERVICES AVAILABLE TO THE SHAREHOLDERS

There are a wide variety of goods and services that can fulfill both legitimate business purposes as well as the personal desires of the shareholders. Automobiles, art and antiques, travel and entertainment, education, and equipment all can and do serve dual purposes. If the corporation provides these goods and services for the shareholders while in pursuit of the corporation's business, these items will be deductible to the corporation and may not be treated as income to the recipient.

Automobiles and Other Equipment

A common example of the shareholders benefiting from deductible corporate expenses is the corporation's purchasing or leasing an automobile and providing it to an employee. To the extent that the automobile is needed for corporate purposes, the corporation may deduct the lease payments or depreciate the purchase price. Rarely is the employee who is given the use of the automobile restricted to using it *only* for business purposes. Thus, the employee may use the automobile for personal use. To the extent the automobile is used for business, the value of the automobile will not be recognized as income to the employee. To the extent that the automobile is used for nonbusiness purposes, the employee will be treated as having received income to the extent of the value of the personal use. He or she will have to pay a tax on that use. It is incumbent on employees to keep careful records of their business and personal use of the automobile. They should keep a daily log indicating the date, the number of miles driven, and the purpose of their various trips.

As an example, assume the value of an automobile purchased by the corporation and provided for the use of an employee is $2,500 per year. Assume further that the employee uses the automobile 50% for business and 50% for personal reasons. The corporation will have a deduction for the full value of the car and the employee will be treated as having income to the extent of $1,250. Assuming the employee is in the 28% bracket, the tax will be $350 per year, a rather small price to pay for the use of an automobile. What is more, many corporations allow their employees to purchase the automobile at book value after it has been fully depreciated or the lease expires. At that point, the book value of the car is minimal while the market value may be somewhat higher. This, too, is a major benefit to shareholder/employees.

The same concept is applicable to other goods and equipment the corporation provides to shareholder/employees. For instance, home computers are often given to employees so that they may work away from the office. Products of the corporation may be provided so that friends and neighbors will see them in use. Furniture, art, antiques, rugs all have been provided for home office use or for the upscale appointment of corporate headquarters. Assuming the business purpose can be shown, the cost of these items may be depreciated or deducted by the corporation while being obtained tax free (or for a relatively small tax in relation to value) by the shareholder.

Travel and Entertainment

Travel and entertainment is another area where the shareholder/employee can obtain significant benefits from the corporation. Assume there are business activities or prospects in interesting locations away from corporate headquarters. You may travel there and have your travel costs, room, board, local transportation, and other related expenses paid for by the corporation, which may deduct these charges. In addition, to the extent the charges were for business purposes, they are not recognized as income to the employee. If a spouse and other family members are employed by the corporation in positions where their presence on the trip would be appropriate, their expenses are similarly deductible to the corporation and not recognized as income to them.

Of course, purely personal activities paid for by the corporation will be treated as income to the shareholder and taxed accordingly. Again, however, the amount actually paid in tax normally bears a disproportionately small relationship to the benefit obtained by the employee. As with automobiles used both for business and personal purposes, the employee should keep a log of activities and expenses. In addition, it should be noted that the Internal Revenue Code § 274 limits the deductibility of meal and entertainment expense to 50% of the cost of such activities.

Finally, the corporation might provide facilities, such as a swimming pool or a gym, for its employees. If these facilities are regularly used by the shareholder/employees, they will have the benefit of them at corporate expense. While the use by the shareholder/employees may not be exclusive, the benefit of having the corporation pay for these activities with deductible dollars is obvious. Moreover, the value of the facilities will not be treated as income for the employees. Thus, the shareholder/employees will obtain the best of both worlds.

Education and Self-Improvement

A corporation generally has an interest in the education of its employees in areas that are likely to improve the on-the-job productivity of those employees. To this end, corporations may offer a variety of formal and informal educational opportunities to its employees. In many cases, the cost of these offerings is deductible to the corporation and not recognized as income of the employee. In order to be deductible, these costs may not be for the purpose of meeting minimal educational requirements for qualifying in one's occupation or a new trade or business. On the other hand, if the shareholder/employee has an interest that is related to the business, the corporation can pay for courses, books, magazines, videotapes, or software for the employee to pursue that interest.

The corporation can also pay dues and memberships in organizations, such as trade associations related to the business's activities or civic associations. This would allow the corporation's representatives to participate in the organization's activities, including travel and education. This goes so far as to permit the payment by the corporation of country club dues if the use of the club is at least 50% for business purposes. As with automobiles, equipment, and travel, employees should keep good records of their activities while at the club as well as outside business activities originating from the club.

From the foregoing brief survey, it should be clear that there are numerous ways in which shareholders can obtain benefits from their corporation at significant tax savings. In the next chapter, we will discuss compensation, fringe benefits, and income splitting that may also provide tax-favored distributions to or for the benefit of shareholders. In each case, the benefits are due to the deductibility of the expense to the corporation and, in many cases, the nonrecognition of income to the shareholder. Of course, these methods are not foolproof and do not work in every case. Moreover, IRS is often on the lookout for dividends masquerading as deductions. Therefore, shareholders should consult with qualified tax professionals before setting up a package for their corporation.

15

EXECUTIVE COMPENSATION

An important question that arises in new closely held corporations is how to compensate managerial employees, many of whom will be shareholders. This question is more difficult to answer than it might at first appear. Employees who are not shareholders in the corporation want the highest possible salaries, whereas shareholders prefer that large amounts be set aside for distribution, in one form or another, to themselves. In addition to these internal tugs of war, the federal and state tax authorities are interested in finding the largest possible taxable income in the corporation from which to derive the greatest possible tax revenue.

Obviously, all these competing factors cannot be met at the same time. Therefore, the ability to maneuver through the maze of interest group desires, legal requirements, and practical realities is a critical skill for the organizers. Indeed, the identification of corporate goals concerning the distribution of its revenue pie is only the first step. The implementation of those goals requires a good grasp of the available options and careful planning as to which ones to utilize in a particular corporate situation. This chapter will present some of the more significant options, along with a discussion of their attributes. Because many of the choices will be heavily influenced by tax considerations, these considerations will be highlighted in the discussion.

Among the most common forms of executive compensation are salaries, bonuses, expense accounts, and fringe benefits such as health, life, and disability insurance. In addition, corporations often provide their employees with pensions, profit-sharing plans, stock options, and other forms of deferred compensation. Before deciding whether to use one or more of these items and in what proportions, the principals of a corporation will need to examine all the factors involved, including:

- Composition of the executive and nonexecutive employees
- Whether management comprises corporate shareholders or outsiders
- Need for and likelihood of securing and retaining nonstockholder employees and executives
- Financial condition of the corporation and its shareholders
- Tax consequences of any particular choice.

As has already been mentioned, tax considerations play a major part in determining how to compensate employees. Many forms of compensation that are tax deductible to the corporation also may not be immediately (if ever) taxable to the employee. If the compensation paid to employees is deductible, the taxable income of the corporation will, of course, be reduced. If the employees who receive the compensation are also its shareholders, they will have successfully reduced or avoided the double taxation that is normally applicable to corporate distributions.

To give an example, suppose a corporation whose shareholders were its only employees took in gross revenue of $200,000 for a particular year. If it had deductible expenses (other than employee compensation) of $90,000, the corporation would have a taxable income of $110,000. This would result in a tax obligation of $26,150, leaving $83,850 for distribution as dividends to shareholders. If, however, the corporation provided salaries and fringe benefits for its shareholder employees in the amount of $75,000, the corporation could also deduct the $75,000 from its gross income. This would leave a taxable income of only $35,000 ($200,000 gross income − $90,000 noncompensation expense − $75,000 compensation expense = $35,000). The tax would be only $5,250, as opposed to the $26,150 in tax owed without the deduction. This would leave $29,750 available for distribution as dividends to shareholders. When this amount is added to the $75,000 they received as compensation, the shareholders could potentially take $104,750 out of the corporation and save $20,900 in corporate taxation in the process.

Of course, not all corporations are as simply constructed as the one in the previous example. Many times, the shareholders are not employees, or there are employees in addition to the shareholders. In such cases, the compensation paid to the employees will still generally be deductible to the corporation and, therefore, beneficial to the shareholders. They will not, however, receive the direct dollar-for-dollar benefit indicated in the example.

Two final points ought to be raised before going into a description of individual forms of compensation. First, state corporation laws often prescribe who may be compensated, for what services they may receive compensation, and in what form the compensation may be provided. In earlier days, for instance, directors were often prohibited from receiving any compensation from the corporation, even if they also served as corporate officers. It was thought that directors were insiders with significant financial interests in the corporation that they were protecting. No additional compensation beyond the profits generated by good management was deemed to be necessary. In addition, the performance by directors of the duties of officers was considered merely to be part of their obligation to the corporation and, again, not separately compensable. As more and more companies utilized the services of "outside" directors, those without substantial (or any) stock holdings in the corporation, the rules concerning the compensation of directors changed. Today, many state corporation laws permit compensation of directors, and clauses providing for compensation frequently appear in Articles of Incorporation and bylaws.

The second preliminary item involves the tax treatment of compensation. In order for any compensation to be deductible, it must be "reasonable" in amount. The Internal Revenue Service is entitled to review any deduction claimed by the corporation for compensation to employees. This issue only arises when the compensation is being paid to shareholders. Because dividends are not deductible and compensation generally is, many corporations have attempted to use a compensation format for what was really a distribution of corporate profits. The purpose of the review is to determine whether the compensation is really a form of disguised dividend to shareholders.

In determining what is *reasonable compensation,* the IRS will look at the amount of compensation paid in relation to a variety of factors, including:

- Size and nature of the corporation
- Services performed by the shareholder
- Qualifications of the shareholder to perform the required services
- Compensation paid for comparable services by similarly situated corporations in the geographic area
- General economic conditions
- Relationship of shareholder salaries to the salaries of other employees of the corporation

- Relationship of salaries to shareholdings (i.e., Is the salary of a 50% shareholder twice as large as the salary of a 25% shareholder?)
- Whether the corporation pays any dividends.

Even in the early days of a corporation's existence, there should be a provision for executive compensation. Many times, there is not enough money to pay the principals a salary. Nevertheless, it may be a good idea to allow a salary to accrue on the books of the corporation, even if it is not paid, in order to create a history of compensation for when times improve. This is because as conditions change, so may the compensation paid to shareholder employees. As the corporation's sales or product line grows, or the managers take on more responsibility, their compensation can increase accordingly.

If the IRS determines that the amounts paid by the corporation to its shareholders as compensation are unreasonably high, it will disallow some or all of the deduction. When this occurs, the tax obligation of the corporation increases. In addition, the corporation becomes liable for interest and penalties on the additional tax. The tax due from the shareholder, on the other hand, generally remains unchanged because he or she pays a tax on the amount received, regardless of whether it was called a dividend or compensation.

SALARIES, FEES, AND BONUSES

The most basic form of compensating employees is providing salaries for their services. When the payments are made to employees who are neither shareholders nor related to the shareholders, there is rarely a question about their reasonableness. This issue does arise, however, in closely held corporations where the main employees are the shareholders or their relatives. Where these corporations are taxed under Subchapter C of the Code, the IRS has been on the alert for attempts to disguise dividends by casting corporate profits in the form of executive compensation paid to shareholder/employees.

Among the most important issues that the IRS examines is whether there really were services performed for the corporation. This is because the deductibility of compensation depends, initially, on there having been something done for the benefit of the corporation. In order to be deductible, the tax law requires a payment to be "ordinary and necessary" within the business and reasonable in amount. The "ordinary and necessary" restriction means that the item being deducted must be necessary for the proper conduct of the business and must be ordinarily expended by businesses of the same kind.

Salaries for management personnel are clearly deductible if reasonable. Shareholders who are employees of their corporations are entitled to pay themselves at the highest reasonable rate, given the financial condition of the corporation and the rate paid by other businesses to their employees with comparable duties. This means that a shareholder should do some investigating before arbitrarily setting a salary level for himself or herself. The investigation can take place through other local businesspeople, the chamber of commerce or a trade association, or with an accountant or attorney familiar with the local business community.

Another way that shareholders can legitimately take deductible dollars out of the corporation is by hiring family members to fill corporate positions. As long as the family member is actually performing a job and the amounts being paid are reasonable for the position, the compensation paid is deductible. This is particularly useful when the employee is an unemancipated child of a shareholder (assuming that this does not violate local child labor laws). If the child does not earn significant amounts from the corporation, he or she might not be required to file a tax return. Even if a return is required, the child may claim available deductions, including the standard deduction, to offset his or her income. Thus, even when there is taxable income, it will be taxed at a rate that is probably lower than that of his or her parents. This form of *income splitting* keeps income in the family while probably taxing it at a lower rate than if it were earned by the shareholder parents.

Since income splitting may draw the attention of the IRS, it is important for the corporation to protect itself against IRS attempts to disallow such deductions. Among the precautions that the corporation may take are the following:

- Making all salary or wage payments directly to the employee or to the employee's bank account
- Having documentation of the employee's hours of employment
- Having at least a general description of the employee's position or of the tasks performed
- Being able to show that the tasks and expenditures were ordinary and necessary
- Having an articulated basis for having established the rate of pay for the employee.

In closely held corporations where the shareholders are also the directors, shareholders often take payments from the corporation in the form of director's fees. These are fees paid to the directors of the corporation for serving in that capacity and for attending directors' meetings. The fees, of course, are income to the recipient, but they may be deductible to the corporation. In order to be deductible, they must, as with other forms of shareholder compensation, be reasonable in light of the size and nature of the corporation, the director's involvement in its affairs, the frequency of meetings, and the difficulty of the tasks the director is asked to perform.

In addition, shareholders who have professional skills, such as accountants or attorneys, often provide their service to the corporation. If these services are outside the scope of their employment with the corporation, these shareholders may generally charge the corporation a fee for the services. Once again, the fee must be reasonable in light of the task and what it would cost to obtain the service elsewhere. This practice is not unlike a shareholder leasing property to his or her corporation at the fair market rental price of the item. It provides a method of taking funds from the corporation, paying them to the shareholder and deducting them from corporate income. Even though the shareholder will have to pay tax on the income, he or she has eliminated the double tax that would apply if the distribution were a dividend.

It is also possible to compensate employees through the use of *bonuses*. These are payments made in excess of the normal compensation obligation of the employer. They are usually distributed when a corporation has a particularly good year or as a reward for a particularly good performance by one or more employees. Often, whether to provide bonuses and, if provided, their amounts are not determined until the end of a tax year. At that time, the financial and tax condition of the corporation is more readily discernible, which provides the principals with the opportunity to adjust corporate finances by eliminating some profit in the form of bonuses to shareholder/employees. The IRS is, again, particularly sensitive to this ploy, especially when the amount of the bonus to each shareholder is proportionate to his or her percentage of stock ownership.

HEALTH AND LIFE INSURANCE

Health, life, and disability insurance are among the most valuable and sought-after fringe benefits employers provide to their employees. The cost of these benefits if the employee had to pay for them individually would be extremely high and, under current law, would generally not be deductible. When provided by the corporate employer, however, the value of the benefits is normally deductible to it, and the cost is generally excluded from the income of the employee. The premiums or other costs of these plans are deductible if they are "ordinary and necessary" business expenses and are reasonable in amount. They also must meet certain nondiscrimination rules established pursuant to the Tax Reform Act of 1986. Since these are commonly provided benefits by employers to their employees, the ordinary and necessary element of the deductibility test should be easily met. The issue of the reasonableness of the amount implicates the same considerations discussed previously in relation to salaries. The nondiscrimination rules will be discussed in some detail later in this chapter.

As has already been mentioned, the costs to employers of providing these benefits are generally not includable in the income of the employee. In addition, amounts received by the beneficiaries of employees are also excludable, in most cases, from their income. The factors that must be examined in determining whether the proceeds of these plans are excludable from the income of the recipient vary, depending on the nature of the plan. With medical and accident reimbursement plans, the exclusion applies to amounts paid or reimbursed not in excess of the cost of care and not attributable to amounts taken by the employee as a medical expense deduction in the prior year. For instance, if an employee had medical costs of $5,000 in 1992 that he or she claimed as a deduction on his or her 1992 tax return, the reimbursement in 1993 of that $5,000 expense will be treated as income in 1993. If the employee was able to deduct (due to limitations on medical expense deductions) only $2,000 of the medical expense in 1992, the reimbursement of the full $5,000 in 1993 would result in only $2,000 of income (the amount of the prior year's deduction), with the remaining $3,000 being excluded.

With group term life insurance, the premiums paid by an employer are, once again, normally deductible from its gross income. They are also excluded from the income of the employee to the extent that the amount of coverage provided in the group policy does not exceed $50,000 for that employee. If an employee has coverage in excess of that amount, the premium for the excess will be treated as income to the employee and, as such, is subject to tax. For a group term life insurance plan to qualify for the employee exclusion, it must cover at least 10 full-time employees or, if the company has fewer than 10 employees, the plan must cover all insurable employees of the company. It must also meet the nondiscrimination requirements set up under the Code.

In order for a corporation to deduct the premiums of group term life insurance, the policy must be designed to cover employees. This is true even if the real purpose is to cover the shareholders. When there are shareholder/employees, the policy must cover them as *employees*. If it appears that the coverage is for the shareholders as shareholders, it will look as if the premium is merely a distribution of a dividend disguised as a business expense.

Life insurance premiums (outside of the group term context) on the life of corporate officers or key employees, are considered additional compensation of the insured. To the extent that the amount of total compensation to the insured is reasonable, and if the corporation is not the beneficiary of the policy, the premium is deductible to the corporation. The premium amount is, however, treated as income of the insured and subject to taxation. As with the proceeds of health insurance policies, the proceeds of a life insurance policy are not includable as income of the beneficiary if they were paid because of the death of the insured.

QUALIFICATION AND NONDISCRIMINATION REQUIREMENTS

To keep corporations from setting up tax-preferred benefit plans that discriminate in favor of highly compensated employees, the tax code, in Section 414, provides for several rules to reduce the advantages of such plans. A *highly compensated employee* is defined as an employee who, at any point during the tax year in question or the preceding tax year, either:

- Owned at least 5% of the employer (i.e., owned at least 5% of the stock of the corporation)
- Received from the employer more than $75,000 annual compensation (with annual adjustments based on an inflation index)
- Received from the employer more than $50,000 annual compensation (with index adjustments) and was among the employer's top 20% employees by compensation
- Was an officer of the employer and earned more than 150% of the amount allowed to be added by the employee to a defined contribution pension plan.

Qualification Requirements

In order for a benefit plan to qualify for favorable tax treatment, it must meet certain threshold requirements. The value of employer-provided benefits must be *included* in an employee's income unless:

- The plan is in writing.
- The employees' rights under the plan are legally enforceable.
- The employees receive reasonable notice of the benefits available to them under the plan.
- The plan is maintained for the exclusive benefit of the employees.
- The plan was established with the intention of its being indefinitely maintained.

The obvious purpose of these qualification rules is to reduce the possibility of an employer establishing an illusory plan that benefits only the shareholders or other favored persons. The requirement of a written plan with enforceable employee rights speaks directly to that issue. Similarly, employees must know about the benefits available in order to take advantage of them. If the employer fails to notify all but a few selected employees of the plan's benefits or existence, the plan is of limited value to the unnotified employees. The fact that the plan must be designed to benefit employees also keeps employers from providing tax-favored benefits to shareholders who do not work for the corporation. Finally, the requirement that the plan be intended to last indefinitely will reduce the likelihood of annual manipulation of finances and employment.

Assuming a benefit plan meets these general requirements, at least some of the benefits provided to employees may be excluded from the employee's income. An important factor in determining how much of the benefit may be excluded is whether the plan discriminates in favor of highly compensated employees.

Nondiscrimination Requirements

The nondiscrimination rules were designed to discourage employers from setting up benefit plans that favor highly compensated employees over rank-and-file workers. In many closely held corporations, where the shareholders are the most highly compensated employees, a discriminatory plan would have the effect of favoring the shareholders. If not restricted, such a plan would allow shareholders to make tax-free distributions to themselves of amounts that would otherwise be treated as dividends and taxed at both the corporate level and in the hands of the shareholders. The rules, therefore, treat as income to the highly compensated employee the discriminatory amount of the coverage or benefits provided under an otherwise qualified benefit plan.

In order to avoid this undesirable consequence and be found to be nondiscriminatory, a plan must meet two tests: an eligibility test and a benefits test. To be nondiscriminatory, a plan must meet the following eligibility requirements:

- At least 50% of all eligible employees must not be highly compensated.

- At least 90% of all not highly compensated employees must be eligible for coverage under the plan.

- The not highly compensated employees would receive a benefit that is at least 50% of the largest benefit available to highly compensated employees.

- There is nothing in the plan as to eligibility that discriminates in favor of highly compensated employees.

The nondiscriminatory benefits test is met if the average employer provided benefit received in a plan year by not highly compensated employees is at least 75% of the average benefit received during that period by highly compensated employees.

There are a variety of rules to determine how to calculate these percentages and which employees may be disregarded in making the calculations. There are also alternative rules that can be elected by small employers in order to mitigate the application of the nondiscrimination rules. Finally, an employer who has only highly compensated employees is excused from the application of the nondiscrimination rules for any year in which it has no nonhighly compensated employees.

OTHER FRINGE BENEFITS

An employer may also provide a variety of other tax-favored benefits to employees, such as:

- Employee discounts
- "Working condition" fringe benefits
- "No additional cost" services
- De minimus benefits.

These benefits are all typical of items that may be included by employers in employee compensation packages. Furthermore, assuming the nondiscrimination rules are observed and certain other tests are met, each of these items may be deductible (or merely not taxed) to the employer as well as excluded from the income of the employee.

Employee discounts are a well-known form of benefit. Many employers, particularly retailers, permit their employees to purchase the goods or services of the employer at a discount from the price charged to the general public. Theoretically, the amount saved by the employee could be treated as income in that the employee obtained an item of a certain value, say $100, for only $75. After the transaction, the employee is $25 ahead. Nevertheless, no income will be recognized, and no tax will be assessed.

Working condition fringe benefits are property or services provided by an employer to an employee for business use. Basically, if the employee could have taken a deduction for the item if he or she had paid for it, it will qualify as a working condition fringe. A common item that fits this category is a company car provided to an employee for business purposes. To the extent the car is used for business, the value of the use of the car is not included in the employee's income, and the cost of providing it is deductible from the income of the employer. To the extent the employee uses the car (or any provided property) for personal reasons, the value of that use will be treated as income to the employee and is subject to tax.

No additional cost services involve services that the employer provides to the public for a fee that an employee is entitled to use at a reduced cost or for free. If, in allowing an employee to use this service, the employer incurs no substantial additional cost over what it would incur without such use, the value of the service will not be treated as income to the employee. An example of this might be an employer who operates a private bus line in the city for which it charges riders a fare but lets its employees ride for free. If this benefit for employees does not result in substantial additional costs to the employer, the benefit will qualify for exclusion from employee income.

De minimus benefits are those incidental benefits that are too small or too costly and inconvenient to monitor. Typical ones include using the office phone for personal calls or copying personal papers on the office copying machine. The cost and effort to monitor and report these items are deemed to be unreasonably high, and, therefore, the value of these benefits is not included in income.

Each element of compensation and fringe benefit discussed up to this point can be found in the structure of many closely held corporations. They help to attract and retain employees for the corporation at a cost that is partially subsidized by the government through the tax savings attached to them. When the employees are also the shareholders of the corporation, these devices help to turn a part of the corporation's taxable income into a tax-free distribution to shareholders. Keep in mind that in order for these deductions to be allowed by the IRS, they must be ordinary and necessary expenses of the corporation and reasonable in amount. If they are, the problem of the double taxation of corporations can be greatly reduced while giving the shareholders the benefits of corporate earnings. It is also important to note that many of the benefits discussed in this chapter would not be deductible if the principals ran their business as a partnership or sole proprietorship. In addition, much of the tax benefit of these compensation devices is lost for the holders of more than 2% of the stock in an S corporation. Therefore, in deciding on a choice of form for your business, consider carefully the tax advantages and disadvantages of incorporation.

EMPLOYEE BENEFIT PLANS

The remainder of this chapter will deal with somewhat more sophisticated forms of executive compensation, known generically as *employee benefits plans* or *deferred compensation*. Deferred compensation is designed to put off some of an employee's compensation until a future time. Often a means to fund one's retirement or other future activities, it is also a way, if done properly, to reduce the tax obligations of both the employee and the corporation. Deferring compensation can be achieved in many ways but the most common include:

- Pension plans
- Profit-sharing plans
- Stock bonus plans
- Cash or deferred arrangements.

Each type of plan is different in substantial ways from each other type and may also have significant internal variations. The rules applicable to the qualification of these plans for tax-favored treatment are very complex and would take a whole volume to describe and explain. The goals for this section are less ambitious than a complete analysis of the law concerning each type of plan. Instead, this section will focus on the nature of each plan, its advantages and disadvantages, on the basic rules pertaining to its operation and on the tax treatment accorded it. Choosing which plan, if any, is appropriate for your corporation and deciding how to implement it depend on a number of factors unique to your business. You will need an experienced hand to guide you through the maze of rules found in the Employee Retirement Income Security Act (ERISA) and the tax regulations. Meeting these requirements, however, is crucial so that your plan will receive the tax treatment that makes it such a valuable compensation device.

General Qualification Requirements

There are several requirements that apply to all tax-favored employee benefit plans. Some of these have already been encountered in relation to other employee fringe benefits; others are specifically related to the investment aspect of these plans. Among the basic requirements for tax-favored treatment are the following:

- The plan must be in writing.
- Its terms must be communicated to the employees.

- It must be exclusively for the benefit of employees or their beneficiaries—this means that there must be predetermined contributions by the employer or predetermined benefits for the employee and that investments made by the plan administrator must be prudent.
- The plan must be established to be permanent and continuing.
- Any trust administering the plan must be a U.S. entity.

If an employee benefit plan is "qualified," the employer's contributions to the plan will be deductible, and they will not be included in the income of the employee. The value of qualification, therefore, cannot be overestimated, nor can the disadvantage of not qualifying. Most employers who are about to establish a new plan or amend an existing one seek an advance ruling from the IRS to determine whether their proposed action will meet the requirements for a tax-favored plan. The request for a determination letter from the IRS may be made on IRS Form 5300 if the plan is a defined benefit plan or Form 5301 if it is a defined contribution plan. There are a number of additional forms and schedules that must be attached to the application for an advance ruling but the time and effort required are well spent in exchange for the knowledge that your plan qualifies or specific information as to how it fails to qualify.

Plan Descriptions

As mentioned previously, each type of employee benefit plan is different and often serves different purposes. This section will describe the basic elements of the major types of plans and the internal variations possible within a plan type. It will also discuss some of the benefits and drawbacks of each plan or variation.

Pension Plans

Pension plans were designed specifically to provide a fund for employee retirement. They are often administered by the employer, by a trust established for that purpose, or by an insurance company. The employer makes a predetermined annual contribution that is invested and allowed to accumulate. An employee is usually entitled to contribute additional amounts to the plan, on a tax-favored basis, from his or her pay. Then, when an employee covered by the plan retires, he or she may draw out his or her share of the accumulated funds, either in a lump sum or as an annuity payable over the rest of his or her life. As opposed to the funding of a profit-sharing plan, the employer's pension plan contribution cannot depend on the profits of the company. Instead, in order to receive tax-favored treatment, the contributions must be calculable in advance. In this regard, there are two basic forms for a "qualified" pension plan: a defined contribution plan and a defined benefit plan.

A *defined contribution plan* is, as its name suggests, a plan in which the employer's contribution is defined for each year. The contribution may be a fixed amount or an amount determined by a preestablished formula. One formula that is often used is a contribution based on a uniform percentage of each employee's salary. Each employee will have a separate "account" in his or her name from which his or her retirement benefits will be derived. Unlike a defined benefit plan, the amount of retirement benefits in a defined contribution plan cannot be determined in advance. They are a function of the amount contributed to each employee's account, the investment success of the contributed funds, and the number of years the employee is a participant in the plan.

The *defined benefit plan* operates on a somewhat different premise. Here, the amount of the benefit is defined in advance, and the employer must make an annual contribution that varies, depending on actuarial information. This information, compiled and analyzed by an actuary hired by the corporation, will indicate how much the employer has to contribute in any year in order to meet the vested retirement rights of employees in the plan. The factors to be considered include the number and age of the employees, the compensation levels, and the projected earnings of the contributed funds.

For example, a plan might provide for employees to receive at the normal retirement age an annual payment of 15% of their highest average salary for any three consecutive years of employment. Assume a corporation has two employees with similar salaries for the three-year period. This would mean that, barring future salary changes, each would be entitled to approximately the same pension benefit. If one employee has 30 years of employment left before retirement, and the other has only 10 years until retirement, the current contribution necessary to give the older employee the same retirement benefit as the younger one would be much greater because there is less time to accumulate the funds necessary to meet the pension obligation.

There are, of course, advantages and disadvantages to each form of pension plan. With a defined contribution plan, the employer knows exactly what has to be contributed each year (in order for the contribution to be deductible, there is an upper limit of the lesser of $30,000 or 25% of the employee's compensation). Because there are no surprises based on the profitability of the company or on actuarial determinations, the plan is relatively simple to establish and maintain. On the other hand, the participants in such a plan will not know how much they will receive upon retirement until they retire. This is a function, in part, of the investment success of the fund. The investment aspect of the plan means that a plan administrator will have to choose and follow the fund's investments and assume liability for inappropriate investments that have failed.

Alternatively, the defined benefit plan leaves an employer at some risk. Because the size of a particular year's contribution can fluctuate, depending on factors beyond the employer's control, there may be an unexpectedly large payment to be made in a year when such a contribution would be damaging to the corporation. Employees, however, know exactly what they will receive upon retirement, which makes retirement planning easier for them. These plans are often funded by the purchase of annuities, which insures that participants do not run the risk of an unexpectedly small pension due to the investment reversals of the fund. On the other hand, they do not have the possibility of surprisingly large pensions due to the investment success of the fund. Moreover, there are limits on the benefit that can be provided to any employee. The limit is the lesser of $90,000 (adjusted for inflation) or 100% of the employee's average annual compensation for his or her highest three-year period of employment. Finally, the defined benefit plan is more closely regulated by ERISA, which requires, among other things, that such plans be insured by the Pension Benefit Guaranty Corporation. This corporation was designed to insure that employees receive what they were promised by defined benefit plans. Plans must pay an annual premium to the corporation for this protection.

Profit-sharing Plans

Profit-sharing plans are different from pensions in several ways. Perhaps the most fundamental difference is that profit sharing plans are not necessarily designed to provide retirement income for the participant. They are devices that let employees share in the profits of the company through employer contributions to a trust fund set up for the benefit of employees. Distributions from the fund *may* come at the time of an employee's retirement, but there may be an earlier distribution of the fund, such as at the time of the employee's leaving his or her employment. As such, it may tide an employee over between jobs, or it may be the capital he or she needs to purchase a home or go on a trip or start his or her own business.

The second major difference between profit-sharing plans and pensions is that contributions to pension plans are based on a predetermined contribution by the employer or on a predetermined benefit to the employee. Profit-sharing plans, on the other hand, do not have such fixed requirements. They are usually funded out of the corporation's profits, although the Tax Reform Act of 1986 allows a corporation to contribute to the plan regardless of the existence of current or accumulated profits. The limit on the amount of contribution that an employer can deduct in any year is 15% of the aggregate compensation paid to all plan participants for that year. The employer's contributions are allocated to the accounts of individual employees, and while there is no required formula for the amount of employer contributions, there is a requirement of a definite, predetermined formula for the allocation of those contributions among the plan participants. The goal of this requirement, of course, is to avoid discrimination in favor of highly compensated employees. There must also be a predetermined formula for the distribution of funds from the plan to employees or their beneficiaries. Employees are permitted to make additional contributions to the plan from their income, but these contributions are not deductible to the employee.

Profit-sharing plans offer many of the same advantages to the corporation and the employee as do pension plans. Employer contributions to a qualified plan are deductions for the corporation and are not taxable to the employee. There are some added benefits to each side as well as some disadvantages to the employee. For the company, there is the added flexibility of no predetermined amount that must be contributed or benefit that must be paid. This allows the company to gear its contribution to the performance of the company on a year-to-year basis. Employees benefit because, unlike pension plans whose funds can be withdrawn before retirement only for limited and specific reasons, profit-sharing plans permit any number of events to trigger a distribution to an employee. For instance, severance of the employment relationship is a common basis for a distribution.

Employees may also suffer a disadvantage in comparison to their rights under a pension plan. With a defined contribution plan, they know what will be contributed each year, even though they cannot predict their pension benefit at the time of their retirement. With defined benefit plans, employees know what their pension will be when they retire. With a profit-sharing plan, employees need not know what will be contributed on their behalf nor what their ultimate benefit will be. The contribution will depend on company performance, and their benefit will depend on the investment experience of the fund into which the employer's contributions are placed.

Stock Bonus Plans

Stock bonus plans are common forms of executive compensation, although they are of limited value in closely held corporations where the existing shareholders are also the employees who would participate in the plan. This is because the payment to the employee is in the form of shares of the company's stock. If the employees already own 100% of the shares, adding shares to their holding does them little good. On the other hand, if a company has a need for outside employees, a stock bonus plan is one way to provide relatively inexpensive benefits. The most widely known type of stock plan is called an *Employee Stock Ownership Plan (ESOP)*. What is more, an ESOP is flexible enough to be used as a pension plan, a profit-sharing plan, or a stock bonus plan.

An ESOP is a trust designed primarily to invest in and hold *employer securities*—stock issued by the employer or a member of the same controlled group as the employer. The stock must be easily tradable on an established market. Because a closely held corporation could not, by definition, meet such a requirement, the law allows employer stock with voting and dividend rights at least equal to the highest rights available on the common stock of the employer to be used instead even if that stock is not traded on a national exchange. The employer contributes cash or employer securities to the ESOP, for which the employer obtains a tax deduction. If the employer contributes cash, the ESOP will use the cash to buy employer securities. The securities, in either case, are credited to and held in an account for each participating employee, who is generally entitled to control the voting of his or her shares.

An employer is entitled to a deduction for contributions to a qualified stock bonus plan. The amount of the additions for any employee is limited generally to the lesser of 25% of the employee's compensation or $30,000. These limits may be increased for particular years to the lesser of $60,000 or the amount of employer securities contributed to the plan. This increase is permissible if no more than one-third of the employer contributions for the year in question were allocated to highly compensated employees. As is typical with qualified employee benefit plans, the amount contributed by the employer for the employee's account will not be treated as income to the employee. Finally, the rules concerning plan eligibility were recently changed to encourage wider coverage and participation of employees.

Generally speaking, small corporations run by their shareholders would have little use for a plan such as this. In addition, similar results could be had with a general profit-sharing plan or with a pension. The main advantage accrues to larger closely held corporations that are in competition for executive employees or that are trying to boost productivity through worker participation in ownership. If a corporation could use a stock bonus plan, an ESOP could be very beneficial. The corporation could contribute shares of its stock rather than cash and, so long as the stock was independently appraised, deduct its value. This means a corporation would be getting a tax deduction without the necessity of a cash outlay, a very enviable position. Of course, the corporation is giving up some of its stock that represents an ownership and control interest in the corporation. The employees are now, at least indirectly through the trust, shareholders, with all the rights that this status entails. This, in turn reduces the control and freedom of action of the original corporate principals.

Cash or Deferred Arrangements

A *Cash or Deferred Arrangement (CODA)* is permitted under Section 401(k) of the Internal Revenue Code and has become known as a *401(k) plan*. A 401(k) plan, basically, is an arrangement that may be a part of a qualified profit-sharing or stock bonus plan. Under the arrangement, an employee participant may elect to take his or her compensation in cash or to defer a part of it through contributions to a trust. To the extent elective contributions (that is, contributions that are at the employee's option) are deferred, there is a limit on the amount of annual deferrals. The limit is $7,000 indexed for inflation per year per employee. Within the limit, however, the amount deferred will not be treated as income to the employee.

The employer and employee may each make contributions to the employee's account. Employer contributions are deductible to it and are not included in employee income. The limit on employer contributions is the same as would be the case with straight profit-sharing or bonus plans. The combination of employee and employer contributions makes this a valuable benefit to the employee at a relatively low cost to the employer. The employer must report to each employee the total amount of the employee's elective contributions to the plan and the total deferred compensation to his or her credit. Distributions from the plan are allowed for death, disability, separation from employment, and plan termination.

Summary of Plans

Each of these plans has some advantages for a closely held corporation. They permit deductible expenditures by the corporation that may inure to the benefit of the shareholders as employees. The benefits may also be tax free or tax deferred to the recipient. As we have seen, for these benefits to accrue, the plans must meet several tests. In each case, the plan:

- Must be for the exclusive benefit of the employees
- Must be reasonable in amount
- May not discriminate in favor of highly compensated employees
- Must provide for the vesting of the plan benefits at various times during the employment.

The Vesting of Plan Benefits

Vesting basically means that at some time during the employment the employee's right to some or all of the benefits under a plan becomes fixed and cannot be forfeited. The tax law sets out a number of rules concerning vesting that must be met in order for a plan to receive tax-favored treatment. We will now turn to a short discussion of the vesting rules.

The law requires the complete vesting of an employee's retirement benefit upon the employee reaching the normal retirement age. In addition, there must be complete vesting of benefits due to the employee's contributions as well as vesting of accrued benefits due to the employer's contributions pursuant to one of two schedules relating to years of service. One of the schedules calls for complete vesting of benefits derived from employer contributions after the employee has completed five years of employment. The other schedule requires 20% vesting per year from the third through the seventh year of service. An employer can create a plan with more rapid vesting of employer-derived benefits, but there can be no slower vesting requirement if a plan is to qualify for favorable tax treatment.

There are also rules concerning how to determine years of service and the normal retirement age. Normal retirement age may be specified in the plan, but it may not be later than age 65 or after 10 years of service, whichever is later. To determine years of service, any years before an employee reaches 18 years of age need not be counted for benefit vesting purposes. Neither must the employer count years of service for years before the plan was established. Special rules apply for employees who have breaks in service. If an employee leaves the employment for one year or more and then returns, the employer need not count any prebreak service until the employee has completed one year of service after his or her return.

As you can see, the use of employee benefit plans can go a long way toward eliminating the double taxation problem of corporations while providing significant benefits to the shareholders. They can also be a major financial burden, especially to a corporation that employs many nonshareholders. The different forms of plans should be evaluated in light of the corporation's cash and tax situation and in light of shareholder needs to determine whether any plan is appropriate and, if so, which one offers the best fit with those needs. The appropriate plan should then be established with the assistance of an experienced professional. In this way the financial and tax benefits that these plans can provide will be within the reach of the corporation and its principals.

16

SECURITIES

No discussion of corporations would be complete without some comment about the securities laws. Securities, which include stocks, bonds, notes, debentures, and so forth, are regulated both by the federal government and the various states. The primary federal statutes involved are the Securities Act of 1933 and the Securities Exchange Act of 1934. The main function of each Act is to require the disclosure of information to potential investors and the prevention of fraud in securities transactions.

Similarly, all the states have laws regulating, in one way or another, the purchase and sale of securities. These laws are known generically as "blue sky" laws and operate independently of the federal laws. A company proposing to sell securities in several states would have to comply with the blue sky laws of each state in which the security was to be sold.

This chapter will not give complete and detailed coverage of this complex field. Rather, it will give an overview of the major requirements and common exceptions to them. The primary focus of this discussion will be the federal law, both because it is a standard for much of the state legislation and because it is one body of law that is applicable throughout the nation. State law, on the other hand, may vary greatly from state to state and each state's law is applicable only to activities in that jurisdiction.

Despite this, the typical corporation will never be subject to the federal statutes concerning the disclosure of information. This is because the federal disclosure laws generally apply only to larger, publicly traded corporations where the securities transactions involve interstate activities. On the other hand, the antifraud provisions of the federal laws do apply to the purchase or sale of securities, even of smaller local corporations.

THE 1933 ACT: REGISTRATION AND EXEMPTION

The 1933 Act had as its main purpose the disclosure to the investing public of complete and accurate information about securities and the companies issuing them. It accomplished this goal by requiring that any person (including an issuing corporation) who made any sale of a security file a registration statement disclosing a wide variety of information about the security being issued, the company itself and the seller of the security (if other than the company). The same Act provides several exemptions from the registration requirement. These exemptions concern who must register and what types of transactions are covered.

For instance, exemptions found in Section 4 of the Act remove from coverage *most* sales of securities unless conducted by an "issuer" (generally, the company creating the security and selling it). Similarly, even some sales conducted by the issuer are removed from coverage. Among the main exemptions are the following:

1. *Private Placements.* This includes the sale of securities to not more than 35 persons and where there is no general advertising or widespread solicitation of purchasers.

2. *Small Offerings.* This exemption, which is simpler to apply than the private placement exemption, concerns the value of the offering rather than the number of investors. Currently sales of not more than $5 million worth of securities need not register.

3. *Intrastate (as opposed to Interstate) Offerings.* Where a corporation is incorporated by and doing business in only one state and sells its securities only to residents of that state, it need not register. This exemption carries strict rules concerning even an offer by the issuer to a nonresident of the state as well as the subsequent sale of these securities by a resident purchaser to a nonresident. These rules make it difficult to use this exemption except in the most clearly local situations.

Offerings of securities falling within these exemptions need not be registered. Determining the availability of any of these exemptions is, however, a very difficult issue requiring the assistance of a professional advisor.

THE 1934 ACT

The 1934 Act is broader in scope than the 1933 Act. The 1934 Act has its own separate registration requirements together with a series of provisions intended to reduce manipulation, based on superior knowledge, of the securities markets and of sellers or buyers of securities.

The registration requirement is limited to companies listed on a national securities exchange and to unlisted companies that have more than 500 shareholders and more than $3 million in assets (this latter group typically includes companies listed in the "over-the-counter" markets, a somewhat less centralized national trading system). Here, rather than registering each new issue of securities as it is about to be sold, whole classes of securities are described in the registration statement and updated information is provided through annual reports.

The states, under specific authority from various federal laws, have been able to maintain regulation of securities. States have used this authority to develop their own laws prohibiting fraud in securities transactions and requiring disclosure through state registration. Thus, if a company wishes to sell its securities in several states, that company must comply with the securities laws of each of those states or qualify for an exemption under them. In doing so, the companies are said to have "blue skied" their issue of securities. As mentioned previously, state laws may vary greatly from each other and from the federal laws. Thus it is critical that any corporation contemplating selling securities in any state hire a securities lawyer in that state in order to obtain information and advice.

SAMPLE PREINCORPORATION AGREEMENT

AGREEMENT made this _____ day of _____, 1992, between _____, _____, and _____.

WHEREAS the parties hereto wish to organize a corporation upon the terms and conditions hereinafter set forth; and

WHEREAS the parties wish to establish their mutual rights and responsibilities in relation to their organizational activities;

NOW, THEREFORE in consideration of the premises and mutual covenants contained herein, it is agreed by and between the parties as follows:

FIRST: The parties will forthwith cause a corporation to be formed and organized under the laws of _____.

SECOND: The proposed Articles of Incorporation shall be attached hereto as Exhibit A.

THIRD: Within 7 days after the issuance of the corporation's certificate of incorporation, the parties agree that the corporation's authorized stock shall be distributed, and consideration paid, as follows:

1. _____ shares of _____ (insert either common or preferred) stock shall be issued to _____ in consideration of his payment to the corporation of $_____ cash.

2. _____ shares of _____ stock shall be issued to
_____ in consideration of her transfer to the corporation of
_____ [list property, real or personal, to be transferred].

3. . . .

4. . . .

FOURTH: The corporation shall employ _____ as its
manager for a term of _____ years and at a salary of $_____ per
annum, such employment not to be terminated without cause and such
salary not to be increased or decreased without the approval of _____%
of the directors.

FIFTH: The parties agree not to transfer, sell, assign, pledge, or otherwise dispose of their shares until they have first offered them for sale to
the corporation, and then, should the corporation refuse such offer, to the
other shareholders on a pro rata basis. The shares shall be offered at their
book value and the corporation, and in the event the corporation refuses,
the other shareholders shall have thirty (30) days to purchase the shares.
If the corporation or other shareholders do not purchase all the offered
shares, the remaining shares may be freely transferred by their owner
without price restrictions.

SIXTH: The parties to this agreement promise to use their best efforts
to incorporate the organization and to commence its business.

_____

_____

_____

APPLICATION FOR RESERVATION OF CORPORATE NAME

To: Secretary of State

Pursuant to the provisions of the Business Corporation Law of
_____, the undersigned hereby applies for
reservation of _____* for a period of sixty (60) days.
If a foreign corporation, name of state where organized _____
_____.

Date _____   _____

                                            Applicant

By _____

Its _____

Address _____

* Insert corporate name to be reserved.

ARTICLES OF INCORPORATION (GENERAL)

_____
(Name of Corporation)

The undersigned, being a natural person, does hereby act as incorporator in adopting the following articles of incorporation for the purpose of organizing a stock corporation pursuant to the provisions of the _____ [name of state] Stock Corporation Act:

FIRST: The name of the corporation (hereinafter called the corporation) is _____ , Inc.

SECOND: The duration of the corporation shall be perpetual.

THIRD: The purpose for which the corporation is organized, which shall include the transaction of any or all lawful business for which corporations may be incorporated under the provisions of the _____ _____ Stock Corporation Act, are as follows: [list, in general terms, the corporation's purposes, such as:]

To provide computer and accounting consulting services and to market and sell computer software.

To have, in furtherance of the corporate purposes, all of the powers conferred upon business corporations organized under the _____ Stock Corporation Act.

FOURTH: The total number of shares of capital stock which the corporation has authority to issue is 2000 divided into 1000 shares of Class A common stock with $.01 par value and 1000 shares of Class B common stock with $.01 par value.

The following is a description of each class of stock of the corporation with the preferences, conversion, and other rights, restrictions, voting powers, and qualifications of each class:

1. Except as hereinafter provided with respect to voting powers, the Class A common stock and the Class B common stock of the corporation shall be identical in all respects.

2. With respect to voting powers, except as otherwise required by the laws of the State of _____ , the holders of Class A common stock shall possess all voting powers for all purposes including, by way of illustration and not of limitation, the election of directors, and holders of Class B common stock shall have no voting power whatsoever, and no holder of Class B common stock shall vote on or otherwise participate in any proceedings in which actions shall be taken by the corporation or the stockholders thereof or be entitled to notification as to any meeting of the Board of Directors or the stockholders.

FIFTH: No holder of any of the shares of any class of the corporation shall be entitled as of right to subscribe for, purchase, or otherwise acquire any shares of any class of the corporation which the corporation proposes to issue or any rights or options which the corporation proposes to grant for the purchase of shares of any class of the corporation or for the purchase of any shares, bonds, securities, or obligations of the corporation which are convertible into or exchangeable for, or which carry any rights, to subscribe for, purchase, or otherwise acquire shares of any class of the corporation; and any and all of such shares, bonds, securities, or obligations of the corporation, whether now or hereafter authorized or created, may be issued, or may be reissued or transferred if the same have been reacquired and have treasury status, and any and all of such rights and options may be granted by the Board of Directors to such persons, firms, corporations, and associations, and for such lawful consideration, and on such terms, as the Board of Directors in its discretion may determine, without first offering the same, or any thereof, to any said holder.

SIXTH: 1. The corporation shall, to the fullest extent permitted by the provisions of the _____ Stock Corporation Act, as the same may be amended and supplemented, indemnify any and all persons whom it shall have power to indemnify under said provisions from and against any and all of the expenses, liabilities, or other matters referred to in or covered by said provisions, and the indemnification provided for herein shall not be deemed exclusive of any other rights to which those indemnified may be entitled under any Bylaw, vote of stockholders, or disinterested directors, or otherwise, both as to action in his or her official capacity and as to action while holding such office, and shall continue as to a person who has ceased to be a director, officer, employee, or agent and shall inure to the benefit of the heirs, executors, and administrators of such a person.

2. The stated capital of the corporation may be reduced by the Board of Directors, without the assent of the stockholders.

SEVENTH: The post office address of the initial registered office of the corporation in the State of _____ is _____, _____, _____. The name of the county or city in the State of _____ in which the said registered office of the corporation is located is the county or city of _____.

The name of the initial registered agent of the corporation at such address is _____. His [her] business office is identical with the initial registered office of the corporation as set forth above.

EIGHTH: The number of directors constituting the initial Board of Directors of the corporation is one (1).

The names and the addresses of the persons who are to serve as members of the initial Board of Directors of the corporation are as follows:

Name	Address
_____	_____
_____	_____
_____	_____

NINTH: The provisions for the regulation of the internal affairs of the corporation shall be as set forth in the bylaws.

Signed on _____.

_____
Incorporator

ARTICLES OF INCORPORATION (CALIFORNIA)

_____
(Name of Corporation)

ONE: The name of this corporation is _____.

TWO: The purpose of the corporation is to engage in any lawful act or activity for which a corporation may be organized under the General Corporation Law of California other than the banking business, the trust company business, or the practice of a profession permitted to be incorporated by the California Corporations Code.

THREE: The name and address in this state of the corporation's initial agent for service of process is _____,
_____, California, _____.

FOUR: This corporation is authorized to issue _____ shares.

DATED: _____

_____
, Incorporator

I declare that I am the person who executed the above articles of incorporation, and that this instrument is my act and deed.

_____
, Incorporator

CERTIFICATE OF INCORPORATION (DELAWARE)

(Name of Corporation)
A CLOSE CORPORATION

FIRST: The name of this corporation is _____.

SECOND: Its registered office in the State of Delaware is to be located at _____ County of _____. The registered agent in charge thereof is _____, address same as above.

THIRD: The nature of the business and the objects and purposes proposed to be transacted, promoted, and carried on are to engage in any lawful act or activity for which corporations may be organized under the General Corporation Law of Delaware.

FOURTH: The amount of total authorized capital stock of the corporation is divided into _____ shares of *no par value*.

FIFTH: The name and mailing address of the incorporator is as follows:

_____.

SIXTH: The powers of the incorporators are to terminate upon filing of the certificate of incorporation, and the name and mailing addresses of the persons who are to serve as directors until their successors are elected are as follows:

Name   Address

_____   _____

_____   _____

_____   _____

SEVENTH: All of the corporation's issued stock, exclusive of treasury shares, shall be held of record by not more than thirty (30) persons.

EIGHTH: All of the issued stock of all classes shall be subject to the following restriction on transfer permitted by Section 202 of the General Corporation Law.

Each stockholder shall offer to the corporation or to other stockholders of the corporation a thirty (30) day "first refusal" option to purchase his or her stock should he or she elect to sell his or her stock.

NINTH: The corporation shall make no offering of any of its stock of any class which would constitute a "public offering" within the meaning of the Securities Act of 1933, as it may be amended from time to time.

I, THE UNDERSIGNED, for the purpose of forming a corporation under the laws of the State of Delaware do make, file, and record this certificate, and do certify that the facts herein stated are true; and I have accordingly hereunto set my hand.

DATED AT: _____

_____

ARTICLES OF INCORPORATION (WASHINGTON, D.C.)

We, the undersigned natural persons of the age of twenty-one (21) years or more, acting as incorporators of a corporation under Title 29, Chapter 3 of the Code of Laws of the District of Columbia, adopt the following Articles of Incorporation for such corporation:

FIRST: The name of the corporation is _____ .
SECOND: The period of its duration is perpetual.
THIRD: The purpose or purposes for which the corporation is organized are _____ ;

To engage in and carry on any other purposes which may conveniently and consistently be conducted in conjunction with any of the purposes of the corporation;

To employ such persons as it deems necessary and proper to carry out these purposes;

To lease personal and real property, as it deems necessary, to carry on these purposes;

To acquire all or any part of the good will, rights, property, and business of any person, firm, association, or corporation heretofore and hereafter engaged in any activity similar to or in furtherance of any purposes which the corporation has the power to conduct, and to hold, utilize, enjoy, and in any manner dispose of the whole or any part of the rights, property, and business so acquired, and to assume in connection therewith any liabilities of any such person, firm, association, or corporation;

To apply for, obtain, purchase, or otherwise acquire any patents, copyrights, licenses, trademarks, trade names, rights, processes, formulas, and the like, which are or may seem capable of being used for any of the purposes of the corporation, and to use, exercise, develop, grant licenses and franchises in respect of, sell, and otherwise turn to account, the same;

To carry out all or any part of the foregoing objects as principal, factor, agent, contractor, or otherwise, either alone or through or in conjunction with any person, firm, association, or corporation, and in carrying on its purposes and for the purpose of attaining or furthering any of its objects and purposes, to make and perform any contracts and to do any acts and things, and to exercise any powers suitable, convenient or proper for the accomplishment of any of the objects and purposes herein enumerated or incidental to the powers herein specified, or which at any time may appear conducive to or expedient for the accomplishment of any such objects and purposes;

To carry out all or any part of the aforesaid objects and purposes, and to conduct its activities in all or any part of its branches, in any or all states, territories, districts, and possessions of the United States of America and in foreign countries, and to maintain offices and agencies in the aforesaid jurisdictions;

The foregoing objects and purposes shall, except when otherwise expressed, be in no way limited or restricted by reference to or inference from the terms of any other clause of this or any other article of these articles of incorporation or any amendment thereto, and shall each be regarded as independent, and construed as powers as well as objects and purposes.

The Corporation shall be authorized to exercise and enjoy all of the powers, rights, and privileges granted to or conferred upon corporations of similar character by the General Laws of the District of Columbia now or hereafter in force, and the enumeration of the foregoing powers shall not be deemed to exclude any powers, rights, or privileges so granted or conferred.

FOURTH: The aggregate number of shares which the corporation is authorized to issue is one class of 1000 at $.01 par value.

FIFTH: The preferences, qualifications, limitations, restrictions, and special or relative rights in respect to the shares of each class are set forth in the bylaws.

SIXTH: The corporation will not commence business until at least one thousand dollars ($1,000) has been received by it as consideration for the issuance of shares.

SEVENTH: The provisions for the regulation of the internal affairs of the corporation are set forth in the bylaws.

EIGHTH: The address, including street and number, of the initial registered office of the corporation is _____ and the name of the initial registered agent at such address is _____ . The address, including street and number, if any, where it conducts its principal business is _____ .

NINTH: The number of directors constituting the initial board of directors of the corporation is one (1) and the name and address, including street and number, if any, of the person who is to serve as director until the first annual meeting of shareholders or until his or her successor is elected and shall qualify is as follows:

Name   Address

_____   _____

TENTH: The name and address, including street and number, if any, of the incorporator is as follows:

Name   Address

_____   _____

DATE: _____

ARTICLES OF INCORPORATION
(MARYLAND)

A Maryland Close Corporation,
Organized Pursuant to Title 4 of the
Corporations and Associations Article of the
Annotated Code of Maryland

FIRST: I, _____ , whose post office address is
_____ , being at least eighteen (18) years of age,
hereby form a corporation under and by virtue of the General Laws of the
State of Maryland.

SECOND: The name of the corporation (which is hereafter called the
"Corporation") is _____ .

THIRD: The Corporation shall be a close corporation as authorized by
Title 4 of the Corporations and Associates Article of the Annotated Code
of Maryland, as amended.

FOURTH: The purposes for which the Corporation is formed are:

1. _____
_____
_____ ; and to engage in any other lawful purpose and business; and

2. To have all power and do anything permitted by Section 2-103 of
the Corporations and Associations Article of the Annotated Code of
Maryland.

FIFTH: The post office address of the principal office of the Corporation in this State is _____

_____ .

The name and post office address of the Resident Agent of the Corporation in this State are_____

_____ .

Said Resident Agent is an individual actually residing in this State.

SIXTH: The total number of shares of capital stock which the Corporation has authority to issue is _____ (_____) shares of common stock, without par value.

SEVENTH: The number of directors shall be (1), which number may be increased or decreased pursuant to the By-Laws of the Corporation. The name of the director, who shall act until the first annual meeting or until his or her successor is duly chosen and qualified is: _____

_____ .

[It should be noted that Maryland permits a close corporation to have no Board of Directors. All power would thus reside with the shareholders. If the organizers of a close corporation choose this option, they should substitute the following for the Seventh Paragraph above]

EIGHTH: The corporation elects to have no Board of Directors. Until the election to have no Board of Directors becomes effective, there shall be one (1) director, whose name is _____ .

IN WITNESS WHEREOF, I have signed these Articles of Incorporation this _____ day of _____, 19____, and I acknowledge the same to be my act.

_____

CERTIFICATE OF INCORPORATION (NEW YORK)

(Name of Corporation)

Under Section 402 of the Business Corporation Law IT IS HEREBY CERTIFIED THAT:

1. The name of the corporation is: _____.

2. The purpose or purposes for which the corporation is formed are as follows, to wit:

To buy, sell, repair, recondition, import, export, and deal in photographic equipment and supplies, parts, and accessories of every kind. To own, operate, manage, and do everything normally associated with conducting the business of a camera and photography business.

To engage in any lawful act or activity for which corporations may be formed under the Business Corporation Law. The corporation is not formed to engage in any act or activity requiring the consent or approval of any state official, department, board, agency, or other body without such consent or approval first being obtained.

To own, operate, manage, acquire, and deal in property, real and personal, which may be necessary to the conduct of the business.

The corporation shall have all of the powers enumerated in Section 202 of the Business Corporation Law, subject to any limitation provided in the business Corporation Law or any other statute in the State of New York.

3. The county in which the office of the corporation is to be located in the State of New York is: _____ .

4. The aggregate number of shares which the corporation shall have authority to issue is 200 shares, no par value.

5. The Secretary of State is designated as agent of the corporation upon whom process against it may be served. The post office address to which the Secretary of State shall mail a copy of any process against the corporation served upon him or her is: _____

_____ .

IN WITNESS WHEREOF, the undersigned incorporator, being at least eighteen (18) years of age, has executed and signed this Certificate of Incorporation this _____ day of June, 19____ .

STATE OF NEW YORK)   _____
)ss.
COUNTY OF _____)

On this _____ day of June 19____ , before me personally came _____ to me known to be the individual described in and who executed the foregoing instrument, and he or she duly acknowledged to me that he or she executed the same.

                              _____
                              Notary

My Commission Expires: _____ .

ARTICLES OF INCORPORATION
(WISCONSIN)

Form 2 - Sec. State 1973

ARTICLES OF INCORPORATION

Executed by the undersigned for the purpose of forming a Wisconsin corporation under the "Wisconsin Business Corporation Law", Chapter 180 of the Wisconsin Statutes:

Article 1.   The name of the corporation is

Article 2.   The period of existence shall be

Article 3.   The purposes shall be

Article 4.   The number of shares which it shall have authority to issue, itemized by classes, par value of shares, shares without par value, and series, if any, within a class, is:

Class	Series (if any)	Number of Shares	Par value per share or statement that shares are without par value

Article 5.   The preferences, limitations, designation, and relative rights of each class or series of stock, are

Article 6.   Address of initial registered office is
The complete address, including street and number, if assigned, and the ZIP Code, must be stated.

Article 7.   Name of initial registered agent at such address is

Article 8.   The number of directors constituting the board of directors shall be fixed by by-law.

OR

Article 8.   The number of directors constituting the board of directors shall be _____ .

Strike out the Article 8 you do not use.

Article 9.   The names of the initial directors are:

Use of Article 9 is optional

Article 10.   (Other provisions)

Article 11.   These articles may be amended in the manner authorized by law at the time of amendment.

Article 12.   The name(s) and address(es) of incorportor(s) are:

<table>
<tr><td align="center">NAME</td><td align="center">ADDRESS
(number, street, city and ZIP Code)</td></tr>
<tr><td>_____</td><td>_____</td></tr>
<tr><td>_____</td><td>_____</td></tr>
<tr><td>_____</td><td>_____</td></tr>
<tr><td>_____</td><td>_____</td></tr>
</table>

Executed in duplicate on the _____ day of _____ , 19____

_____

_____

_____

STATE OF WISCONSIN

County of

Personally came before me this _____ day of _____ A.D. 19____
the above named _____

_____

to me known to be the person(s) who executed the foregoing instrument, and acknowledged the same.

_____
Notary Public

My Commission expires _____

This document was drafted by

_____
(Name of Person)
Please print or type

APPENDIX **10**

STOCK CERTIFICATE

EXPLANATION OF ABBREVIATIONS

The following abbreviations, when used in the inscription of ownership on the face of this certificate, shall be construed as if they were written out in full according to applicable laws or regulations. Abbreviations, in addition to those appearing below, may be used.

JT TEN	As joint tenants with right of survivorship and not as tenants in common	TEN ENT	As tenants by the entireties
TEN COM	As tenants in common	UNIF GIFT MIN ACT	Uniform Gifts to Minors Act
		CUST	Custodian for

For Value Received, _____ *hereby sell, assign and transfer unto*

PLEASE INSERT SOCIAL SECURITY OR OTHER
IDENTIFYING NUMBER OF ASSIGNEE

_____

_____ *Shares represented by the within Certificate, and do hereby irrevocably constitute and appoint*

_____ *Attorney to transfer the said Shares on the books of the within named Corporation with full power of substitution in the premises.*

Dated _____ *19* ___

In presence of

_____   _____

NOTICE THE SIGNATURE OF THIS ASSIGNMENT MUST CORRESPOND WITH THE NAME AS WRITTEN UPON THE FACE OF THE CERTIFICATE, IN EVERY PARTICULAR WITHOUT ALTERATION OR ENLARGEMENT OR ANY CHANGE WHATEVER

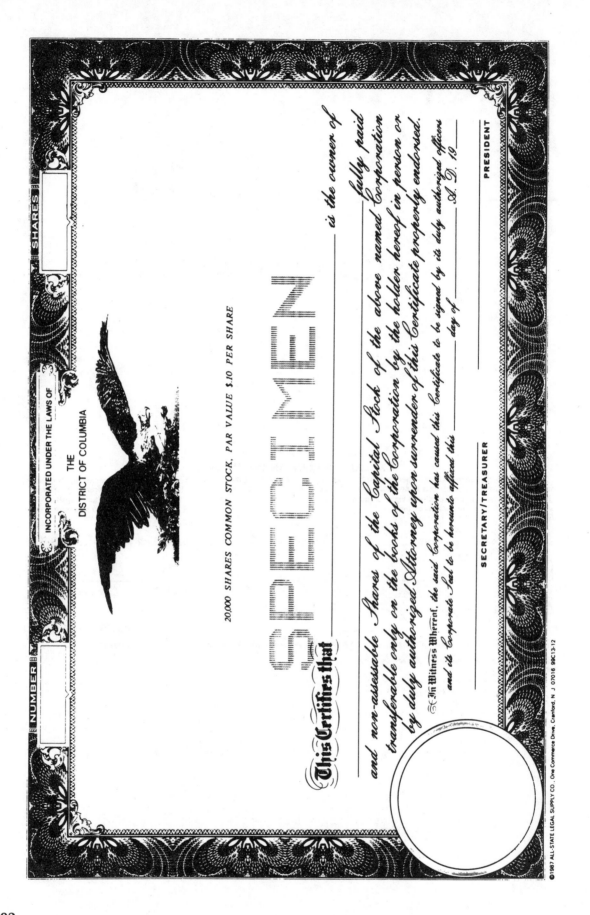

NUMBER

SHARES

INCORPORATED UNDER THE LAWS OF

THE
DISTRICT OF COLUMBIA

20,000 SHARES COMMON STOCK, PAR VALUE $.10 PER SHARE

SPECIMEN

This Certifies that _____ is the owner of

fully paid
and non-assessable Shares of the Capital Stock of the above named Corporation
transferable only on the books of the Corporation by the holder hereof in person or
by duly authorized Attorney upon surrender of this Certificate properly endorsed.

In Witness Whereof, the said Corporation has caused this Certificate to be signed by its duly authorized officers
and its Corporate Seal to be hereunto affixed this _____ day of _____ A. D. 19 _____

_____
SECRETARY/TREASURER

_____
PRESIDENT

© 1987 ALL-STATE LEGAL SUPPLY CO., One Commerce Drive, Cranford, N. J. 07016 99C13-12

202

BYLAWS

ARTICLE I

Offices

SECTION 1. *Registered Office.*   The registered office of the Corporation within the [State of corporation] shall be at _____
_____ .

SECTION 2. *Other Offices.*   The corporation may also have an office or offices other than said registered office at such place or places, either within or without the State, as the Board of Directors shall from time to time determine or the business of the corporation may require.

ARTICLE II

Meetings of Stockholders

SECTION 1. *Place of Meetings.*   All meetings of the stockholders for the election of directors or for any other purpose shall be held on [date] at _____ o'clock _____.м., at such place as may be fixed from time to time by the Board of Directors, or at such other place, either within or without the State, as shall be designated from time to time by the Board of Directors.

SECTION 2. *Annual Meeting.* The annual meeting of stockholders, commencing with the year 1987, shall be held on the second Tuesday of March, if not a legal holiday, and if a legal holiday, then on the next succeeding day not a legal holiday, at 10:00 A.M., or at such other date and time as shall be designated from time to time by the Board of Directors. At such annual meeting, the stockholders shall elect, by a plurality vote, a Board of Directors and transact such other business as may properly be brought before the meeting.

SECTION 3. *Special Meetings.* Special meetings of stockholders, unless otherwise prescribed by statute, may be called at any time by the Board of Directors or the Chairperson of the Board, if one shall have been elected, or the President, and shall be called by the Secretary upon the request in writing of a stockholder or stockholders holding of record at least 20% of the voting power of the issued and outstanding shares of stock of the Corporation entitled to vote at such meeting.

SECTION 4. *Notice of Meetings.* Written notice of each annual and special meeting of stockholders stating the date, place, and hour of the meeting, and, in the case of a special meeting, the purpose or purposes for which the meeting is called, shall be given to each stockholder of record entitled to vote thereat not less than ten (10) nor more than fifty (50) days before the date of the meeting. Business transacted at any special meeting of stockholders shall be limited to the purposes stated in the notice. Notice shall be given personally or by mail and, if by mail, shall be sent in a postage prepaid envelope, addressed to the stockholder at his or her address as it appears on the records of the Corporation. Notice by mail shall be deemed given at the time when the same shall be deposited in the United States mail, postage prepaid. Notice of any meeting shall not be required to be given to any person who attends such meeting, except when such person attends the meeting in person or by proxy for the express purpose of objecting, at the beginning of the meeting, to the transaction of any business because the meeting is not lawfully called or convened, or who, either before or after the meeting, shall submit a signed written waiver of notice, in person or by proxy. Neither the business to be transacted at, nor the purpose of, an annual or special meeting of stockholders need be specified in any written waiver of notice.

SECTION 5. *List of Stockholders.* The officer who has charge of the stock ledger of the Corporation shall prepare and make, at least ten (10) days before each meeting of stockholders, a complete list of the stockholders entitled to vote at the meeting, arranged in alphabetical order, showing the address of and the number of shares registered in the name of each stockholder. Such list shall be open to the examination of any stockholder, for any purpose germane to the meeting, during ordinary business hours, for a period of at least ten (10) days prior to the meeting, either at a place within the city, town or village where the meeting is to be held, which place shall be specified, in the notice of meeting, or if not specified, at the place where the meeting is to be held. The list shall be produced and kept at the time and place of the meeting during the whole time thereof, and may be inspected by any stockholder who is present.

SECTION 6. *Quorum, Adjournments.*   The holders of a majority of the voting power of the issued and outstanding stock of the Corporation entitled to vote thereat, present in person or represented by proxy, shall constitute a quorum for the transaction of business at all meetings of stockholders, except as otherwise provided by statute or by the Articles of Incorporation. If, however, such a quorum shall not be present or represented at any meeting of stockholders, the stockholders entitled to vote thereat, present in person or represented by proxy, shall have power to adjourn the meeting from time to time, without notice other than announcement at the meeting, until a quorum shall be present or represented. At such adjourned meeting at which a quorum shall be present or represented, any business may be transacted that might have been transacted at the meeting as originally called. If the adjournment is for more than thirty (30) days, or, if after adjournment a new record date is set, a notice of the adjourned meeting shall be given to each stockholder of record entitled to vote at the meeting.

SECTION 7. *Organization.*   At each meeting of stockholders the Chairperson of the Board, if one shall have been elected, or, in the Chairperson's absence or if one has not been elected, the President, shall act as chairperson of the meeting. The Secretary, or in his or her absence or inability to act, the person whom the chair of the meeting shall appoint, shall act as secretary of the meeting and keep the minutes thereof.

SECTION 8. *Order of Business.*   The order of business at all meetings of the stockholders shall be as determined by the chair of the meeting.

SECTION 9. *Voting.*   Except as otherwise provided by statute or the Articles of Incorporation, each stockholder of the Corporation shall be entitled at each meeting of stockholders to one vote for each share of capital stock of the Corporation standing in his or her name on the record of stockholders of the Corporation:

(a)   on the date fixed pursuant to the provisions of Section 7 of Article V of these bylaws as the record date for the determination of the stockholders who shall be entitled to notice of and to vote at such meeting; or

(b) if no such record date shall have been so fixed, then at the close of business on the day next preceding the day on which notice thereof shall be given, or, if notice is waived, at the close of business on the date next preceding the day on which the meeting is held.

Each stockholder entitled to vote at any meeting of stockholders may authorize another person or persons to act for him or her by a proxy signed by such stockholder or his or her attorney-in-fact, but no proxy shall be voted after three (3) years from its date, unless the proxy provides for a longer period. Any such proxy shall be delivered to the secretary of the meeting at or prior to the time designated in the order of business for so delivering such proxies. When a quorum is present at any meeting, the vote of the holders of a majority of the voting power of the issued and outstanding stock of the Corporation entitled to vote thereon, present in person or represented by proxy, shall decide any question brought before such meeting, unless the question is one upon which by express provision of statute or of the Articles of Incorporation or of these bylaws, a different vote is required, in which case such express provision shall govern and control the decision of such question. Unless required by statute, or determined by the chair of the meeting to be advisable, the vote on any question need not be by ballot. On a vote by ballot, each ballot shall be signed by the stockholder voting, or by his proxy, if there be such proxy, and shall state the number of shares voted.

SECTION 10. *Inspectors.*   The Board of Directors may, in advance of any meeting of stockholders, appoint one or more inspectors to act at such meeting or any adjournment thereof. If any of the inspectors so appointed shall fail to appear or act, the chair of the meeting shall, or if inspectors shall not have been appointed, the chair of the meeting may, appoint one or more inspectors. Each inspector, before entering upon the discharge of his or her duties, shall take and sign an oath faithfully to execute the duties of inspector at such meeting with strict impartiality and according to the best of his or her ability. The inspectors shall determine the number of shares of capital stock of the Corporation outstanding and the voting power of each, the number of shares represented at the meeting, the existence of a quorum, the validity and effect of proxies, and shall receive votes, ballots, or consents, hear and determine the results, and do such acts as are proper to conduct the election or vote with fairness to all stockholders. On request of the chair of the meeting, the inspectors shall make a report in writing of any challenge, request, or matter determined by them and shall execute a certificate of any fact found by them. No director or candidate for the office of director shall act as an inspector of an election of directors. Inspectors need not be stockholders.

SECTION 11. *Action by Consent.*   Whenever the vote of stockholders at a meeting thereof is required or permitted to be taken for or in connection with any corporate action, by a statute or provision of the Articles of Incorporation or of these bylaws, the meeting and vote of stockholders may be dispensed with, and the action taken without such meeting and vote, if a consent in writing, setting forth the action so taken, shall be signed by the holders of all the outstanding stock entitled to vote thereon.

ARTICLE III

Board of Directors

SECTION 1. *General Powers.*   The business and affairs of the Corporation shall be managed by or under the direction of the Board of Directors. The Board of Directors may exercise all such authority and powers of the Corporation and do all such lawful acts and things as are not by statute or the Articles of Incorporation directed or required to be exercised or done by the stockholders.

SECTION 2. *Number, Qualifications, Election, and Term of Office.* The number of directors constituting the initial Board of Directors shall be _____ (   ). Thereafter, the number of directors may be fixed, from time to time, by the affirmative vote of a majority of the entire Board of Directors or by action of the stockholders of the Corporation. Any decrease in the number of directors shall be effective at the time of the next succeeding annual meeting of stockholders unless there shall be vacancies in the Board of Directors, in which case such decrease may become effective at any time prior to the next succeeding annual meeting to the extent of the number of such vacancies. Directors need not be stockholders. Each director shall hold office until his or her successor shall have been elected and qualified, or until his or her death, resignation, or removal as hereinafter provided in these bylaws.

SECTION 3. *Place of Meetings.*   Meetings of the Board of Directors shall be held at such place or places, within or without the State, as the Board of Directors may from time to time determine or as shall be specified in the notice of any such meeting.

SECTION 4. *First Meeting.*   The Board of Directors shall meet for the purpose of organization, the election of officers and the transaction of other business, as soon as practicable after each annual meeting of stockholders, on the same day and at the same place where such annual meeting shall be held. Notice of such meeting need not be given. Such meeting may be held at any other time or place (within or without the State) which shall be specified in a notice thereof given as hereinafter provided in Section 7 of this Article III.

SECTION 5. *Regular Meetings.* Regular meetings of the Board of Directors shall be held at such time and place as the Board of Directors may fix. If any day fixed for a regular meeting shall be a legal holiday at the place where the meeting is to be held, then the meeting which would otherwise be held on that day shall be held at the same hour on the next succeeding business day. Notice of regular meetings of the Board of Directors need not be given except as otherwise required by statute or these bylaws.

SECTION 6. *Special Meetings.* Special meetings of the Board of Directors may be called by the Chairperson of the Board, if one shall have been elected, or by two or more directors of the Corporation, or by the President.

SECTION 7. *Notice of Meetings.* Notice of each special meeting of the Board of Directors (and of each regular meeting for which notice shall be required) shall be given by the Secretary as hereinafter provided in this Section 7, in which notice shall be stated the time and place of the meeting. Except as otherwise required by these bylaws, such notice need not state the purpose of such meeting. Notice of each such meeting shall be mailed, postage prepaid, to each director, addressed to his or her residence or usual place of business, by first-class mail, at least five (5) days before the day on which such meeting is to be held, or shall be sent addressed to him or her at such place by telegraph, cable, telex, telecopier, or other similar means, or be delivered personally or be given by telephone or other similar means, at least twenty-four (24) hours before the time at which such meeting is to be held. Notice of any such meeting need not be given to any director who shall, either before or after the meeting, submit a signed waiver of notice or who shall attend such meeting, except when he or she shall attend for the express purpose of objecting, at the beginning of the meeting, to the transaction of any business because the meeting is not lawfully called or convened.

SECTION 8. *Quorum and Manner of Acting.* A majority of the Board of Directors then in office shall constitute a quorum for the transaction of business at any meeting of the Board of Directors, and, except as otherwise expressly required by statute or the Articles of Incorporation or these bylaws, the act of a majority of the directors present at any meeting at which a quorum is present shall be the act of the Board of Directors. In the absence of a quorum at any meeting of the Board of Directors, a majority of the directors present thereat may adjourn such meeting to another time and place. Notice of the time and place of any such adjourned meeting shall be given to the directors unless such time and place were announced, at the meeting at which the adjournment was taken, to the other directors. At any adjourned meeting at which a quorum is present, any business may be transacted which might have been transacted at the meeting as originally called. The directors shall act only as a Board and the individual directors shall have no power as such.

SECTION 9. *Organization.*   At each meeting of the Board of Directors, the Chairperson of the Board, if one shall have been elected, or, in the absence of the Chairperson of the Board or if one shall not have been elected, the President (or, in his or her absence, another director chosen by a majority of the directors present) shall act as Chair of the meeting and preside thereat. The Secretary (or, in his or her absence, any person appointed by the chair) shall act as secretary of the meeting and keep the minutes thereof.

SECTION 10. *Resignations.*   Any director of the Corporation may resign at any time by giving written notice of his or her resignation to the Corporation. Any such resignation shall take effect at the time specified therein or, if the time when it shall become effective shall not be specified therein, immediately upon its receipt. Unless otherwise specified therein, the acceptance of such resignation shall not be necessary to make it effective.

SECTION 11. *Vacancies.*   Any vacancy in the Board of Directors, whether arising from death, resignation, removal (with or without cause), an increase in the number of directors, or any other cause, may be filled by the vote of a majority of the directors then in office, though less than a quorum, or by the sole remaining director, or by the stockholders at the next annual meeting thereof or at a special meeting thereof. Each director so elected shall hold office until his or her successor shall have been elected and qualified.

SECTION 12. *Removal of Directors.*   Any director may be removed, either with or without cause, at any time by the holders of a majority of the voting power of the issued and outstanding capital stock of the Corporation entitled to vote at an election of directors. Any director may be removed for cause by the Board of Directors.

SECTION 13. *Compensation.* The Board of Directors shall have authority to fix the compensation, including fees and reimbursement of expenses, of directors for services to the Corporation.

SECTION 14. *Committees.* The Board of Directors may, by resolution passed by a majority of the entire Board of Directors, designate one or more committees, including an Executive Committee, each committee to consist of one or more of the directors of the Corporation. The Board of Directors may designate one or more directors as alternate members of any committee, who may replace any absent or disqualified member at any meeting of the committee. Except to the extent restricted by statute or the Articles of Incorporation, each such committee, to the extent provided in the resolution creating it, shall have and may exercise all the powers and authority of the Board of Directors and may authorize the seal of the Corporation to be affixed to all papers which require it. Each such committee shall serve at the pleasure of the Board of Directors and have such name as may be determined from time to time by resolution adopted by the Board of Directors. Each committee shall keep regular minutes of its meetings and report the same to the Board of Directors.

SECTION 15. *Action by Consent.* Unless restricted by the Articles of Incorporation, any action required or permitted to be taken by the Board of Directors or any committee thereof may be taken without a meeting if all members of the Board of Directors or such committee, as the case may be, consent thereto in writing, and the writing or writings are filed with the minutes of the proceedings of the Board of Directors or such committee, as the case may be.

ARTICLE IV

Officers

SECTION 1. *Number and Qualifications.* The officers of the Corporation shall be elected by the Board of Directors [or by the stockholders] and shall include the President, one or more Vice-Presidents, the Secretary, and the Treasurer. If the Board of Directors wishes, it may also elect as an officer of the Corporation a Chairperson of the Board, and may elect other officers (including one or more Assistant Treasurers and one or more Assistant Secretaries) as may be necessary or desirable for the business of the Corporation. Any two or more offices may be held by the same person except the offices of President and Secretary. Each officer shall hold office until his or her successor shall have been duly elected and shall have qualified, or until his or her death, resignation, or removal, as hereinafter provided in these bylaws.

SECTION 2. *Resignations.*   Any officers of the Corporation may resign at any time by giving written notice of his or her resignation to the Corporation. Any such resignation shall take effect at the time specified therein or, if the time when it shall become effective shall not be specified, immediately upon receipt. Unless otherwise specified therein, the acceptance of any such resignation shall not be necessary to make it effective.

SECTION 3. *Removal.*   Any officer of the corporation may be removed, either with or without cause, at any time by the Board of Directors at any meeting thereof.

SECTION 4. *Chairperson of the Board.*   The Chairperson of the Board, if one shall have been elected, shall be a member of the Board, an officer of the Corporation, and, if present, shall preside at each meeting of the Board of Directors or of the stockholders. He or she shall advise and counsel with the President, and, in his or her absence, with other executives of the Corporation, and shall perform such other duties as may from time to time be assigned by the Board of Directors.

SECTION 5. *The President.*   The President shall be the chief executive officer of the Corporation. He or she shall, in the absence of the Chairperson of the Board or if a Chairperson shall not have been elected, preside at each meeting of the Board of Directors or the stockholders. He or she shall perform all duties incident to the office of the President and chief executive officer and such other duties as may from time to time be assigned by the Board of Directors.

SECTION 6. *Vice-President.*   Each Vice-President shall perform all such duties as from time to time may be assigned to him or her by the Board of Directors or the President. At the request of the President, or in his or her absence or in the event of his or her inability or refusal to act, the Vice-President, or if there shall be more than one, the Vice-Presidents in the order determined by the Board of Directors (or if there be no such determination, the Vice-Presidents in the order of their election), shall perform the duties of the President, and, when so acting, shall have the powers of and be subject to the restrictions placed upon the President in respect of the performance of such duties.

SECTION 7. *Treasurer.* The Treasurer shall

a. Have charge and custody of, and be responsible for, all the funds and securities of the Corporation;

b. Keep full and accurate accounts of receipts and disbursements in books belonging to the Corporation;

c. Deposit all moneys and other valuables to the credit of the Corporation in such depositories as may be designated by the Board of Directors or pursuant to its direction;

d. Receive, and give receipts for, moneys due and payable to the Corporation from any source whatsoever;

e. Disburse the funds of the Corporation and supervise the investments of its funds, taking proper vouchers therefore;

f. Render to the Board of Directors, whenever the Board of Directors may require, an account of the financial condition of the Corporation; and

g. In general, perform all duties incident to the office of Treasurer and such other duties as from time to time may be assigned by the Board of Directors.

SECTION 8. *Secretary.* The Secretary shall

a. Keep or cause to be kept, in one or more books provided for that purpose, the minutes of all meetings of the Board of Directors, the committees of the Board of Directors, and the stockholders;

b. See that all notices are duly given in accordance with the provisions of these bylaws and as required by law;

c. Be custodian of the records and the seal of the Corporation and affix and attest the seal to all certificates for shares of the Corporation (unless the seal of the Corporation on such certificates shall be a facsimile, as hereinafter provided) and affix and attest the seal to all other documents to be executed on behalf of the Corporation under its seal;

d. See that the books, reports, statements, certificates and other documents and records required by law to be kept and filed are properly kept and filed; and

e. In general, perform all duties incident to the office of Secretary and such other duties as from time to time may be assigned by the Board of Directors.

SECTION 9. *The Assistant Treasurer.* The Assistant Treasurer, or if there shall be more than one, the Assistant Treasurers in the order determined by the Board of Directors (or if there be no such determination, then in the order of their election) shall, in the absence of the Treasurer or in the event of his or her inability or refusal to act, perform the duties and exercise the powers of the Treasurer and shall perform such other duties as from time to time may be assigned by the Board of Directors.

SECTION 10. *The Assistant Secretary.* The Assistant Secretary, or if there be more than one, the Assistant Secretaries in the order determined by the Board of Directors (or if there be no such determination, then in the order of their election) shall, in the absence of the Secretary or in the event of his or her inability or refusal to act, perform the duties and exercise the powers of the Secretary and shall perform such other duties as from time to time may be assigned by the Board of Directors.

SECTION 11. *Officers' Bonds or Other Security.* If required by the Board of Directors, any officer of the Corporation shall give a bond or other security for the faithful performance of his or her duties, in such amount and with such surety as the Board of Directors may require.

SECTION 12. *Compensation.* The compensation of the Officers of the Corporation for their services as such officers shall be fixed from time to time by the Board of Directors. An officer of the Corporation shall not be prevented from receiving compensation by reason of the fact that he or she is also a director of the Corporation.

ARTICLE V

Stock Certificates and Their Transfer

SECTION 1. *Stock Certificates.* Every holder of stock in the corporation shall be entitled to have a certificate, signed by or in the name of the Corporation, by the President or a Vice-President and by the Secretary or an Assistant Secretary of the Corporation, certifying the number of shares owned by him or her in the Corporation. If the Corporation shall be authorized to issue more than one class of stock or more than one series of any class, the designations, preferences, and relative, participating, optional, or other special rights of each class of stock or series thereof, and the qualifications, limitations, or restriction of such preferences and/or rights shall be set forth in full or summarized on the face or back of the certificate which the Corporation shall issue to represent such class or series of stock, provided that, except as otherwise provided in the Business Corporation Law of _____, in lieu of the foregoing requirements, there may be set forth on the face or back of the certificate which the Corporation shall issue to represent such class or series of stock, a statement that the Corporation will furnish without charge to each stockholder who so requests the designations, preferences, and relative, participating, optional, or other special rights of each class of stock or series thereof and the qualifications, limitations, or restrictions of such preferences and/or rights.

SECTION 2. *Facsimile Signatures.*   Any or all of the signatures on a certificate may be a facsimile. In case any officer, transfer agent, or registrar who has signed or whose facsimile signature has been placed upon a certificate shall have ceased to be such officer, transfer agent, or registrar before such certificate is issued, it may be issued by the Corporation with the same effect as if he or she were such officer, transfer agent, or registrar at the date of issue.

SECTION 3. *Lost Certificates.*   The Board of Directors may direct a new certificate or certificates to be issued in place of any certificate or certificates theretofore issued by the Corporation alleged to have been lost, stolen, or destroyed. When authorizing such issue of a new certificate or certificates, the Board of Directors may, in its discretion and as a condition precedent to the issuance thereof, require the owner of such lost, stolen, or destroyed certificate or certificates, or his or her legal representative, to give the Corporation a bond, in such sum as it may direct, sufficient to indemnify it against any claim that may be made against the corporation on account of the alleged loss, theft, or destruction of any certificate or the issuance of such new certificate.

SECTION 4. *Transfers of Stock.*   Upon surrender to the Corporation or the transfer agent of the Corporation of a certificate for shares duly endorsed or accompanied by proper evidence of succession, assignment, or authority to transfer, it shall be the duty of the Corporation to issue a new certificate to the person entitled thereto, cancel the old certificate, and record the transaction upon its records, provided, however, that the Corporation shall be entitled to recognize and enforce any lawful restriction on transfer. Whenever any transfer of stock shall be made for collateral security, and not absolutely, it shall be so expressed in the entry of transfer if, when the certificates are presented to the Corporation for transfer, both the transferor and the transferee request the Corporation to do so.

SECTION 5. *Transfer Agents and Registrars.*   The Board of Directors may appoint, or authorize any officer or officers to appoint, one or more transfer agents and one or more registrars.

SECTION 6. *Regulations.*   The Board of Directors may make such additional rules and regulations, not inconsistent with these bylaws, as it may deem expedient concerning the issue, transfer, and registration of certificates for shares of stock of the Corporation.

SECTION 7. *Fixing Record Date.*   In order that the Corporation may determine the stockholders entitled to notice of or to vote at any meeting of stockholders or any adjournment thereof, or to express consent to corporate action in writing without a meeting, or entitled to receive payment of any dividend or other distribution or allotment of any rights, or entitled to exercise any rights in respect of any change, conversion, or exchange of stock, or for the purpose of any other lawful action, the Board of Directors may fix, in advance, a record date, which shall not be more than fifty (50) nor fewer than ten (10) days before the date of such meeting, nor more than sixty (60) days prior to any other action. A determination of stockholders of record entitled to notice of or to vote at a meeting of stockholders shall apply to any adjournment of the meeting, provided, however, that the Board of Directors may fix a new record date for the adjourned meeting.

SECTION 8. *Registered Stockholders.*   The Corporation shall be entitled to recognize the exclusive right of a person registered on its records as the owner of shares of stock to receive dividends and to vote as such owner, shall be entitled to hold liable for calls and assessments a person registered on its records as the owner of shares of stock, and shall not be bound to recognize any equitable or other claim to or interest in such share or shares or stock on the part of any other person, whether or not it shall have express or other notice thereof, except as otherwise provided by the laws of _____ .

ARTICLE VI

Indemnification of Directors and Officers

SECTION 1. *General.*   The Corporation shall indemnify any person who was or is a party or is threatened to be made a party to any threatened, pending, or completed action, suit, or proceeding, whether civil, criminal, administrative, or investigative (other than an action by or in the right of the Corporation) by reason of the fact that he or she is or was a director, officer, employee, or agent of the Corporation, or is or was serving at the request of the Corporation as a director, officer, employee, or agent of another corporation, partnership, joint venture, trust, or other enterprise, against expenses (including attorneys' fees), judgments, fines, and amounts paid in settlement actually and reasonably incurred by him or her in connection with such action, suit, or proceeding if such person acted in good faith and in a manner reasonably believed to be in or not opposed to the best interests of the Corporation, and, with respect to any criminal action or proceeding, had no reasonable cause to believe the conduct was unlawful. The termination of any action, suit, or proceeding by judgment, order, settlement, conviction, or upon a plea of nolo contendere or its equivalent, shall not, of itself, create a presumption that the person did not act in good faith and in a manner which he or she reasonably believed to be in or not opposed to the best interests of the Corporation, and, with respect to any criminal action or proceeding, had reasonable cause to believe that the conduct was unlawful.

SECTION 2. *Derivative Actions.* The Corporation shall indemnify any person who was or is a party or is threatened to be made a party to any threatened, pending, or completed action or suit by or in the right of the Corporation to procure a judgment in its favor by reason of the fact that he or she is or was a director, officer, employee or agent of the Corporation, or is or was serving at the request of the Corporation as director, officer, employee, or agent of another corporation, partnership, joint venture, trust, or other enterprise against expenses (including attorneys' fees) actually and reasonably incurred by him or her in connection with the defense or settlement of such action or suit if he or she acted in good faith and in a manner he or she reasonably believed to be in or not opposed to the best interests of the Corporation. No indemnification shall be made in respect of any claim, issue, or matter as to which such person shall have been adjudged to be liable for negligence or misconduct in the performance of his or her duty to the Corporation unless and only to the extent that the court in which such action or suit was brought shall determine upon application that, despite the adjudication of liability but in view of all the circumstances of the case, such person is fairly and reasonably entitled to indemnity for such expenses which the court shall deem proper.

SECTION 3. *Indemnification in Certain Cases.* To the extent that a director, officer, employee, or agent of the Corporation has been successful on the merits or otherwise in defense of any action, suit, or proceeding referred to in Sections 1 and 2 of this Article VI, or in defense of any claim, issue, or matter therein, he or she shall be indemnified against expenses (including attorneys' fees) actually and reasonably incurred in connection therewith.

SECTION 4. *Procedure.* Any indemnification under Section 1 and 2 of this Article VI (unless ordered by a court) shall be made by the Corporation only as authorized in the specific case upon a determination that indemnification of the director, officer, employee, or agent is proper in the circumstances because he or she has met the applicable standard of conduct set forth in such Section 1 and 2. Such determination shall be made: (a) by the Board of Directors by a majority vote of a quorum consisting of directors who were not parties to such action, suit, or proceeding; or (b) if such a quorum is not obtainable, or, even if obtainable and a quorum of disinterested directors so directs, by independent legal counsel in a written opinion; or (c) by the stockholders.

SECTION 5. *Advances for Expenses.*   Expenses incurred in defending a civil or criminal action, suit, or proceeding may be paid by the Corporation in advance of the final disposition of such action, suit, or proceeding as authorized by the Board of Directors in the specific case, upon receipt of an undertaking by or on behalf of the director, officer, employee, or agent to repay such amount, unless it shall ultimately be determined that he or she is entitled to be indemnified by the Corporation as authorized in this Article VI.

SECTION 6. *Rights Not Exclusive.*   The indemnification provided by this Article VI shall not be deemed exclusive of any other rights to which those seeking indemnification may be entitled under any law, bylaw, agreement, vote of stockholders, or disinterested directors, or otherwise, both as to action in his or her official capacity and as to action in another capacity while holding such office, and shall continue as to a person who has ceased to be a director, officer, employee, or agent and shall inure to the benefit of the heirs, executors, and administrators of such a person.

SECTION 7. *Insurance.*   The Corporation shall have power to purchase and maintain insurance on behalf of any person who is or was a director, officer, employee or agent of the Corporation, or is or was serving at the request of the Corporation as a director, officer, employee, or agent of another corporation, partnership, joint venture, trust, or other enterprise, against any liability asserted against him or her and incurred by him or her in any capacity, or arising out of his or her status as such, whether or not the Corporation would have the power to indemnify him or her against such liability under the provisions of this Article VI.

SECTION 8. *Definition of Corporation.*   For the purposes of this Article VI, references to "the Corporation" include all constituent corporations absorbed in a consolidation or merger as well as the resulting or surviving corporation, so that any person who is or was a director, officer, employee, or agent of such a constituent corporation as a director, officer, employee, or agent of another corporation, partnership, joint venture, trust, or other enterprise shall stand in the same position under the provisions of this Article VI with respect to the resulting or surviving corporation as he or she would if he or she had served the resulting or surviving corporation in the same capacity.

ARTICLE VII

General Provisions

SECTION 1. *Dividends.*   Subject to statute and the Articles of Incorporation, dividends upon the shares of stock of the Corporation may be declared by the Board of Directors. Dividends may be paid in cash, in property, or in shares of stock of the Corporation, unless otherwise provided by statute or the Articles of Incorporation.

SECTION 2. *Reserves.*   Before payment of any dividend, there may be set aside out of any funds of the Corporation available for dividends such sum or sums as the Board of Directors may, from time to time, in its absolute discretion, think proper as a reserve or reserves to meet contingencies, or for equalizing dividends, or for repairing or maintaining any property of the Corporation, or for such other purpose as the Board of Directors may think conducive to the interest of the Corporation. The Board of Directors may modify or abolish any such reserves in the manner in which the reserves were created.

SECTION 3. *Seal.*   The seal of the Corporation shall be in such form as shall be approved by the Board of Directors.

SECTION 4. *Fiscal Year.*   The fiscal year of the Corporation shall be fixed, and once fixed, may thereafter be changed by resolution of the Board of Directors.

SECTION 5. *Checks, Notes, Drafts, and So Forth.*   All checks, notes, drafts, or other order for the payment of money of the Corporation shall be signed, endorsed, or accepted in the name of the Corporation by such officer, officers, person, or persons as from time to time may be designated by the Board of Directors or by an officer or officers authorized by the Board of Directors to make such designation.

SECTION 6. *Execution of Contracts, Deeds, and So Forth.*   The Board of Directors may authorize any officer or officers, agent or agents, in the name and on behalf of the Corporation, to enter into or execute and deliver any and all deeds, bonds, mortgages, contracts, and other obligations or instruments, and such authority may be general or confined to specific instances.

SECTION 7. *Voting of Stock in Other Corporations.* Unless otherwise provided by resolution of the Board of Directors, the Chairperson of the Board or the President, from time to time, may (or may appoint one or more attorneys or agents to) cast the votes which the Corporation may be entitled to cast as a shareholder or otherwise in any other corporation, any of whose shares or securities may be held by the Corporation, at meetings of the holders of the shares or other securities of such other corporation, or to consent in writing to any action by any such other corporation. In the event one or more attorneys or agents are appointed, the Chairperson of the Board or the President may instruct the person or persons so appointed as to the manner of casting such votes or giving such consent. The Chairperson of the Board or the President may, or may instruct the attorneys or agents appointed to, execute or cause to be executed in the name and on behalf of the Corporation and under its seal or otherwise, such written proxies, consents, waivers, or other instruments as may be necessary or proper in the premises.

ARTICLE VIII

Amendments

These bylaws may be amended or repealed or new bylaws adopted (a) by action of the stockholders entitled to vote thereon at any annual or special meeting of stockholder, or (b) by action of the Board of Directors. Any bylaw made by the Board of Directors may be amended or repealed by the stockholders.

MINUTES OF ORGANIZATION MEETING OF BOARD OF DIRECTORS

The organization meeting of the Board of Directors of the _____ Corporation was held on the date, time, and at the place set forth in the written Waiver of Notice signed by all the Directors, fixing the time and place, and attached to the minutes of this meeting.

The following directors were present:

_____

_____

_____

being all the members of the Board of Directors.

The meeting was called to order by _____.

It was moved, seconded, and unanimously carried, that _____ _____ act as Temporary Chairperson, and that _____ act as Temporary Secretary.

The Chairperson reported that the Articles of Incorporation were filed in the Office of the Secretary of State and that the incorporation was effective as of the date of filing. The Secretary was then instructed to insert the duplicate original of the Articles of Incorporation together with the Certificate of Incorporation in the corporate minute book.

The Secretary then presented a form of bylaws governing the business affairs of the Corporation. After review, upon motion duly made, seconded and unanimously carried, it was

RESOLVED, that the form of bylaws submitted to this meeting be, and it hereby is, approved, and adopted as the bylaws of this Corporation and that the Secretary is hereby instructed to insert the bylaws in the Corporate minute book immediately following the Articles of Incorporation and the Certificate of Incorporation.

The meeting proceeded to the election of officers. Upon nominations duly made and seconded, the following were elected and qualified:

President   _____

Vice-President   _____

Secretary   _____

Treasurer   _____

The President of the Corporation thereupon assumed the Chair and the Secretary of the corporation assumed the duties of secretary of the meeting.

There was presented to the meeting a specimen of a proposed certificate to represent the shares of the Corporation. Upon motion duly made, seconded, and unanimously carried, it was

RESOLVED, that the specimen form of certificate be, and the same hereby is, approved and adopted as the certificate to represent the shares of this Corporation; and further

RESOLVED, that the specimen certificate so presented to the meeting be annexed to the minutes thereof.

The Secretary submitted to the meeting a seal proposed for use as the corporate seal of the corporation. Upon motion duly made, seconded, and unanimously carried, it was

RESOLVED, that the form of seal submitted to this meeting be, and it hereby is, approved and adopted as and for the Corporate seal of this corporation.

The banking arrangements of the Corporation were then discussed. After discussion, on motion duly made, seconded, and carried, a proposed Secretarial Certificate to be furnished by the Secretary of the Corporation to [*name of banking institution*] was unanimously approved, and the resolutions set forth in such Secretarial Certificate were unanimously adopted. A conformed copy of such Secretarial Certificate was ordered annexed to the minutes of the meeting.

The Chairperson presented to the meeting a certain written offer addressed to the Corporation by _____ , dated _____ , 19____, pertaining to the issuance of the shares of the Corporation. A discussion followed. Upon motion duly made, seconded, and unanimously carried, it was

RESOLVED, that the written offer dated _____ , pertaining to the issuance of shares by _____ be, and the same hereby is in all respects, approved for and on behalf of the Corporation; and further

RESOLVED, that a copy of such written offer be annexed to the minutes of this meeting; and further

RESOLVED, that the Corporation issue and deliver to _____ _____ upon receipt of the consideration therefor pursuant to the terms of the aforesaid proposal, a certificate representing _____ shares of the Corporation, _____ par value per share; and further

RESOLVED, that the shares so issued shall be fully paid and nonassessable, and that the value of the aforesaid consideration and the stated capital with respect to such shares shall be _____ ; and further

RESOLVED, that the officers of the Corporation be, and they hereby are, authorized, empowered, and directed to take any and all steps, and to execute and deliver any and all instruments in connection with consummating the transaction contemplated by the aforesaid proposal and in connection with carrying the foregoing resolutions into effect.

There being no further business to come before the meeting, upon motion duly made, seconded, and unanimously carried, the same was adjourned.

_____
Secretary

ATTEST:
Board of Directors

_____ _____

OFFER TO
PURCHASE SHARES

_____
[Date]

To the Board of Directors of

_____

The undersigned hereby offers to purchase _____
[Number]

shares of _____ stock at purchase price of $_____ per share
[class]

for a total payment of $_____ .

_____
[Name of Purchaser]

BOARD RESOLUTION ACCEPTING OFFER TO PURCHASE SHARES

The Chairperson presented to the meeting a written offer from _____
_____ , dated
_____ , 19____ , to purchase _____ shares of the
_____ stock of this corporation.

Upon motion duly made, seconded, and unanimously carried, it was

RESOLVED, that the written offer from _____ ,
dated _____ , 19____ , and attached hereto, to purchase
_____ shares of the _____
                        [class]

stock of this corporation is hereby accepted on behalf of the Corporation; and further

RESOLVED, that upon receipt of the consideration therefore, the Secretary is directed to issue to _____ , a certificate representing
_____ shares of the _____ stock of this Corporation; and further
                  [class]

RESOLVED, that the shares so issued shall be treated as fully paid and nonassessable.

ATTEST:

_____   _____
Secretary   President

WAIVER OF NOTICE OF ANNUAL MEETING OF SHAREHOLDERS

The undersigned, being all of the shareholders of the _____ Corporation, hereby agree that the annual meeting of shareholders of the corporation be held on the_____[date]_____ , at_____[time]_____ and at _____[address]_____ designated in this waiver. We hereby waive all notice whatsoever of such meeting and of any adjournment or adjournments thereof.

We further agree that any and all lawful business may be transacted at such meeting or at any adjournment or adjournments thereof as may be deemed appropriate as determined by any shareholder present thereat and that any such business transacted at such meeting or at any adjournment or adjournments thereof shall be of the same force and effect as if such meeting or adjourned meeting were held after notice.

Dated: _____

_____
Shareholder

_____
Shareholder

_____
Shareholder

PROXY FOR ANNUAL MEETING OF SHAREHOLDERS

KNOW ALL PERSONS BY THESE PRESENTS, that I am the owner of _____ shares of the _____ stock of _____ Corporation, and I hereby appoint and constitute my true and lawful attorney and proxy with full power of substitution and revocation to attend and represent me at the annual meeting of shareholders of the corporation to be held on _____, 19____. _____ may vote my shares on any question, proposition, or resolution, or any other matter which may come before the meeting or any adjournment thereof upon which I would be entitled to vote if personally present.

This proxy shall be void if I personally attend said meeting.

IN WITNESS WHEREOF, I have executed this proxy on the day of _____, 19____.

_____
Shareholder

MINUTES OF FIRST MEETING
OF SHAREHOLDERS

The first meeting of shareholders of the _____ Corporation was held on the date, time, and at the place set forth in the written Waiver of Notice signed by the shareholders, fixing such time and place, and attached to the minutes of this meeting.

The meeting was called to order by the President, heretofore elected by the Board of Directors, and the following shareholders, being all of the shareholders of the Corporation, were present:

_____

_____

_____

There was presented to the meeting the following:

1. Certificate of Incorporation
2. Articles of Incorporation
3. Copy of bylaws of the corporation, duly adopted by the directors
4. Minutes of organization meeting of directors
5. Corporate certificate book
6. Corporate certificate record book

Upon motion duly made, seconded, and unanimously carried, it was

> RESOLVED, that the items listed above have been examined by all shareholders, and are all approved and adopted, and that all acts taken and decisions reached, as set forth in such documents, be, and they hereby are, ratified and approved by the shareholders of the corporation.

There being no further business to come before the meeting, upon motion duly made, seconded, and unanimously carried, the same was adjourned.

_____

Secretary

ATTEST:

_____

_____

_____

SHAREHOLDERS' AGREEMENT

AGREEMENT made this _____ day of _____, 19____, between _____[name of corporation]_____, having its principal office at _____, _____[State]_____, and _____[shareholder's name]_____ , of _____[shareholder's address]_____, and _____[shareholder's name]_____, of _____[shareholder's address]_____, and _____[shareholder's name]_____, _____[shareholder's address]_____.

WHEREAS, the parties desire to promote their mutual interests and the interests of the Corporation by making provision to avoid future differences,

NOW, THEREFORE, it is mutually agreed as follows:

1. Each of the undersigned shareholders agrees that so long as he or she shall remain a shareholder in [name of corporation], he or she will vote his or her respective shares of stock in the corporation for each of the following named persons as a director, so long as that person remains a shareholder of the Corporation:

1. _____

2. _____

3. _____

Any of the foregoing directors who ceases to be a shareholder in the Corporation shall submit to the Corporation his or her resignation as a director when he or she transfers his or her shares.

2. For the best interest of [name of corporation], the undersigned shareholders agree to have each of the following persons appointed and elected as an officer of [name of corporation], as long as he or she remains a shareholder and performs faithfully, efficiently, and competently for the Corporation.

President _____

Vice-President _____

Secretary _____

Treasurer _____

Any of the foregoing officers who ceases to be a shareholder in the Corporation shall submit to the Corporation his or her resignation as an officer when he or she transfers his or her shares.

3. Each of the undersigned persons agrees that he or she will devote his or her best efforts to develop the best interests of the Corporation.

4.(a) The undersigned shareholders agree that if any action be taken at a meeting of the shareholders or directors of the Corporation by a vote of less than _____% of the shareholders or directors, as the case may be, the dissenting shareholder may require the other shareholders or directors within _____ days either to (1) rescind the action dissented from, or (2) purchase the shares owned by the dissenter at a price per share computed on a pro rata basis according to Section 4(d) of this agreement. The individual shareholders party to this agreement agree that should their vote in favor of the action be dissented from, they will either (1) rescind it, or (2) purchase the dissenter's shares within _____ days.

(b) The undersigned shareholders agree that they will not transfer, assign, sell, pledge, hypothecate, or otherwise dispose of the shares of stock owned by any of them, or the certificates of stock representing their interests, unless such shares of stock shall have been first offered to the Corporation at a price per share computed on a pro rata basis according to the provisions of Section 4(d) of this agreement. Such offer shall be made in writing and shall remain open for the Corporation's acceptance for a period of _____ days. In the event the Corporation wishes to accept the offer, it must agree in writing to purchase the entire amount of stock offered and shall at that time make a down payment of _____% of the purchase price. The balance of the purchase price shall be paid as provided in section 4(e) of this agreement. If the Corporation should not choose to purchase the shares within _____ days, they shall then be offered to the remaining stockholder's on a pro rata basis. Such offer shall be made in writing and shall remain open for a period of _____ days. In the event the stockholders wish to accept the offer, they must agree in writing to purchase any or all of their pro rata portion of shares, and make a down payment in the amount of _____% of the purchase price. The balance of the purchase price shall be paid as provided in Section 4(e) of this agreement. If any shareholder should elect not to purchase his or her pro rata portion, or should purchase less than the full amount, the remainder shall be offered to the other shareholders on a pro rata basis. The amount of stock that remains unpurchased after this offering to the shareholders shall be freely transferable and no longer subject to the provisions and limitations of this agreement. This agreement shall not bar a transfer, assignment, bequest, or sale of shares of stock by one of the undersigned shareholders to a member of his or her immediate family, who shall, however, take his or her stock subject to all the limitations of this agreement as if he or she were a party to it.

(c) The parties to this agreement agree that upon the death of [name of shareholders], _____ , or _____ , the executors, administrators, or legal representatives of the deceased shall, within _____ days after qualification as such, sell to [name of corporation], and the corporation agrees to buy, all the shares of stock in [name of corporation], owned by the deceased at the time of his or her death. It is the wish of the parties to this agreement that within the period specified above after the death of the shareholder, his or her family shall terminate all interest in the corporation, and all members of the family to whom any shares of stock have been or shall be transferred shall sell to the corporation all shares of its stock owned by them, within _____ days. The price per share shall be computed on a pro rata basis according to the provisions of Section 4(d) of this agreement.

(d) The parties to this agreement agree that as of the date hereof one share of stock in the corporation shall be worth $_____. It is the intention of the parties to review this figure _____ times a year, on _____ [date] _____ , and that the last agreed-upon figure prior to a transfer described in Sections 4(a), (b), or (c) shall be conclusive as to the value of the stock for such purposes.

(e) The purchase price shall be paid as follows: _____% in cash within _____ days after the qualification of the legal representatives of the deceased shareholder. _____% of the unpaid balance shall be paid within the succeeding _____ days, and _____% of the still remaining unpaid balance within _____ days. Interest at the rate of _____% shall be calculated on the outstanding unpaid balance. The corporation reserves the right to prepay the whole or any part of the amount owed without the imposition of a premium or penalty therefore.

5. The parties hereto agree that they will take no action or dispose of their stock in such a way as to cause the termination of the corporation's ability to be taxed as an electing small business corporation under Subchapter S of the Internal Revenue Code of 1954.

6. Each stock certificate of the corporation shall contain the following information:

> Transfer or pledge of these shares is restricted under a shareholders' agreement dated _____, 19____. A copy of the agreement, which affects other rights of the holder of these shares, is on file at the office of the corporation at [address of corporate offices].

7. Should any dispute arise between any one or more of the parties to this agreement as to their rights under any provisions of this agreement, the parties hereby agree to refer such dispute to the American Arbitration Association, whose decision on the questions shall be binding on the parties and shall be without appeal.

8. The corporation is authorized to enter into this agreement by a resolution adopted by the shareholders and directors, dated _____ _____, 19____.

9. This agreement or any of its provisions may be changed only by the mutual consent of the parties hereto, and unless so changed it remains binding upon all the parties, their heirs, executors, administrators, legal representatives, and assigns, who shall execute and deliver all necessary documents required to carry out the terms of this agreement.

IN WITNESS WHEREOF, the individual parties hereto set their hands and seals, and the corporation has caused this agreement to be signed by its duly authorized officers and the corporate seal affixed.

NAME OF CORPORATION

BY: _____
                   President

[Names of shareholders] _____

_____

_____

ATTEST:

_____
          Secretary

VOTING TRUST AGREEMENT

An agreement made this _____ day of _____, 19____, between stockholders of _____[name of corporation]_____, a corporation organized under the laws of _____, whose names are hereunto subscribed and all other stockholders of the said company who shall join in and become parties to this agreement as hereinafter provided, all of which stockholders are hereinafter called subscribers, and _____, who is hereinafter called the trustee(s):

Whereas, the subscribers are respectively owners of shares of common stock in the corporation and the amounts set out opposite their signatures hereto;

And whereas, with a view to the safe and competent management of the corporation, in the interest of all the stockholders thereof, the subscribers are desirous of creating a trust in the following manner;

Now, it is hereby agreed and declared as follows:

1. The subscribers shall forthwith endorse, assign, and deliver to the trustee(s) the certificates representing the shares of stock owned by them respectively, and shall do all things necessary for the transfer of their respective shares to the trustee(s) on the books of the corporation.

2. Every other stockholder in the corporation may become a party to this agreement by signing it and assigning and delivering the certificate(s) of his or her shares to the trustee(s).

3. The trustee(s) shall hold the shares of stock transferred to them, under the terms and conditions hereinafter set forth.

4. The trustee(s) shall surrender to the proper officer of the corporation the certificates of the subscribers, and shall receive for them new certificates issued to them as trustee(s) under this agreement.

5. The trustee(s) shall issue to each of the subscribers a trust certificate for the number of shares transferred by the subscriber to the trustees. Each trust certificate shall state that it is issued under this agreement, and shall set forth each subscriber's proportional interest in the trust. The trustee(s) shall keep a list of the shares of stock transferred to them, and shall keep a record of all trust certificates issued or transferred on their books, which records shall contain the names and addresses of the trust certificate holders and the number of shares represented by each trust certificate. Such list and record shall be open at all reasonable times to the inspection of the trust certificate holders.

6. It shall be the duty of the trustee(s), and they, or a majority of them, shall have the power to represent the holders of such trust certificates and the stock transferred to the trustee(s) as aforesaid, and vote upon such stock, as in the judgment of the trustee(s), or of a majority of them, may be for the best interest of the corporation, in the election of directors and upon any and all matters and questions which may be brought before them, as fully as any stockholder might do.

7. The trustee(s) shall collect and receive all dividends that may accrue upon the shares of stock subject to this trust, and shall pay the same to the trust certificate holders in proportion to the number of shares respectively represented by their trust certificates.

8. The trustee(s) shall be entitled to be fully indemnified out of the dividends coming into their hands for all costs, changes, expenses, and other liabilities properly incurred by them in the exercise of any power conferred upon them by this agreement; and the subscribers hereby covenant with the trustee(s) that in the event of the monies and securities in their hands being insufficient for that purpose, the subscribers and each of them will, in proportion to the amounts of their respective shares and interests, indemnify the trustee(s) of and from all loss or damage which they may sustain or be put to, by reason of anything they may lawfully do in the execution of this trust.

9. In the event that the holder of any trust certificate shall desire to sell or pledge his or her beneficial interest in the shares of stock represented thereby, he or she shall first give to the trustee(s) notice in writing of such desire, and the trustee(s) shall have the right to purchase the trust certificates at the book value of the stock represented by such certificates at the time of such purchase. If the trustee(s) shall exercise such option to

purchase, they shall hold the beneficial interest thereof for the benefit of all the remaining trust certificate holders who shall, upon _____ days' notice given by the trustee(s) before exercising such option, contribute their respective proportionate share of the purchase money to be paid by the trustee(s). In the event that the trustee(s) shall not exercise such option to purchase the subscriber's interest, and only in that event, the holder of such trust certificate shall have the right to sell the same to such person and for such price as he or she sees fit.

10. In the event of any trustee dying, resigning, refusing, or becoming unable to act, the surviving or other trustee(s), if any, shall appoint a trustee or trustees to fill the vacancy or vacancies, and any person so appointed shall thereupon be vested with all the duties, powers, and authority of a trustee as if originally named herein.

11. This trust shall continue for _____ years from the date hereof, and shall then terminate, provided, however, that the beneficial owners of _____% of the shares of stock subject to this agreement may at any time terminate this trust by resolution adopted at a meeting of the trust certificate holders called by any one of them, upon notice of _____ days, stating the purpose of such meeting, in writing, mailed to the trust certificate holders at their respective addresses as they appear in the records of the trustee(s). Upon the termination of the trust, the trustee(s) shall, upon the surrender of the trust certificates by the respective holders thereof, assign and transfer to them the number of shares of stock thereby represented.

IN WITNESS WHEREOF, the individual parties hereto set their hands and seals, and the corporation has caused this agreement to be signed by its duly authorized officers.

ATTEST: NAME OF CORPORATION

_____   By: _____
Secretary   President

                         Name of Shareholders

                         _____

                         _____

                         Name of Trustee(s)

                         _____

                         _____

COMPARISON CHART—MODEL ACT AND STATE STATUTES

The following chart compares selected sections of the Model Business Corporation Act with similar provisions in state statutes. The chart is intended as a general guide and not as a substitute for research and/or professional advice. The sections compared are those of more general significance where there are differences with the Model Act. Sections were left out of the chart because of their more esoteric nature or their close similarity with the Model Act. Always check your state's law for precise information.

COMPARISON CHART: MODEL ACT SECTIONS

State	2	3	6	7	9	14	15	25	29	31	34	36	38	43	44	45	48	50	52	54	58	59	85 86 87	92 93	106	115	144	146
Alabama	C	C	C	I	I	E	A	I	B	C	B	B	C	C	I	I	J	J	B	A	A	A	A	N	J	A	I	J
Alaska	C	C	C	I	I	C	A	C	G	B	C	B	K	A	C	I	B	B	B	L	I	B	I	I	C	C	C	J
Arizona	C	C	I	C	E	A	C	I	D	C	D	H	K	C	A	B	I	A	L	A	L	A	A	N	C	O	C	J
Arkansas	C	A	C	I	C	A	C	G	B	C	B	K	J	C	A	B	A	I	A	L	C	B	M	A	O	C	J
California	C	A	C	I	D	E	A	C	J	C	C	B	K	A	C	C	B	I	A	L	A	A	M	A	A	O	C	J
Colorado	C	A	C	C	D	C	A	I	G	B	A	C	K	A	C	C	B	I	B	L	C	A	C	A	O	I	I
Connecticut	C	A	C	C	D	E	A	C	B	C	C	B	A	C	C	C	B	A	C	A	A	M	N	C	C	C	C	J
Delaware	C	A	C	C	D	E	A	C	G	C	C	H	K	A	C	C	B	A	C	A	A	A	N	A	C	C	C	J
Florida	C	A	C	C	D	E	A	C	G	D	D	H	K	A	C	C	A	C	A	L	A	A	N	C	O	C	P	J
Georgia	C	A	C	C	D	C	A	C	G	G	D	B	K	J	C	A	C	A	A	L	A	A	M	N	C	C	P	J
Hawaii	C	A	C	J	D	E	A	C	G	D	H	K	A	J	C	J	A	C	A	L	A	M	N	I	O	P	P	J
Idaho	C	A	I	J	D	E	A	C	G	G	D	H	K	A	J	A	C	A	A	L	A	A	M	N	C	O	P	J
Illinois	C	A	A	I	D	C	A	C	G	D	B	K	C	C	A	C	I	A	L	A	C	C	C	C	C	C	I	J
Indiana	C	A	A	I	D	E	A	C	G	G	D	B	K	I	C	A	C	C	A	L	A	M	N	A	A	O	C	J
Iowa	C	A	A	A	D	C	A	C	I	G	D	B	K	C	J	A	C	C	B	L	A	A	C	I	I	I	I	I
Kansas	C	A	A	A	I	E	A	C	G	G	D	B	K	C	J	A	C	A	A	C	A	M	N	A	A	O	J	J
Kentucky	C	A	A	A	D	E	A	C	G	J	D	H	K	C	C	A	C	A	C	A	A	M	N	A	A	O	P	J
Louisiana	C	A	A	A	D	E	A	C	G	G	D	H	K	C	A	C	C	A	C	A	A	M	N	A	A	O	P	J
Maine	C	A	A	C	E	E	A	C	G	J	D	H	K	C	J	A	C	A	C	A	A	M	N	A	A	O	P	J
Maryland	C	A	A	I	C	E	A	C	G	J	D	H	K	C	C	A	B	C	C	A	A	M	N	C	C	O	C	J
Massachusetts	C	A	A	A	D	C	A	C	G	J	D	H	K	C	C	A	C	A	C	A	A	M	N	A	A	O	C	J
Michigan	C	A	A	A	D	E	A	C	G	J	D	H	K	C	C	A	C	A	C	A	A	M	N	A	A	O	C	J
Minnesota	C	A	A	A	D	E	A	C	G	J	D	H	K	C	A	C	C	A	C	A	A	M	N	A	A	O	C	J
Mississippi	C	A	C	I	C	I	A	I	I	B	D	H	K	C	C	C	B	A	B	C	I	A	I	C	C	C	I	I
Missouri	C	A	I	D	C	A	C	I	G	B	C	H	K	C	C	A	C	I	C	L	A	C	A	I	C	C	I	J
Montana	C	A	C	I	E	A	C	I	G	C	B	K	C	C	A	A	C	I	C	L	A	C	I	C	C	C	I	J
Nebraska	C	A	C	I	E	A	C	I	B	C	B	B	K	C	I	B	A	C	L	A	A	C	C	A	C	C	I	J
Nevada	C	A	A	I	D	E	A	C	G	J	C	H	K	C	C	A	C	A	C	L	A	M	N	O	I	I	O	J

244

State	Codes
New Hampshire	C A A A D E A C G J C H J C A A A L A A M N A C J
New Jersey	C A I D E A C G B C H J C A A I A A I N C O A J
New Mexico	C A C I I I B C C I C H B K C C I L I A M I C O I I
New York	C A C I D E A C G B C H K C C A A L A A M N C A J
North Carolina	C C C I C A C I B C .C H K C C A B C L A A M A C I J
North Dakota	C A I I C A I C B C H J I B I C L I A I C I I
Ohio	C A C A D E A C G B C H K C C A B A L A A M A O C J
Oklahoma	C A C A D E A C I B C H K C C A C L A C N C C C J
Oregon	C I A I I C A I G B C H K C C I B L I A C C I C J
Pennsylvania	C C C I D E A C G B C H J C C A A M C C J M C C J
Rhode Island	C C C A C E A C G B C H K C C A C N A I A C N I A J
South Carolina	C C A C C G B D H K C C I C C A I A C A J
South Dakota	C A A I I C A I I B C B K A C I B L A A C C C I J
Tennessee	C A I C D A C G B C H K A J I B C C L A A M C C J
Texas	C A C C D C I I B C B K A I A B I C L A C C C I J
Utah	C A A A I E A I I B C B K A J I B I C L C A M I C I I
Vermont	C A C A D E A C G B C H K A C A A L A A C N C C J
Washington	C A C A D E A I I B C B K A C I B L C A C I I I J
West Virginia	C A C I D E I C G I C B K A C A A L A C C I C C J
Wisconsin	C C C I D E A C G B C B K A J I B A C L A A E I C C J
Wyoming	C I C I I I A C G B C B K A C C I C L I A C I A I J
Washington D.C.	C C C C A C G B C B K A C C B I

A Many technical differences (check state laws).
B Uses older version of Model Act (1962, 1969).
C Essentially the same as Model Act with some technical differences.
D Sets specific time limit on duration.
E May have officer or agents.
F Power lies in director or shareholder to appeal, adopt, or amend.
G Requires prior notice by specified number of days in advance.
H Require at least one director.

I Identical to Model Act.
J No state provision.
K Vacancy may be filled by Board.
L Minimum dollar amount—before start of operation ($1,000).
M Must provide notice to creditor of intent to dissolve.
N Has one-step provision for dissolution.
O May serve process on registered agent.
P No provision for waiver by directors.

APPLICATION FOR EMPLOYER IDENTIFICATION NUMBER, FORM SS-4

Form **SS-4** (Rev. April 1991) Department of the Treasury Internal Revenue Service	**Application for Employer Identification Number** (For use by employers and others. Please read the attached instructions before completing this form.)	**EIN** OMB No. 1545-0003 Expires 4-30-94

Please type or print clearly.

1 Name of applicant (True legal name) (See instructions.)

2 Trade name of business, if different from name in line 1	**3** Executor, trustee, "care of" name

4a Mailing address (street address) (room, apt., or suite no.)	**5a** Address of business (See instructions.)
4b City, state, and ZIP code	**5b** City, state, and ZIP code

6 County and state where principal business is located

7 Name of principal officer, grantor, or general partner (See instructions.) ▶

8a Type of entity (Check only one box.) (See instructions.)

☐ Individual SSN _____   ☐ Estate   ☐ Trust
☐ REMIC   ☐ Personal service corp.   ☐ Plan administrator SSN _____   ☐ Partnership
☐ State/local government   ☐ National guard   ☐ Other corporation (specify) _____   ☐ Farmers' cooperative
☐ Other nonprofit organization (specify) _____   ☐ Federal government/military   ☐ Church or church controlled organization
☐ Other (specify) ▶ _____   If nonprofit organization enter GEN (if applicable) _____

8b If a corporation, give name of foreign country (if applicable) or state in the U.S. where incorporated ▶

Foreign country	State

9 Reason for applying (Check only one box.)
☐ Started new business   ☐ Changed type of organization (specify) ▶ _____
☐ Hired employees   ☐ Purchased going business
☐ Created a pension plan (specify type) ▶ _____   ☐ Created a trust (specify) ▶ _____
☐ Banking purpose (specify) ▶   ☐ Other (specify) ▶

10 Date business started or acquired (Mo., day, year) (See instructions.)	**11** Enter closing month of accounting year. (See instructions.)

12 First date wages or annuities were paid or will be paid (Mo., day, year). **Note:** *If applicant is a withholding agent, enter date income will first be paid to nonresident alien. (Mo., day, year)* . . . . ▶

13 Enter highest number of employees expected in the next 12 months. **Note:** *If the applicant does not expect to have any employees during the period, enter "0."* . . . . ▶

Nonagricultural	Agricultural	Household

14 Principal activity (See instructions.) ▶

15 Is the principal business activity manufacturing? . . . . ☐ Yes   ☐ No
If "Yes," principal product and raw material used ▶

16 To whom are most of the products or services sold? Please check the appropriate box.   ☐ Business (wholesale)
☐ Public (retail)   ☐ Other (specify) ▶   ☐ N/A

17a Has the applicant ever applied for an identification number for this or any other business? . . . . ☐ Yes   ☐ No
Note: *If "Yes," please complete lines 17b and 17c.*

17b If you checked the "Yes" box in line 17a, give applicant's true name and trade name, if different than name shown on prior application.

True name ▶   Trade name ▶

17c Enter approximate date, city, and state where the application was filed and the previous employer identification number if known.

Approximate date when filed (Mo., day, year)	City and state where filed	Previous EIN

Under penalties of perjury, I declare that I have examined this application, and to the best of my knowledge and belief, it is true, correct, and complete | Telephone number (include area code)

Name and title (Please type or print clearly.) ▶

Signature ▶   Date ▶

Note: *Do not write below this line.   For official use only.*

Please leave blank ▶	Geo.	Ind.	Class	Size	Reason for applying

For Paperwork Reduction Act Notice, see attached instructions.   Cat. No. 16055N   Form **SS-4** (Rev. 4-91)

INSTRUCTIONS FOR FORM SS-4

Form SS-4 (Rev. 4-91)

General Instructions

(Section references are to the Internal Revenue Code unless otherwise noted.)

Paperwork Reduction Act Notice.—We ask for the information on this form to carry out the Internal Revenue laws of the United States. You are required to give us this information. We need it to ensure that you are complying with these laws and to allow us to figure and collect the right amount of tax.

The time needed to complete and file this form will vary depending on individual circumstances. The estimated average time is:

Recordkeeping	7 min.
Learning about the law or the form	21 min.
Preparing the form	42 min.
Copying, assembling, and sending the form to IRS	20 min.

If you have comments concerning the accuracy of these time estimates or suggestions for making this form more simple, we would be happy to hear from you. You can write to both the **Internal Revenue Service,** Washington, DC 20224, Attention: IRS Reports Clearance Officer, T:FP; and the **Office of Management and Budget,** Paperwork Reduction Project (1545-0003), Washington, DC 20503. **DO NOT** send the tax form to either of these offices. Instead, see **Where To Apply.**

Purpose.—Use Form SS-4 to apply for an employer identification number (EIN). The information you provide on this form will establish your filing requirements.

Who Must File.—You must file this form if you have not obtained an EIN before and

● You pay wages to one or more employees.

● You are required to have an EIN to use on any return, statement, or other document, even if you are not an employer.

● You are required to withhold taxes on income, other than wages, paid to a nonresident alien (individual, corporation, partnership, etc.). For example, individuals who file **Form 1042,** Annual Withholding Tax Return for U.S. Source Income of Foreign Persons, to report alimony paid to nonresident aliens must have EINs.

Individuals who file **Schedule C,** Profit or Loss From Business, or **Schedule F,** Profit or Loss From Farming, of **Form 1040,** U.S. Individual Income Tax Return, must use EINs if they have a Keogh plan or are required to file excise, employment, or alcohol, tobacco, or firearms returns.

The following must use EINs even if they do not have any employees:

● Trusts, except an IRA trust, unless the IRA trust is required to file **Form 990-T,** Exempt Organization Business Income Tax Return, to report unrelated business taxable income or is filing Form 990-T to obtain a refund of the credit from a regulated investment company.

● Estates

● Partnerships

● REMICS (real estate mortgage investment conduits)

● Corporations

● Nonprofit organizations (churches, clubs, etc.)

● Farmers' cooperatives

● Plan administrators

New Business.—If you become the new owner of an existing business, **DO NOT** use the EIN of the former owner. If you already have an EIN, use that number. If you do not have an EIN, apply for one on this form. If

you become the "owner" of a corporation by acquiring its stock, use the corporation's EIN.

If you already have an EIN, you may need to get a new one if either the organization or ownership of your business changes. If you incorporate a sole proprietorship or form a partnership, you must get a new EIN. However, **DO NOT** apply for a new EIN if you change only the name of your business.

File Only One Form SS-4.—File only one Form SS-4, regardless of the number of businesses operated or trade names under which a business operates. However, each corporation in an affiliated group must file a separate application.

If you do not have an EIN by the time a return is due, write "Applied for" and the date you applied in the space shown for the number. **DO NOT** show your social security number as an EIN on returns.

If you do not have an EIN by the time a tax deposit is due, send your payment to the Internal Revenue service center for your filing area. (See **Where To Apply** below.) Make your check or money order payable to Internal Revenue Service and show your name (as shown on Form SS-4), address, kind of tax, period covered, and date you applied for an EIN.

For more information about EINs, see **Pub. 583,** Taxpayers Starting a Business.

How To Apply.—You can apply for an EIN either by mail or by telephone. You can get an EIN immediately by calling the Tele-TIN phone number for your service center for your state, or you can send the completed Form SS-4 directly to the service center to receive your EIN in the mail.

Application by Tele-TIN.—The Tele-TIN program is designed to assign EINs by telephone. Under this program, you can receive your EIN over the telephone and use it immediately to file a return or make a payment.

To receive an EIN by phone, complete Form SS-4, then call the Tele-TIN phone number listed for your state under **Where To Apply.** The person making the call must be authorized to sign the form (see **Signature block** on page 3).

An IRS representative will use the information from the Form SS-4 to establish your account and assign you an EIN. Write the number you are given on the upper right-hand corner of the form, sign and date it, and promptly mail it to the Tele-TIN Unit at the service center address for your state.

Application by mail.—Complete Form SS-4 at least 4 to 5 weeks before you will need an EIN. Sign and date the application and mail it to the service center address for your state. You will receive your EIN in the mail in approximately 4 weeks.

Note: *The Tele-TIN phone numbers listed below will involve a long-distance charge to callers outside of the local calling area, and should only be used to apply for an EIN. Use 1-800-829-1040 to ask about an application by mail.*

Where To Apply.—

If your principal business, office or agency, or legal residence in the case of an individual, is located in: ▼	Call the Tele-TIN phone number shown or file with the Internal Revenue service center at: ▼
Florida, Georgia, South Carolina	Atlanta, GA 39901 (404) 455-2360
New Jersey, New York City and counties of Nassau, Rockland, Suffolk, and Westchester	Holtsville, NY 00501 (516) 447-4955
New York (all other counties), Connecticut, Maine, Massachusetts, New Hampshire, Rhode Island, Vermont	Andover, MA 05501 (508) 474-9717
Illinois, Iowa, Minnesota, Missouri, Wisconsin	Kansas City, MO 64999 (816) 926-5999
Delaware, District of Columbia, Maryland, Pennsylvania, Virginia	Philadelphia, PA 19255 (215) 961-3980
Indiana, Kentucky, Michigan, Ohio, West Virginia	Cincinnati, OH 45999 (606) 292-5467
Kansas, New Mexico, Oklahoma, Texas	Austin, TX 73301 (512) 462-7845
Alaska, Arizona, California (counties of Alpine, Amador, Butte, Calaveras, Colusa, Contra Costa, Del Norte, El Dorado, Glenn, Humboldt, Lake, Lassen, Marin, Mendocino, Modoc, Napa, Nevada, Placer, Plumas, Sacramento, San Joaquin, Shasta, Sierra, Siskiyou, Solano, Sonoma, Sutter, Tehama, Trinity, Yolo, and Yuba), Colorado, Idaho, Montana, Nebraska, Nevada, North Dakota, Oregon, South Dakota, Utah, Washington, Wyoming	Ogden, UT 84201 (801) 625-7645
California (all other counties), Hawaii	Fresno, CA 93888 (209) 456-5900
Alabama, Arkansas, Louisiana, Mississippi, North Carolina, Tennessee	Memphis, TN 37501 (901) 365-5970

If you have no legal residence, principal place of business, or principal office or agency in any Internal Revenue District, file your form with the Internal Revenue Service Center, Philadelphia, PA 19255 or call (215) 961-3980.

Specific Instructions

The instructions that follow are for those items that are not self-explanatory. Enter N/A (nonapplicable) on the lines that do not apply.

Line 1.—Enter the legal name of the entity applying for the EIN.

Individuals.—Enter the first name, middle initial, and last name.

Trusts.—Enter the name of the trust.

Estate of a decedent.—Enter the name of the estate.

Partnerships.—Enter the legal name of the partnership as it appears in the partnership agreement.

Corporations.—Enter the corporate name as set forth in the corporation charter or other legal document creating it.

Plan administrators.—Enter the name of the plan administrator. A plan administrator who already has an EIN should use that number.

Line 2.—Enter the trade name of the business if different from the legal name.

Note: *Use the full legal name entered on line 1 on all tax returns to be filed for the entity. However, if a trade name is entered on line 2, use only the name on line 1 or the name on line 2 consistently when filing tax returns.*

Line 3.—Trusts enter the name of the trustee. Estates enter the name of the executor, administrator, or other fiduciary. If the entity applying has a designated person to receive tax information, enter that person's name as the "care of" person. Print or type the first name, middle initial, and last name.

Lines 5a and 5b.—If the physical location of the business is different from the mailing address (lines 4a and 4b), enter the address of the physical location on lines 5a and 5b.

Line 7.—Enter the first name, middle initial, and last name of a principal officer if the business is a corporation; of a general partner if a partnership; and of a grantor if a trust.

Line 8a.—Check the box that best describes the type of entity that is applying for the EIN. If not specifically mentioned, check the "other" box and enter the type of entity. Do not enter N/A.

Individual.—Check this box if the individual files Schedule C or F (Form 1040) and has a Keogh plan or is required to file excise, employment, or alcohol, tobacco, or firearms returns. If this box is checked, enter the individual's SSN (social security number) in the space provided.

Plan administrator.—The term plan administrator means the person or group of persons specified as the administrator by the instrument under which the plan is operated. If the plan administrator is an individual, enter the plan administrator's SSN in the space provided.

New withholding agent.—If you are a new withholding agent required to file Form 1042, check the "other" box and enter in the space provided "new withholding agent."

REMICs.—Check this box if the entity is a real estate mortgage investment conduit (REMIC). A REMIC is any entity

1. To which an election to be treated as a REMIC applies for the tax year and all prior tax years,

2. In which all of the interests are regular interests or residual interests,

3. Which has one class of residual interests (and all distributions, if any, with respect to such interests are pro rata),

4. In which as of the close of the 3rd month beginning after the startup date and at all times thereafter, substantially all of its assets consist of qualified mortgages and permitted investments,

5. Which has a tax year that is a calendar year, and

6. With respect to which there are reasonable arrangements designed to ensure that: (a) residual interests are not held by disqualified organizations (as defined in section 860E(e)(5)), and (b) information necessary for the application of section 860E(e) will be made available.

For more information about REMICs see the Instructions for **Form 1066,** U. S. Real Estate Mortgage Investment Conduit Income Tax Return.

Personal service corporations.—Check this box if the entity is a personal service corporation. An entity is a personal service corporation for a tax year only if

1. The entity is a C corporation for the tax year.

2. The principal activity of the entity during the testing period (as defined in Temporary Regulations section 1.441-4T(f)) for the tax year is the performance of personal service.

3. During the testing period for the tax year, such services are substantially performed by employee-owners.

4. The employee-owners own 10 percent of the fair market value of the outstanding stock in the entity on the last day of the testing period for the tax year.

For more information about personal service corporations, see the instructions to **Form 1120,** U.S. Corporation Income Tax Return, and Temporary Regulations section 1.441-4T.

Other corporations.—This box is for any corporation other than a personal service corporation. If you check this box, enter the type of corporation (such as insurance company) in the space provided.

Other nonprofit organizations.—Check this box if the nonprofit organization is other than a church or church-controlled organization and specify the type of nonprofit organization (for example, an educational organization.)

Group exemption number (GEN).—If the applicant is a nonprofit organization that is a subordinate organization to be included in a group exemption letter under Revenue Procedure 80-27, 1980-1 C.B. 677, enter the GEN in the space provided. If you do not know the GEN, contact the parent organization for it. GEN is a four-digit number. Do not confuse it with the nine-digit EIN.

Line 9.—Check only one box. Do not enter N/A.

Started new business.—Check this box if you are starting a new business that requires an EIN. If you check this box, enter the type of business being started. **DO NOT** apply if you already have an EIN and are only adding another place of business.

Changed type of organization.—Check this box if the business is changing its type of organization, for example, if the business was a sole proprietorship and has been incorporated or has become a partnership. If you check this box, specify in the space provided the type of change made, for example, "from sole proprietorship to partnership."

Purchased going business.—Check this box if you acquired a business through purchase. Do not use the former owner's EIN. If you already have an EIN, use that number.

Hired employees.—Check this box if the existing business is requesting an EIN because it has hired or is hiring employees and is therefore required to file employment tax return for which an EIN is required. **DO NOT** apply if you already have an EIN and are only hiring employees.

Created a trust.—Check this box if you created a trust, and enter the type of trust created.

Created a pension plan.—Check this box if you have created a pension plan and need this number for reporting purposes. Also, enter the type of plan created.

Banking purpose.—Check this box if you are requesting an EIN for banking purpose only and enter the banking purpose (for example, checking, loan, etc.).

Other (specify).—Check this box if you are requesting an EIN for any reason other than those for which there are checkboxes and enter the reason.

Line 10.—If you are starting a new business, enter the starting date of the business. If the business you acquired is already operating, enter the date you acquired the business. Trusts should enter the date the trust was legally created. Estates should enter the date of death of the decedent whose name appears on line 1.

Line 11.—Enter the last month of your accounting year or tax year. An accounting year or tax year is usually 12 consecutive months. It may be a calendar year or a fiscal year (including a period of 52 or 53 weeks). A calendar year is 12 consecutive months ending on December 31. A fiscal year is either 12 consecutive months ending on the last day of any month other than December or a 52-53 week year. For more information

on accounting periods, see **Pub. 538,** Accounting Periods and Methods.

Individuals.—Your tax year generally will be a calendar year.

Partnerships.—Partnerships generally should conform to the tax year of either (1) its majority partners; (2) its principal partners; (3) the tax year that results in the least aggregate deferral of income (see Temporary Regulations section 1.706-1T); or (4) some other tax year, if (a) a business purpose is established for the fiscal year, or (b) the fiscal year is a "grandfather" year, or (c) an election is made under section 444 to have a fiscal year. (See the Instructions for **Form 1065,** U.S. Partnership Return of Income, for more information.)

REMICs.—Remics must have a calendar year as their tax year.

Personal service corporations.—A personal service corporation generally must adopt a calendar year unless:

1. It can establish to the satisfaction of the Commissioner that there is a business purpose for having a different tax year, or

2. It elects under section 444 to have a tax year other than a calendar year.

Line 12.—If the business has or will have employees, enter on this line the date on which the business began or will begin to pay wages to the employees. If the business does not have any plans to have employees, enter N/A on this line.

New withholding agent.—Enter the date you began or will begin to pay income to a nonresident alien. This also applies to individuals who are required to file Form 1042 to report alimony paid to a nonresident alien.

Line 14.—Generally, enter the exact type of business being operated (for example, advertising agency, farm, labor union, real estate agency, steam laundry, rental of coin-operated vending machine, investment club, etc.).

Governmental.—Enter the type of organization (state, county, school district, or municipality, etc.)

Nonprofit organization (other than governmental).—Enter whether organized for religious, educational, or humane purposes, and the principal activity (for example, religious organization—hospital, charitable).

Mining and quarrying.—Specify the process and the principal product (for example, mining bituminous coal, contract drilling for oil, quarrying dimension stone, etc.).

Contract construction.—Specify whether general contracting or special trade contracting. Also, show the type of work normally performed (for example, general contractor for residential buildings, electrical subcontractor, etc.).

Trade.—Specify the type of sales and the principal line of goods sold (for example, wholesale dairy products, manufacturer's representative for mining machinery, retail hardware, etc.).

Manufacturing.—Specify the type of establishment operated (for example, sawmill, vegetable cannery, etc.).

Signature block.—The application must be signed by: (1) the individual, if the person is an individual, (2) the president, vice president, or other principal officer, if the person is a corporation, (3) a responsible and duly authorized member or officer having knowledge of its affairs, if the person is a partnership or other unincorporated organization, or (4) the fiduciary, if the person is a trust or estate.

ELECTION BY A SMALL BUSINESS CORPORATION, FORM 2553

Form **2553**
(Rev. December 1990)
Department of the Treasury
Internal Revenue Service

Election by a Small Business Corporation

(Under section 1362 of the Internal Revenue Code)
▶ For Paperwork Reduction Act Notice, see page 1 of Instructions.
▶ See separate instructions.

OMB No. 1545-0146
Expires 11-30-93

Notes: 1. *This election, to be treated as an "S corporation," can be accepted only if all the tests in General Instruction B are met; all signatures in Parts I and III are originals (no photocopies); and the exact name and address of the corporation and other required form information are provided.*

2. *Do not file Form 1120S until you are notified that your election is accepted. See General Instruction E.*

Part I Election Information

Please Type or Print

Name of corporation (see instructions)	**A Employer identification number** (see instructions)
Number, street, and room or suite no. (If a P.O. box, see instructions.)	**B** Name and telephone number (including area code) of corporate officer or legal representative who may be called for information
City or town, state, and ZIP code	**C** Election is to be effective for tax year beginning (month, day, year)

D Is the corporation the outgrowth or continuation of any form of predecessor? . . ☐ **Yes** ☐ **No**
If "Yes," state name of predecessor, type of organization, and period of its existence ▶

E Date of incorporation

F Check here ▶ ☐ if the corporation has changed its name or address since applying for the employer identification number shown in item A above.

G State of incorporation

H If this election takes effect for the first tax year the corporation exists, enter month, day, and year of the **earliest** of the following: (1) date the corporation first had shareholders, (2) date the corporation first had assets, or (3) date the corporation began doing business. ▶

I Selected tax year: Annual return will be filed for tax year ending (month and day) ▶
If the tax year ends on any date other than December 31, except for an automatic 52-53-week tax year ending with reference to the month of December, you **must** complete Part II on the back. If the date you enter is the ending date of an automatic 52-53-week tax year, write "52-53-week year" to the right of the date. See Temporary Regulations section 1.441-2T(e)(3).

J Name of each shareholder, person having a community property interest in the corporation's stock, and each tenant in common, joint tenant, and tenant by the entirety. (A husband and wife (and their estates) are counted as one shareholder in determining the number of shareholders without regard to the manner in which the stock is owned.)	**K** Shareholders' Consent Statement. We, the undersigned shareholders, consent to the corporation's election to be treated as an "S corporation" under section 1362(a). (Shareholders sign and date below.)*		**L** Stock owned		**M** Social security number or employer identification number (see instructions)	**N** Shareholder's tax year ends (month and day)
	Signature	Date	Number of shares	Dates acquired		

*For this election to be valid, the consent of each shareholder, person having a community property interest in the corporation's stock, and each tenant in common, joint tenant, and tenant by the entirety must either appear above or be attached to this form. (See instructions for Column K if continuation sheet or a separate consent statement is needed.)

Under penalties of perjury, I declare that I have examined this election, including accompanying schedules and statements, and to the best of my knowledge and belief, it is true, correct, and complete.

Signature of officer ▶ **Title ▶** **Date ▶**

See Parts II and III on back. Form **2553** (Rev. 12-90)

Form 2553 (Rev. 12-90)   Page **2**

Part II   **Selection of Fiscal Tax Year (All corporations using this Part must complete item O and one of items P, Q, or R.)**

O   Check the applicable box below to indicate whether the corporation is:

1. ☐ A new corporation adopting the tax year entered in item I, Part I.

2. ☐ An existing corporation retaining the tax year entered in item I, Part I.

3. ☐ An existing corporation changing to the tax year entered in item I, Part I.

P   Complete item P if the corporation is using the expeditious approval provisions of Revenue Procedure 87-32, 1987-2 C.B. 396, to request: **(1)** a natural business year (as defined in section 4.01(1) of Rev. Proc. 87-32), or **(2)** a year that satisfies the ownership tax year test in section 4.01(2) of Rev. Proc. 87-32. Check the applicable box below to indicate the representation statement the corporation is making as required under section 4 of Rev. Proc. 87-32.

1. Natural Business Year ▶ ☐ I represent that the corporation is retaining or changing to a tax year that coincides with its natural business year as defined in section 4.01(1) of Rev. Proc. 87-32 and as verified by its satisfaction of the requirements of section 4.02(1) of Rev. Proc. 87-32. In addition, if the corporation is changing to a natural business year as defined in section 4.01(1), I further represent that such tax year results in less deferral of income to the owners than the corporation's present tax year. I also represent that the corporation is not described in section 3.01(2) of Rev. Proc. 87-32. (See instructions for additional information that must be attached.)

2. Ownership Tax Year ▶ ☐ I represent that shareholders holding more than half of the shares of the stock (as of the first day of the tax year to which the request relates) of the corporation have the same tax year or are concurrently changing to the tax year that the corporation adopts, retains, or changes to per item I, Part I. I also represent that the corporation is not described in section 3.01(2) of Rev. Proc. 87-32.

Note: *If you do not use item P and the corporation wants a fiscal tax year, complete either item Q or R below. Item Q is used to request a fiscal tax year based on a business purpose and to make a back-up section 444 election. Item R is used to make a regular section 444 election.*

Q   Business Purpose—To request a fiscal tax year based on a business purpose, you must check box Q1 and pay a user fee. See instructions for details. You may also check box Q2 and/or box Q3.

1. Check here ▶ ☐ if the fiscal year entered in item I, Part I, is requested under the provisions of section 6.03 of Rev. Proc. 87-32. Attach to Form 2553 a statement showing the business purpose for the requested fiscal year. See instructions for additional information that must be attached.

2. Check here ▶ ☐ to show that the corporation intends to make a back-up section 444 election in the event the corporation's business purpose request is not approved by the IRS. (See instructions for more information.)

3. Check here ▶ ☐ to show that the corporation agrees to adopt or change to a tax year ending December 31 if necessary for the IRS to accept this election for S corporation status in the event: (1) the corporation's business purpose request is not approved and the corporation makes a back-up section 444 election, but is ultimately not qualified to make a section 444 election, or (2) the corporation's business purpose request is not approved and the corporation did not make a back-up section 444 election.

R   Section 444 Election—To make a section 444 election, you must check box R1 and you may also check box R2.

1. Check here ▶ ☐ to show the corporation will make, if qualified, a section 444 election to have the fiscal tax year shown in item I, Part I. To make the election, you must complete **Form 8716,** Election To Have a Tax Year Other Than a Required Tax Year, and either attach it to Form 2553 or file it separately.

2. Check here ▶ ☐ to show that the corporation agrees to adopt or change to a tax year ending December 31 if necessary for the IRS to accept this election for S corporation status in the event the corporation is ultimately not qualified to make a section 444 election.

Part III   **Qualified Subchapter S Trust (QSST) Election Under Section 1361(d)(2)****

Income beneficiary's name and address	Social security number
Trust's name and address	Employer identification number

Date on which stock of the corporation was transferred to the trust (month, day, year) ▶

In order for the trust named above to be a QSST and thus a qualifying shareholder of the S corporation for which this Form 2553 is filed, I hereby make the election under section 1361(d)(2). Under penalties of perjury, I certify that the trust meets the definition requirements of section 1361(d)(3) and that all other information provided in Part III is true, correct, and complete.

_____   _____
Signature of income beneficiary or signature and title of legal representative or other qualified person making the election   Date

**Use of Part III to make the QSST election may be made only if stock of the corporation has been transferred to the trust on or before the date on which the corporation makes its election to be an S corporation. The QSST election must be made and filed separately if stock of the corporation is transferred to the trust after the date on which the corporation makes the S election.

INSTRUCTIONS FOR FORM 2553

**Department of the Treasury
Internal Revenue Service**

Instructions for Form 2553
(Revised December 1990)
Election by a Small Business Corporation
(Section references are to the Internal Revenue Code unless otherwise noted.)

Paperwork Reduction Act Notice.—We ask for the information on this form to carry out the Internal Revenue laws of the United States. You are required to give us the information. We need it to ensure that you are complying with these laws and to allow us to figure and collect the right amount of tax.

The time needed to complete and file this form will vary depending on individual circumstances. The estimated average time is:

Recordkeeping . . . . . 6 hrs., 28 min.
Learning about the
law or the form . . . . . 3 hrs., 16 min.
Preparing, copying,
assembling, and sending
the form to IRS . . . . 3 hrs., 31 min.

If you have comments concerning the accuracy of these time estimates or suggestions for making this form more simple, we would be happy to hear from you. You can write to both the **Internal Revenue Service,** Washington, DC 20224, Attention: IRS Reports Clearance Officer, T:FP, and the **Office of Management and Budget,** Paperwork Reduction Project (1545-0146), Washington, DC 20503. **DO NOT** send the tax form to either of these offices. Instead, see the instructions below for information on where to file.

General Instructions

A. Purpose.—To elect to be treated as an "S Corporation," a corporation must file Form 2553. The election permits the income of the S corporation to be taxed to the shareholders of the corporation rather than to the corporation itself, except as provided in Subchapter S of the Code. For more information, see **Publication 589,** Tax Information on S Corporations.

B. Who May Elect.—Your corporation may make the election to be treated as an S corporation only if it meets **all** of the following tests:

1. It is a domestic corporation.

2. It has no more than 35 shareholders. A husband and wife (and their estates) are treated as one shareholder for this requirement. All other persons are treated as separate shareholders.

3. It has only individuals, estates, or certain trusts as shareholders. See the instructions for Part III regarding qualified subchapter S trusts.

4. It has no nonresident alien shareholders.

5. It has only one class of stock. See sections 1361(c)(4) and (5) for additional details.

6. It is not one of the following ineligible corporations:

(a) a corporation that owns 80% or more of the stock of another corporation, unless

the other corporation has not begun business and has no gross income;

(b) a bank or thrift institution;

(c) an insurance company subject to tax under the special rules of Subchapter L of the Code;

(d) a corporation that has elected to be treated as a possessions corporation under section 936; or

(e) a domestic international sales corporation (DISC) or former DISC.

See section 1361(b)(2) for details.

7. It has a permitted tax year as required by section 1378 or makes a section 444 election to have a tax year other than a permitted tax year. Section 1378 defines a permitted tax year as a tax year ending December 31, or any other tax year for which the corporation establishes a business purpose to the satisfaction of the IRS. See Part II for details on requesting a fiscal tax year based on a business purpose or on making a section 444 election.

8. Each shareholder consents as explained in the instructions for Column K.

See sections 1361, 1362, and 1378 for additional information on the above tests.

C. Where To File.—File this election with the Internal Revenue Service Center listed below.

If the corporation's principal business, office, or agency is located in ▼	Use the following Internal Revenue Service Center address ▼
New Jersey, New York (New York City and counties of Nassau, Rockland, Suffolk, and Westchester)	Holtsville, NY 00501
New York (all other counties), Connecticut, Maine, Massachusetts, New Hampshire, Rhode Island, Vermont	Andover, MA 05501
Florida, Georgia, South Carolina	Atlanta, GA 39901
Indiana, Kentucky, Michigan, Ohio, West Virginia	Cincinnati, OH 45999
Kansas, New Mexico, Oklahoma, Texas	Austin, TX 73301
Alaska, Arizona, California (counties of Alpine, Amador, Butte, Calaveras, Colusa, Contra Costa, Del Norte, El Dorado, Glenn, Humboldt, Lake, Lassen, Marin, Mendocino, Modoc, Napa, Nevada, Placer, Plumas, Sacramento, San Joaquin, Shasta, Sierra, Siskiyou, Solano, Sonoma, Sutter, Tehama, Trinity, Yolo, and Yuba), Colorado, Idaho, Montana, Nebraska, Nevada, North Dakota, Oregon, South Dakota, Utah, Washington, Wyoming	Ogden, UT 84201
California (all other counties), Hawaii	Fresno, CA 93888
Illinois, Iowa, Minnesota, Missouri, Wisconsin	Kansas City, MO 64999
Alabama, Arkansas, Louisiana, Mississippi, North Carolina, Tennessee	Memphis, TN 37501
Delaware, District of Columbia, Maryland, Pennsylvania, Virginia	Philadelphia, PA 19255

D. When To Make the Election.—Complete Form 2553 and file it either: **(1)** at any time during that portion of the first tax year the election is to take effect which occurs before the 16th day of the third month of that tax year (if the tax year has 2½ months or less, and the election is made not later than 2 months and 15 days after the first day of the tax year, it shall be treated as timely made during such year), or **(2)** in the tax year before the first tax year it is to take effect. An election made by a small business corporation after the 15th day of the third month but before the end of the tax year is treated as made for the next year. For example, if a calendar tax year corporation makes the election in April 1991, it is effective for the corporation's 1992 calendar tax year. See section 1362(b) for more information.

E. Acceptance or Non-Acceptance of Election.—The Service Center will notify you if your election is accepted and when it will take effect. You will also be notified if your election is not accepted. You should generally receive a determination on your election within 60 days after you have filed Form 2553. If the Q1 box in Part II is checked on page 2, the corporation will receive a ruling letter from IRS in Washington, DC, which approves or denies the selected tax year. When Item Q1 is checked, it will generally take an additional 90 days for the Form 2553 to be accepted.

Do not file Form 1120S until you are notified that your election is accepted. If you are now required to file **Form 1120,** U.S. Corporation Income Tax Return, or any other applicable tax return, continue filing it until your election takes effect.

Care should be exercised to ensure that the election is received by the Internal Revenue Service. If you are not notified of acceptance or nonacceptance of your election within 3 months of date of filing (date mailed), or within 6 months if Part II, Item Q1, is checked, you should take follow-up action by corresponding with the Service Center where the election was filed. If filing of Form 2553 is questioned by IRS, an acceptable proof of filing is: **(1)** certified receipt (timely filed); **(2)** Form 2553 with accepted stamp; **(3)** Form 2553 with stamped IRS received date; or **(4)** IRS letter stating that Form 2553 had been accepted.

F. End of Election.—Once the election is made, it stays in effect for all years until it is terminated. During the 5 years after the election is terminated under section 1362(d), the corporation can make another election on Form 2553 only with IRS consent.

Specific Instructions
Part I

Part I must be completed by all corporations.

Name and Address of Corporation.— Enter the true corporate name as set forth in the corporate charter or other legal document creating it. If the corporation's mailing address is the same as someone else's, such as a shareholder's, please enter this person's name below the name of the corporation. Include the suite, room, or other unit number after the street address. If the Post Office does not deliver to the street address and the corporation has a P.O. box, show the P.O. box number instead of the street address. If the corporation has changed its name or address since applying for its EIN (filing Form SS-4), be sure to check the box in item F of Part I.

A. Employer Identification Number.— If you have applied for an employer identification number (EIN) but have not received it, enter "applied for." If the corporation does not have an EIN, you should apply for one on **Form SS-4,** Application for Employer Identification Number, available from most IRS and Social Security Administration offices.

C. Effective Date of Election.— Enter the beginning effective date (month, day, year) of the tax year that you have requested for the S corporation. Generally, this will be the beginning date of the tax year for which the ending effective date is required to be shown in item I, Part I. For a new corporation (first year the corporation exists) it will generally be the date required to be shown in item H, Part I. The tax year of a new corporation starts on the date that it has shareholders, acquires assets, or begins doing business, whichever happens first. If the effective date for item C for a newly formed corporation is later than the date in item H, the corporation should file Form 1120 or Form 1120-A, for the tax period between these dates.

Column K. Shareholders' Consent Statement.— Each shareholder who owns (or is deemed to own) stock at the time the election is made must consent to the election. If the election is made during the corporation's first tax year for which it is effective, any person who held stock at any time during the portion of that year which occurs before the time the election is made, must consent to the election although the person may have sold or transferred his or her stock before the election is made. Each shareholder consents by signing and dating in column K or signing and dating a separate consent statement described below. If stock is owned by a trust that is a qualified shareholder, the deemed owner of the trust must consent. See section 1361(c)(2) for details regarding qualified trusts that may be shareholders and rules on determining who is the deemed owner of the trust.

An election made during the first 2½ months of the tax year is considered made for the following tax year if one or more of the persons who held stock in the corporation during such tax year and before the election was made did not consent to the election. See section 1362(b)(2).

If a husband and wife have a community interest in the stock or in the income from it, both must consent. Each tenant in common, joint tenant, and tenant by the entirety also must consent.

A minor's consent is made by the minor or the legal representative of the minor, or by a natural or adoptive parent of the minor if no legal representative has been appointed. The consent of an estate is made by an executor or administrator.

Continuation sheet or separate consent statement.— If you need a continuation sheet or use a separate consent statement, attach it to Form 2553. The separate consent statement must contain the name, address, and employer identification number of the corporation and the shareholder information requested in columns J through N of Part I.

If you want, you may combine all the shareholders' consents in one statement.

Column L.— Enter the number of shares of stock each shareholder owns and the dates the stock was acquired. If the election is made during the corporation's first tax year for which it is effective, do not list the shares of stock for those shareholders who sold or transferred all of their stock before the election was made. However, these shareholders must still consent to the election for it to be effective for the tax year.

Column M.— Enter the social security number of each shareholder who is an individual. Enter the employer identification number of each shareholder that is an estate or a qualified trust.

Column N.— Enter the month and day that each shareholder's tax year ends. If a shareholder is changing his or her tax year, enter the tax year the shareholder is changing to, and attach an explanation indicating the present tax year and the basis for the change (e.g., automatic revenue procedure or letter ruling request).

If the election is made during the corporation's first tax year for which it is effective, you do not have to enter the tax year of any shareholder who sold or transferred all of his or her stock before the election was made.

Signature.— Form 2553 must be signed by the president, treasurer, assistant treasurer, chief accounting officer, or other corporate officer (such as tax officer) authorized to sign.

Part II

Complete Part II if you selected a tax year ending on any date other than December 31 (other than a 52-53-week tax year ending with reference to the month of December).

Box P1.— Attach a statement showing separately for each month the amount of gross receipts for the most recent 47 months as required by section 4.03(3) of

Revenue Procedure 87-32, 1987-2 C.B. 396. A corporation that does not have a 47-month period of gross receipts cannot establish a natural business year under section 4.01(1).

Box Q1.— For examples of an acceptable business purpose for requesting a fiscal tax year, see Revenue Ruling 87-57, 1987-2 C.B. 117.

In addition to a statement showing the business purpose for the requested fiscal year, you must attach the other information necessary to meet the ruling request requirements of Revenue Procedure 90-1, 1990-1 C.B. 356 (updated annually). Also attach a statement that shows separately the amount of gross receipts from sales or services (and inventory costs, if applicable) for each of the 36 months preceding the effective date of the election to be an S corporation. If the corporation has been in existence for fewer than 36 months, submit figures for the period of existence.

If you check box Q1, you must also pay a user fee of $200 (subject to change). Do not pay the fee when filing Form 2553. The Service Center will send Form 2553 to the IRS in Washington, DC, who, in turn, will notify the corporation that the fee is due. See Revenue Procedure 90-17, 1990-1 C.B. 479.

Box Q2.— If the corporation makes a back-up section 444 election for which it is qualified, then the election must be exercised in the event the business purpose request is not approved. Under certain circumstances, the tax year requested under the back-up section 444 election may be different than the tax year requested under business purpose. See **Form 8716,** Election To Have a Tax Year Other Than a Required Tax Year, for details on making a back-up section 444 election.

Boxes Q2 and R2.— If the corporation is not qualified to make the section 444 election after making the item Q2 back-up section 444 election or indicating its intention to make the election in item R1, and therefore it later files a calendar year return, it should write "Section 444 Election Not Made" in the top left corner of the 1st calendar year Form 1120S it files.

Part III

Certain Qualified Subchapter S Trusts (QSSTs) may make the QSST election required by section 1361(d)(2) in Part III. Part III may be used to make the QSST election only if corporate stock has been transferred to the trust on or before the date on which the corporation makes its election to be an S corporation. However, a statement can be used in lieu of Part III to make the election.

Note: Part III may be used only in conjunction with making the Part I election (i.e., Form 2553 cannot be filed with only Part III completed).

The deemed owner of the QSST must also consent to the S corporation election in column K, page 1, of Form 2553. See section 1361(c)(2).

*U.S. Government Printing Office: 1992 — 619-071/40536

APPLICATION FOR AUTOMATIC EXTENSION OF TIME TO FILE CORPORATION INCOME TAX RETURN, FORM 7004

Form **7004**
(Rev. October 1991)
Department of the Treasury
Internal Revenue Service

Application for Automatic Extension of Time To File Corporation Income Tax Return

OMB No. 1545-0233
Expires 10-31-94

Name of corporation

Employer identification number

Number, street, and room or suite no. (If a P.O. box, see instructions.)

City or town, state, and ZIP code

Check type of return to be filed:

☐ Form 1120	☐ Form 1120F	☐ Form 1120L	☐ Form 1120-POL	☐ Form 1120S
☐ Form 1120-A	☐ Form 1120-FSC	☐ Form 1120-ND	☐ Form 1120-REIT	☐ Form 990-C
☐ Form 1120-DF	☐ Form 1120-H	☐ Form 1120-PC	☐ Form 1120-RIC	☐ Form 990-T

Form 1120F filers: Check here if you do not have an office or place of business in the United States . . . . ▶ ☐

1a I request an automatic 6-month extension of time until ...., 19......, to file the income tax return of the corporation named above for ▶ ☐ calendar year 19 ...... or ▶ ☐ tax year beginning ...., 19......, and ending ...., 19...... .

b If this tax year is for less than 12 months, check reason:
☐ Initial return   ☐ Final return   ☐ Change in accounting period   ☐ Consolidated return to be filed

2 If this application also covers subsidiaries to be included in a consolidated return, complete the following:

Name and address of each member of the affiliated group	Employer identification number	Tax period

3 Tentative tax (see instructions) . . . . | **3** |

4 Credits:

a Overpayment credited from prior year. | 4a |

b Estimated tax payments for the tax year. . . . . | 4b |

c Less refund for the tax year applied for on Form 4466 . . . . . . | 4c | ( ) | Bal ▶ | 4d |

e Credit from regulated investment companies . . . . | 4e |

f Credit for Federal tax on fuels . . . . | 4f |

5 Total. Add lines 4d through 4f . . . . | **5** |

6 **Balance due.** Subtract line 5 from line 3. **Deposit this amount with a Federal Tax Deposit (FTD) Coupon** (see instructions) . . . . | **6** |

Signature.—Under penalties of perjury, I declare that I have been authorized by the above-named corporation to make this application, and to the best of my knowledge and belief, the statements made are true, correct, and complete.

....
(Signature of officer or agent)   (Title)   (Date)

For Paperwork Reduction Act Notice, see instructions.   Cat. No. 13804A   Form **7004** (Rev. 10-91)

APPENDIX **26**

U.S. CORPORATION INCOME TAX RETURN, FORM 1120

US CORPORATION INCOME TAX RETURN, FORM 1120

Form 1120

Department of the Treasury
Internal Revenue Service

U.S. Corporation Income Tax Return

For calendar year 1994 or tax year beginning .... , 1994, ending .... , 19 ...
▶ Instructions are separate. See page 1 for Paperwork Reduction Act Notice.

OMB No. 1545-0123

1994

A Check if a:	Use IRS label. Otherwise, please print or type.	Name	B Employer identification number
1 Consolidated return (attach Form 851) ☐			
2 Personal holding co. (attach Sch. PH) ☐		Number, street, and room or suite no. (If a P.O. box, see page 6 of instructions.)	C Date incorporated
3 Personal service corp. (as defined in Temporary Regs. sec. 1.441-4T— see instructions)		City or town, state, and ZIP code	D Total assets (see Specific Instructions)

E Check applicable boxes: (1) ☐ Initial return (2) ☐ Final return (3) ☐ Change of address $

Income	1a	Gross receipts or sales _____ b Less returns and allowances _____ c Bal ▶	1c
	2	Cost of goods sold (Schedule A, line 8)	2
	3	Gross profit. Subtract line 2 from line 1c	3
	4	Dividends (Schedule C, line 19)	4
	5	Interest	5
	6	Gross rents	6
	7	Gross royalties	7
	8	Capital gain net income (attach Schedule D (Form 1120))	8
	9	Net gain or (loss) from Form 4797, Part II, line 20 (attach Form 4797)	9
	10	Other income (see instructions—attach schedule)	10
	11	**Total income.** Add lines 3 through 10 . . . . ▶	11

Deductions (See instructions for limitations on deductions.)	12	Compensation of officers (Schedule E, line 4)	12
	13	Salaries and wages (less employment credits)	13
	14	Repairs and maintenance	14
	15	Bad debts	15
	16	Rents	16
	17	Taxes and licenses	17
	18	Interest	18
	19	Charitable contributions (see instructions for 10% limitation) . . .	19
	20	Depreciation (attach Form 4562) 20	
	21	Less depreciation claimed on Schedule A and elsewhere on return . . 21a	21b
	22	Depletion	22
	23	Advertising	23
	24	Pension, profit-sharing, etc., plans	24
	25	Employee benefit programs	25
	26	Other deductions (attach schedule)	26
	27	**Total deductions.** Add lines 12 through 26 . . . . ▶	27
	28	Taxable income before net operating loss deduction and special deductions. Subtract line 27 from line 11	28
	29	**Less:** a Net operating loss deduction (see instructions) 29a	
		b Special deductions (Schedule C, line 20) 29b	29c

Tax and Payments	30	**Taxable income.** Subtract line 29c from line 28	30
	31	**Total tax** (Schedule J, line 10)	31
	32	**Payments: a** 1993 overpayment credited to 1994 32a	
	b	1994 estimated tax payments . . 32b	
	c	Less 1994 refund applied for on Form 4466 32c ( ) d Bal ▶ 32d	
	e	Tax deposited with Form 7004 . . . . 32e	
	f	Credit from regulated investment companies (attach Form 2439) . . . 32f	
	g	Credit for Federal tax on fuels (attach Form 4136). See instructions . . 32g	32h
	33	Estimated tax penalty (see instructions). Check if Form 2220 is attached . . . . . . ▶ ☐	33
	34	**Tax due.** If line 32h is smaller than the total of lines 31 and 33, enter amount owed	34
	35	**Overpayment.** If line 32h is larger than the total of lines 31 and 33, enter amount overpaid . . .	35
	36	Enter amount of line 35 you want: **Credited to 1995 estimated tax** ▶ **Refunded** ▶	36

Please Sign Here

Under penalties of perjury, I declare that I have examined this return, including accompanying schedules and statements, and to the best of my knowledge and belief, it is true, correct, and complete. Declaration of preparer (other than taxpayer) is based on all information of which preparer has any knowledge.

▶ _____   _____   ▶ _____
Signature of officer   Date   Title

Paid Preparer's Use Only

Preparer's signature ▶	Date	Check if self-employed ☐	Preparer's social security number
Firm's name (or yours if self-employed) and address ▶		E.I. No. ▶	
		ZIP code ▶	

Cat. No. 11450Q

Form 1120 (1994)   Page **2**

Schedule A   Cost of Goods Sold (See instructions.)

1	Inventory at beginning of year	**1**
2	Purchases	**2**
3	Cost of labor	**3**
4	Additional section 263A costs (attach schedule)	**4**
5	Other costs (attach schedule)	**5**
6	**Total.** Add lines 1 through 5	**6**
7	Inventory at end of year	**7**
8	**Cost of goods sold.** Subtract line 7 from line 6. Enter here and on page 1, line 2	**8**

9a Check all methods used for valuing closing inventory:

☐ Cost   ☐ Lower of cost or market as described in Regulations section 1.471-4

☐ Writedown of subnormal goods as described in Regulations section 1.471-2(c)

☐ Other (Specify method used and attach explanation.) ▶ ....

b Check if the LIFO inventory method was adopted this tax year for any goods (if checked, attach Form 970) . . . . . ▶ ☐

c If the LIFO inventory method was used for this tax year, enter percentage (or amounts) of closing
inventory computed under LIFO   **9c**

d Do the rules of section 263A (for property produced or acquired for resale) apply to the corporation? . . . . ☐ Yes ☐ No

e Was there any change in determining quantities, cost, or valuations between opening and closing inventory? If "Yes,"
attach explanation . . . . ☐ Yes ☐ No

Schedule C   Dividends and Special Deductions (See instructions.)

		(a) Dividends received	(b) %	(c) Special deductions (a) × (b)
1	Dividends from less-than-20%-owned domestic corporations that are subject to the 70% deduction (other than debt-financed stock)		70	
2	Dividends from 20%-or-more-owned domestic corporations that are subject to the 80% deduction (other than debt-financed stock)		80	
3	Dividends on debt-financed stock of domestic and foreign corporations (section 246A)		see instructions	
4	Dividends on certain preferred stock of less-than-20%-owned public utilities . . .		42	
5	Dividends on certain preferred stock of 20%-or-more-owned public utilities . . .		48	
6	Dividends from less-than-20%-owned foreign corporations and certain FSCs that are subject to the 70% deduction		70	
7	Dividends from 20%-or-more-owned foreign corporations and certain FSCs that are subject to the 80% deduction		80	
8	Dividends from wholly owned foreign subsidiaries subject to the 100% deduction (section 245(b))		100	
9	**Total.** Add lines 1 through 8. See instructions for limitation			
10	Dividends from domestic corporations received by a small business investment company operating under the Small Business Investment Act of 1958		100	
11	Dividends from certain FSCs that are subject to the 100% deduction (section 245(c)(1))		100	
12	Dividends from affiliated group members subject to the 100% deduction (section 243(a)(3))		100	
13	Other dividends from foreign corporations not included on lines 3, 6, 7, 8, or 11 .			
14	Income from controlled foreign corporations under subpart F (attach Form(s) 5471) .			
15	Foreign dividend gross-up (section 78)			
16	IC-DISC and former DISC dividends not included on lines 1, 2, or 3 (section 246(d)) .			
17	Other dividends			
18	Deduction for dividends paid on certain preferred stock of public utilities			
19	**Total dividends.** Add lines 1 through 17. Enter here and on line 4, page 1 . . ▶			
20	**Total special deductions.** Add lines 9, 10, 11, 12, and 18. Enter here and on line 29b, page 1 . . . . . ▶			

Schedule E   Compensation of Officers (See instructions for line 12, page 1.)

Complete Schedule E only if total receipts (line 1a plus lines 4 through 10 on page 1, Form 1120) are $500,000 or more.

	(a) Name of officer	(b) Social security number	(c) Percent of time devoted to business	Percent of corporation stock owned		(f) Amount of compensation
				(d) Common	(e) Preferred	
1			%	%	%	
			%	%	%	
			%	%	%	
			%	%	%	
			%	%	%	

2	Total compensation of officers	
3	Compensation of officers claimed on Schedule A and elsewhere on return	
4	Subtract line 3 from line 2. Enter the result here and on line 12, page 1	

Form 1120 (1994)   Page **3**

Schedule J   Tax Computation (See instructions.)

1 Check if the corporation is a member of a controlled group (see sections 1561 and 1563) . . . . . ▶ ☐

2a If the box on line 1 is checked, enter the corporation's share of the $50,000, $25,000, and $9,925,000 taxable income brackets (in that order):

(1) $ _____   (2) $ _____   (3) $ _____

b Enter the corporation's share of:

(1) Additional 5% tax (not more than $11,750) $ _____

(2) Additional 3% tax (not more than $100,000) $ _____

3 Income tax. Check this box if the corporation is a qualified personal service corporation as defined in section 448(d)(2) (see instructions on page 14). . . . . ▶ ☐ | **3**

4a Foreign tax credit (attach Form 1118) . . . . . . | **4a**

b Possessions tax credit (attach Form 5735) . . . . | **4b**

c Orphan drug credit (attach Form 6765) . . . . . | **4c**

d Check: ☐ Nonconventional source fuel credit ☐ QEV credit (attach Form 8834) | **4d**

e General business credit. Enter here and check which forms are attached:

☐ 3800 ☐ 3468 ☐ 5884 ☐ 6478 ☐ 6765 ☐ 8586 ☐ 8830

☐ 8826 ☐ 8835 ☐ 8844 ☐ 8845 ☐ 8846 ☐ 8847 . . . . | **4e**

f Credit for prior year minimum tax (attach Form 8827) . . . . | **4f**

5 **Total credits.** Add lines 4a through 4f . . . . | **5**

6 Subtract line 5 from line 3 . . . . | **6**

7 Personal holding company tax (attach Schedule PH (Form 1120)) . . . . . | **7**

8 Recapture taxes. Check if from: ☐ Form 4255 ☐ Form 8611 . . . . | **8**

9a Alternative minimum tax (attach Form 4626) . . . . | **9a**

b Environmental tax (attach Form 4626) . . . . | **9b**

10 **Total tax.** Add lines 6 through 9b. Enter here and on line 31, page 1 . . . . | **10**

Schedule K   Other Information (See pages 17 and 18 of instructions.)

	Yes	No
1 Check method of accounting: **a** ☐ Cash		
b ☐ Accrual **c** ☐ Other (specify) ▶ _____		
2 Refer to page 19 of the instructions and state the principal:		
a Business activity code no. ▶ _____		
b Business activity ▶ _____		
c Product or service ▶ _____		
3 Did the corporation at the end of the tax year own, directly or indirectly, 50% or more of the voting stock of a domestic corporation? (For rules of attribution, see section 267(c).)		
If "Yes," attach a schedule showing: (a) name and identifying number, (b) percentage owned, and (c) taxable income or (loss) before NOL and special deductions of such corporation for the tax year ending with or within your tax year.		
4 Is the corporation a subsidiary in an affiliated group or a parent-subsidiary controlled group?		
If "Yes," enter employer identification number and name of the parent corporation ▶ _____		
5 Did any individual, partnership, corporation, estate or trust at the end of the tax year own, directly or indirectly, 50% or more of the corporation's voting stock? (For rules of attribution, see section 267(c).)		
If "Yes," attach a schedule showing name and identifying number. (Do not include any information already entered in **4** above.) Enter percentage owned ▶ _____		
6 During this tax year, did the corporation pay dividends (other than stock dividends and distributions in exchange for stock) in excess of the corporation's current and accumulated earnings and profits? (See secs. 301 and 316.)		
If "Yes," file Form 5452. If this is a consolidated return, answer here for the parent corporation and on **Form 851,** Affiliations Schedule, for each subsidiary.		

	Yes	No
7 Was the corporation a U.S. shareholder of any controlled foreign corporation? (See sections 951 and 957.) . . .		
If "Yes," attach Form 5471 for each such corporation. Enter number of Forms 5471 attached ▶ _____		
8 At any time during the 1994 calendar year, did the corporation have an interest in or a signature or other authority over a financial account in a foreign country (such as a bank account, securities account, or other financial account)? .		
If "Yes," the corporation may have to file Form TD F 90-22.1. If "Yes," enter name of foreign country ▶ _____		
9 Was the corporation the grantor of, or transferor to, a foreign trust that existed during the current tax year, whether or not the corporation has any beneficial interest in it? If "Yes," the corporation may have to file Forms 926, 3520, or 3520-A		
10 Did one foreign person at any time during the tax year own, directly or indirectly, at least 25% of: **(a)** the total voting power of all classes of stock of the corporation entitled to vote, or **(b)** the total value of all classes of stock of the corporation? If "Yes,"		
a Enter percentage owned ▶ _____		
b Enter owner's country ▶ _____		
c The corporation may have to file Form 5472. Enter number of Forms 5472 attached ▶ _____		
11 Check this box if the corporation issued publicly offered debt instruments with original issue discount . ▶ ☐		
If so, the corporation may have to file Form 8281.		
12 Enter the amount of tax-exempt interest received or accrued during the tax year ▶ $ _____		
13 If there were 35 or fewer shareholders at the end of the tax year, enter the number ▶ _____		
14 If the corporation has an NOL for the tax year and is electing to forego the carryback period, check here ▶ ☐		
15 Enter the available NOL carryover from prior tax years (Do not reduce it by any deduction on line 29a.) ▶ $ _____		

Form 1120 (1994)   Page **4**

Schedule L	Balance Sheets	Beginning of tax year		End of tax year	
Assets		**(a)**	**(b)**	**(c)**	**(d)**
1	Cash				
2a	Trade notes and accounts receivable . . .				
b	Less allowance for bad debts	( )		( )	
3	Inventories				
4	U.S. government obligations				
5	Tax-exempt securities (see instructions) . .				
6	Other current assets (attach schedule) . .				
7	Loans to stockholders				
8	Mortgage and real estate loans				
9	Other investments (attach schedule) . . .				
10a	Buildings and other depreciable assets . .				
b	Less accumulated depreciation	( )		( )	
11a	Depletable assets				
b	Less accumulated depletion	( )		( )	
12	Land (net of any amortization)				
13a	Intangible assets (amortizable only) . . .				
b	Less accumulated amortization	( )		( )	
14	Other assets (attach schedule)				
15	Total assets				
Liabilities and Stockholders' Equity					
16	Accounts payable				
17	Mortgages, notes, bonds payable in less than 1 year				
18	Other current liabilities (attach schedule) . .				
19	Loans from stockholders				
20	Mortgages, notes, bonds payable in 1 year or more				
21	Other liabilities (attach schedule)				
22	Capital stock: **a** Preferred stock . . .				
	b Common stock . . .				
23	Paid-in or capital surplus				
24	Retained earnings—Appropriated (attach schedule)				
25	Retained earnings—Unappropriated . . .				
26	Less cost of treasury stock		( )		( )
27	Total liabilities and stockholders' equity . .				

Note: *You are not required to complete Schedules M-1 and M-2 below if the total assets on line 15, column (d) of Schedule L are less than $25,000.*

Schedule M-1	Reconciliation of Income (Loss) per Books With Income per Return (See instructions.)

1	Net income (loss) per books		7	Income recorded on books this year not included on this return (itemize):	
2	Federal income tax			Tax-exempt interest $	
3	Excess of capital losses over capital gains .			....	
4	Income subject to tax not recorded on books this year (itemize):		8	Deductions on this return not charged against book income this year (itemize):	
	....		a	Depreciation . . . . $	
5	Expenses recorded on books this year not deducted on this return (itemize):		b	Contributions carryover $	
a	Depreciation . . . . $			....	
b	Contributions carryover $				
c	Travel and entertainment $				
	....		9	Add lines 7 and 8	
6	Add lines 1 through 5		10	Income (line 28, page 1)—line 6 less line 9	

Schedule M-2	Analysis of Unappropriated Retained Earnings per Books (Line 25, Schedule L)

1	Balance at beginning of year		5	Distributions: **a** Cash	
2	Net income (loss) per books			**b** Stock	
3	Other increases (itemize):			**c** Property	
	....		6	Other decreases (itemize):	
	....			....	
	....		7	Add lines 5 and 6	
4	Add lines 1, 2, and 3		8	Balance at end of year (line 4 less line 7)	

♲ *Printed on recycled paper*   *U.S. Government Printing Office: 1994 — 375-287

U.S. CORPORATION SHORT-FORM INCOME TAX RETURN, FORM 1120-A

Form 1120-A

Department of the Treasury
Internal Revenue Service

U.S. Corporation Short-Form Income Tax Return

See separate instructions to make sure the corporation qualifies to file Form 1120-A.
For calendar year 1994 or tax year beginning ...., 1994, ending ...., 19.....

OMB No. 1545-0890

1994

A Check this box if the corp. is a personal service corp. (as defined in Temporary Regs. section 1.441-4T—see instructions) ▶ ☐

Use IRS label. Otherwise, please print or type.

Name

Number, street, and room or suite no. (If a P.O. box, see page 6 of instructions.)

City or town, state, and ZIP code

B Employer identification number

C Date incorporated

D Total assets (see Specific Instructions)

$

E Check applicable boxes: **(1)** ☐ Initial return **(2)** ☐ Change of address

F Check method of accounting: **(1)** ☐ Cash **(2)** ☐ Accrual **(3)** ☐ Other (specify) . . ▶

Income

1a Gross receipts or sales _____ **b** Less returns and allowances _____ **c** Balance ▶	1c	
2 Cost of goods sold (see instructions)	2	
3 Gross profit. Subtract line 2 from line 1c	3	
4 Domestic corporation dividends subject to the 70% deduction .	4	
5 Interest	5	
6 Gross rents	6	
7 Gross royalties	7	
8 Capital gain net income (attach Schedule D (Form 1120)) . . .	8	
9 Net gain or (loss) from Form 4797, Part II, line 20 (attach Form 4797)	9	
10 Other income (see instructions)	10	
11 **Total income.** Add lines 3 through 10 . . . . . . ▶	11	

Deductions

(See instructions for limitations on deductions.)

12 Compensation of officers (see instructions)	12	
13 Salaries and wages (less employment credits)	13	
14 Repairs and maintenance	14	
15 Bad debts	15	
16 Rents	16	
17 Taxes and licenses	17	
18 Interest	18	
19 Charitable contributions (see instructions for 10% limitation) .	19	
20 Depreciation (attach Form 4562) **20**		
21 Less depreciation claimed elsewhere on return . . . **21a**	21b	
22 Other deductions (attach schedule)	22	
23 **Total deductions.** Add lines 12 through 22 . . . . ▶	23	
24 Taxable income before net operating loss deduction and special deductions. Subtract line 23 from line 11	24	
25 **Less: a** Net operating loss deduction (see instructions) . . . **25a**		
b Special deductions (see instructions) **25b**	25c	

Tax and Payments

26 **Taxable income.** Subtract line 25c from line 24	26	
27 **Total tax** (from page 2, Part I, line 7)	27	
28 **Payments:**		
a 1993 overpayment credited to 1994 **28a**		
b 1994 estimated tax payments . **28b**		
c Less 1994 refund applied for on Form 4466 **28c** ( ) Bal ▶ **28d**		
e Tax deposited with Form 7004 **28e**		
f Credit from regulated investment companies (attach Form 2439) . **28f**		
g Credit for Federal tax on fuels (attach Form 4136). See instructions **28g**		
h Total payments. Add lines 28d through 28g	28h	
29 Estimated tax penalty (see instructions). Check if Form 2220 is attached . . . . . ▶ ☐	29	
30 **Tax due.** If line 28h is smaller than the total of lines 27 and 29, enter amount owed	30	
31 **Overpayment.** If line 28h is larger than the total of lines 27 and 29, enter amount overpaid . .	31	
32 Enter amount of line 31 you want: **Credited to 1995 estimated tax** ▶ Refunded ▶	32	

Please Sign Here

Under penalties of perjury, I declare that I have examined this return, including accompanying schedules and statements, and to the best of my knowledge and belief, it is true, correct, and complete. Declaration of preparer (other than taxpayer) is based on all information of which preparer has any knowledge.

▶ _____ _____ ▶ _____
    Signature of officer   Date   Title

Paid Preparer's Use Only

Preparer's signature ▶	Date	Check if self-employed ▶ ☐	Preparer's social security number
Firm's name (or yours if self-employed) and address		E.I. No. ▶	
		ZIP code ▶	

For Paperwork Reduction Act Notice, see page 1 of the instructions.   Cat. No. 11456E   Form **1120-A** (1994)

Form 1120-A (1994) Page **2**

Part I Tax Computation (See instructions.)

1	Income tax. If the corporation is a qualified personal service corporation (see page 14), check here ▶ ☐	1
2a	General business credit. Check if from: ☐ Form 3800 ☐ Form 3468 ☐ Form 5884	
	☐ Form 6478 ☐ Form 6765 ☐ Form 8586 ☐ Form 8830 ☐ Form 8826 ☐ Form 8835	
	☐ Form 8844 ☐ Form 8845 ☐ Form 8846 ☐ Form 8847 . . . . 2a	
b	Credit for prior year minimum tax (attach Form 8827) 2b	
3	**Total credits.** Add lines 2a and 2b	3
4	Subtract line 3 from line 1	4
5	Recapture taxes. Check if from: ☐ Form 4255 ☐ Form 8611	5
6	Alternative minimum tax (attach Form 4626)	6
7	**Total tax.** Add lines 4 through 6. Enter here and on line 27, page 1	7

Part II Other Information (See instructions.)

1 Refer to page 19 of the instructions and state the principal:

a Business activity code no. ▶ ....

b Business activity ▶ ....

c Product or service ▶ ....

2 Did any individual, partnership, estate, or trust at the end of the tax year own, directly or indirectly, 50% or more of the corporation's voting stock? (For rules of attribution, see section 267(c).) . . . . ☐ Yes ☐ No

If "Yes," attach a schedule showing name and identifying number.

3 Enter the amount of tax-exempt interest received or accrued during the tax year . . . ▶ $ |

4 Enter amount of cash distributions and the book value of property (other than cash) distributions made in this tax year . . . . ▶ $ |

5a If an amount is entered on line 2, page 1, see the worksheet on page 12 for amounts to enter below:

(1) Purchases		
(2) Additional sec. 263A costs (see instructions—attach schedule) .		
(3) Other costs (attach schedule) .		

b Do the rules of section 263A (for property produced or acquired for resale) apply to the corporation? . . . . . . ☐ Yes ☐ No

6 At any time during the 1994 calendar year, did the corporation have an interest in or a signature or other authority over a financial account in a foreign country (such as a bank account, securities account, or other financial account)? If "Yes," the corporation may have to file Form TD F 90-22.1 . . . . ☐ Yes ☐ No

If "Yes," enter the name of the foreign country ▶ ....

Part III Balance Sheets

		(a) Beginning of tax year		(b) End of tax year	
Assets	**1** Cash				
	2a Trade notes and accounts receivable				
	b Less allowance for bad debts	(	)	(	)
	3 Inventories				
	4 U.S. government obligations				
	5 Tax-exempt securities (see instructions)				
	6 Other current assets (attach schedule)				
	7 Loans to stockholders				
	8 Mortgage and real estate loans				
	9a Depreciable, depletable, and intangible assets				
	b Less accumulated depreciation, depletion, and amortization	(	)	(	)
	10 Land (net of any amortization)				
	11 Other assets (attach schedule)				
	12 Total assets				
Liabilities and Stockholders' Equity	**13** Accounts payable				
	14 Other current liabilities (attach schedule)				
	15 Loans from stockholders				
	16 Mortgages, notes, bonds payable				
	17 Other liabilities (attach schedule)				
	18 Capital stock (preferred and common stock)				
	19 Paid-in or capital surplus				
	20 Retained earnings				
	21 Less cost of treasury stock	(	)	(	)
	22 Total liabilities and stockholders' equity				

Part IV Reconciliation of Income (Loss) per Books With Income per Return (You are not required to complete Part IV if the total assets on line 12, column (b), Part III are less than $25,000.)

1 Net income (loss) per books	6 Income recorded on books this year not included on this return (itemize)...................	
2 Federal income tax.		
3 Excess of capital losses over capital gains . .	7 Deductions on this return not charged against book income this year (itemize)................	
4 Income subject to tax not recorded on books this year (itemize)		
5 Expenses recorded on books this year not deducted on this return (itemize)	8 Income (line 24, page 1). Enter the sum of lines 1 through 5 less the sum of lines 6 and 7 . .	

U.S. INCOME TAX RETURN FOR AN S CORPORATION, FORM 1120S

Form **1120S**

Department of the Treasury
Internal Revenue Service

U.S. Income Tax Return for an S Corporation

▶ Do not file this form unless the corporation has timely filed
Form 2553 to elect to be an S corporation.
▶ See separate instructions.

OMB No. 1545-0130

1994

For calendar year 1994, or tax year beginning _____ , 1994, and ending _____ , 19 _____

A Date of election as an S corporation	**Use IRS label. Otherwise, please print or type.**	Name	**C** Employer identification number
		Number, street, and room or suite no. (If a P.O. box, see page 9 of the instructions.)	**D** Date incorporated
B Business code no. (see Specific Instructions)		City or town, state, and ZIP code	**E** Total assets (see Specific Instructions) $

F Check applicable boxes: (1) ☐ Initial return   (2) ☐ Final return   (3) ☐ Change in address   (4) ☐ Amended return

G Check this box if this S corporation is subject to the consolidated audit procedures of sections 6241 through 6245 (see instructions before checking this box) . ▶ ☐

H Enter number of shareholders in the corporation at end of the tax year . . . . ▶

Caution: *Include **only** trade or business income and expenses on lines 1a through 21. See the instructions for more information.*

Income

1a	Gross receipts or sales |_____| **b** Less returns and allowances |_____| **c** Bal ▶	**1c**	
2	Cost of goods sold (Schedule A, line 8)	**2**	
3	Gross profit. Subtract line 2 from line 1c	**3**	
4	Net gain (loss) from Form 4797, Part II, line 20 *(attach Form 4797)*	**4**	
5	Other income (loss) (see instructions) *(attach schedule)* . . .	**5**	
6	**Total income (loss).** Combine lines 3 through 5 . . . . . . ▶	**6**	

Deductions (See instructions for limitations.)

7	Compensation of officers	**7**	
8	Salaries and wages (less employment credits)	**8**	
9	Repairs and maintenance	**9**	
10	Bad debts	**10**	
11	Rents	**11**	
12	Taxes and licenses	**12**	
13	Interest	**13**	
14a	Depreciation (see instructions)	**14a**		
b	Depreciation claimed on Schedule A and elsewhere on return .	**14b**		
c	Subtract line 14b from line 14a	**14c**	
15	Depletion **(Do not deduct oil and gas depletion.)**	**15**	
16	Advertising	**16**	
17	Pension, profit-sharing, etc., plans	**17**	
18	Employee benefit programs	**18**	
19	Other deductions (see instructions) *(attach schedule)*	**19**	
20	**Total deductions.** Add the amounts shown in the far right column for lines 7 through 19 . ▶	**20**	
21	Ordinary income (loss) from trade or business activities. Subtract line 20 from line 6	**21**	

Tax and Payments

22	**Tax: a** Excess net passive income tax *(attach schedule)*. . .	**22a**		
b	Tax from Schedule D (Form 1120S)	**22b**		
c	Add lines 22a and 22b (see instructions for additional taxes) .	**22c**	
23	**Payments: a** 1994 estimated tax payments and amount applied from 1993 return	**23a**		
b	Tax deposited with Form 7004	**23b**		
c	Credit for Federal tax paid on fuels *(attach Form 4136)* . . .	**23c**		
d	Add lines 23a through 23c	**23d**	
24	Estimated tax penalty (see instructions). Check if Form 2220 is attached. . . . . . . ▶☐	**24**	
25	**Tax due.** If the total of lines 22c and 24 is larger than line 23d, enter amount owed. See instructions for depositary method of payment . . . . ▶	**25**	
26	Overpayment. If line 23d is larger than the total of lines 22c and 24, enter amount overpaid ▶	**26**	
27	Enter amount of line 26 you want: **Credited to 1995 estimated tax ▶** _____ **Refunded ▶**	**27**	

Please Sign Here

Under penalties of perjury, I declare that I have examined this return, including accompanying schedules and statements, and to the best of my knowledge and belief, it is true, correct, and complete. Declaration of preparer (other than taxpayer) is based on all information of which preparer has any knowledge.

▶ Signature of officer	Date	▶ Title

Paid Preparer's Use Only

Preparer's signature ▶	Date	Check if self-employed ▶ ☐	Preparer's social security number
Firm's name (or yours if self-employed) and address ▶		E.I. No. ▶	
		ZIP code ▶	

For Paperwork Reduction Act Notice, see page 1 of separate instructions.   Cat. No. 11510H   Form **1120S** (1994)

| Schedule A | Cost of Goods Sold (See instructions.) |

1	Inventory at beginning of year	1		
2	Purchases	2		
3	Cost of labor	3		
4	Additional section 263A costs (see instructions) *(attach schedule)*	4		
5	Other costs *(attach schedule)*	5		
6	**Total.** Add lines 1 through 5	6		
7	Inventory at end of year	7		
8	**Cost of goods sold.** Subtract line 7 from line 6. Enter here and on page 1, line 2	8		

9a Check all methods used for valuing closing inventory:

    (i) ☐ Cost

    (ii) ☐ Lower of cost or market as described in Regulations section 1.471-4

    (iii) ☐ Writedown of "subnormal" goods as described in Regulations section 1.471-2(c)

    (iv) ☐ Other (specify method used and attach explanation) ▶ ....

  b Check if the LIFO inventory method was adopted this tax year for any goods *(if checked, attach Form 970)*. . . . . . . ▶ ☐

  c If the LIFO inventory method was used for this tax year, enter percentage (or amounts) of closing inventory computed under LIFO . . . . | 9c |

  d Do the rules of section 263A (for property produced or acquired for resale) apply to the corporation? . . . . ☐ Yes ☐ No

  e Was there any change in determining quantities, cost, or valuations between opening and closing inventory? . . ☐ Yes ☐ No
    If "Yes," attach explanation.

| Schedule B | Other Information |

		Yes	No
1	Check method of accounting: **(a)** ☐ Cash **(b)** ☐ Accrual **(c)** ☐ Other (specify) ▶		
2	Refer to the list in the instructions and state the corporation's principal:		
	(a) Business activity ▶ .... **(b)** Product or service ▶		
3	Did the corporation at the end of the tax year own, directly or indirectly, 50% or more of the voting stock of a domestic corporation? (For rules of attribution, see section 267(c).) If "Yes," attach a schedule showing: **(a)** name, address, and employer identification number and **(b)** percentage owned.		
4	Was the corporation a member of a controlled group subject to the provisions of section 1561?		
5	At any time during calendar year 1994, did the corporation have an interest in or a signature or other authority over a financial account in a foreign country (such as a bank account, securities account, or other financial account)? (See instructions for exceptions and filing requirements for Form TD F 90-22.1.)		
	If "Yes," enter the name of the foreign country ▶		
6	Was the corporation the grantor of, or transferor to, a foreign trust that existed during the current tax year, whether or not the corporation has any beneficial interest in it? If "Yes," the corporation may have to file Forms 3520, 3520-A, or 926		
7	Check this box if the corporation has filed or is required to file **Form 8264,** Application for Registration of a Tax Shelter . . . . ▶ ☐		
8	Check this box if the corporation issued publicly offered debt instruments with original issue discount . . ▶ ☐		
	If so, the corporation may have to file **Form 8281,** Information Return for Publicly Offered Original Issue Discount Instruments.		
9	If the corporation: **(a)** filed its election to be an S corporation after 1986, **(b)** was a C corporation before it elected to be an S corporation **or** the corporation acquired an asset with a basis determined by reference to its basis (or the basis of any other property) in the hands of a C corporation, and **(c)** has net unrealized built-in gain (defined in section 1374(d)(1)) in excess of the net recognized built-in gain from prior years, enter the net unrealized built-in gain reduced by net recognized built-in gain from prior years (see instructions) . . . . . . ▶ $		
10	Check this box if the corporation had subchapter C earnings and profits at the close of the tax year (see instructions) . . . . ▶ ☐		

Designation of Tax Matters Person (See instructions.)

Enter below the shareholder designated as the tax matters person (TMP) for the tax year of this return:

Name of designated TMP ▶		Identifying number of TMP ▶

Address of designated TMP ▶

Form 1120S (1994)   **Page 3**

Schedule K   Shareholders' Shares of Income, Credits, Deductions, etc.

	(a) Pro rata share items		(b) Total amount	
Income (Loss)	**1** Ordinary income (loss) from trade or business activities (page 1, line 21)	**1**		
	2 Net income (loss) from rental real estate activities *(attach Form 8825)*	**2**		
	3a Gross income from other rental activities	**3a**		
	b Expenses from other rental activities *(attach schedule)*.	**3b**		
	c Net income (loss) from other rental activities. Subtract line 3b from line 3a	**3c**		
	4 Portfolio income (loss):			
	a Interest income	**4a**		
	b Dividend income.	**4b**		
	c Royalty income	**4c**		
	d Net short-term capital gain (loss) *(attach Schedule D (Form 1120S))*	**4d**		
	e Net long-term capital gain (loss) *(attach Schedule D (Form 1120S))* .	**4e**		
	f Other portfolio income (loss) *(attach schedule)*	**4f**		
	5 Net gain (loss) under section 1231 (other than due to casualty or theft) *(attach Form 4797)*	**5**		
	6 Other income (loss) *(attach schedule)*	**6**		
Deductions	**7** Charitable contributions (see instructions) *(attach schedule)*	**7**		
	8 Section 179 expense deduction *(attach Form 4562)*.	**8**		
	9 Deductions related to portfolio income (loss) (see instructions) (itemize)	**9**		
	10 Other deductions *(attach schedule)*	**10**		
Investment Interest	**11a** Interest expense on investment debts	**11a**		
	b (1) Investment income included on lines 4a, 4b, 4c, and 4f above	**11b(1)**		
	(2) Investment expenses included on line 9 above	**11b(2)**		
Credits	**12a** Credit for alcohol used as a fuel *(attach Form 6478)*	**12a**		
	b Low-income housing credit (see instructions):			
	(1) From partnerships to which section 42(j)(5) applies for property placed in service before 1990	**12b(1)**		
	(2) Other than on line 12b(1) for property placed in service before 1990.	**12b(2)**		
	(3) From partnerships to which section 42(j)(5) applies for property placed in service after 1989	**12b(3)**		
	(4) Other than on line 12b(3) for property placed in service after 1989	**12b(4)**		
	c Qualified rehabilitation expenditures related to rental real estate activities *(attach Form 3468)* .	**12c**		
	d Credits (other than credits shown on lines 12b and 12c) related to rental real estate activities (see instructions).	**12d**		
	e Credits related to other rental activities (see instructions)	**12e**		
	13 Other credits (see instructions)	**13**		
Adjustments and Tax Preference Items	**14a** Depreciation adjustment on property placed in service after 1986	**14a**		
	b Adjusted gain or loss	**14b**		
	c Depletion (other than oil and gas)	**14c**		
	d (1) Gross income from oil, gas, or geothermal properties	**14d(1)**		
	(2) Deductions allocable to oil, gas, or geothermal properties	**14d(2)**		
	e Other adjustments and tax preference items *(attach schedule)*	**14e**		
Foreign Taxes	**15a** Type of income ▶			
	b Name of foreign country or U.S. possession ▶			
	c Total gross income from sources outside the United States *(attach schedule)* . . .	**15c**		
	d Total applicable deductions and losses *(attach schedule)*	**15d**		
	e Total foreign taxes (check one): ▶ ☐ Paid ☐ Accrued	**15e**		
	f Reduction in taxes available for credit *(attach schedule)*	**15f**		
	g Other foreign tax information *(attach schedule)*	**15g**		
Other	**16a** Total expenditures to which a section 59(e) election may apply	**16a**		
	b Type of expenditures ▶			
	17 Tax-exempt interest income	**17**		
	18 Other tax-exempt income	**18**		
	19 Nondeductible expenses	**19**		
	20 Total property distributions (including cash) other than dividends reported on line 22 below	**20**		
	21 Other items and amounts required to be reported separately to shareholders (see instructions) *(attach schedule)*			
	22 Total dividend distributions paid from accumulated earnings and profits	**22**		
	23 Income (loss). (Required only if Schedule M-1 must be completed.) Combine lines 1 through 6 in column (b). From the result, subtract the sum of lines 7 through 11a, 15e, and 16a	**23**		

Form 1120S (1994)   Page **4**

Schedule L	**Balance Sheets**	Beginning of tax year		End of tax year	
	Assets	(a)	(b)	(c)	(d)
1	Cash				
2a	Trade notes and accounts receivable . .				
b	Less allowance for bad debts				
3	Inventories				
4	U.S. Government obligations.				
5	Tax-exempt securities				
6	Other current assets (attach schedule). .				
7	Loans to shareholders				
8	Mortgage and real estate loans . . .				
9	Other investments (attach schedule) . .				
10a	Buildings and other depreciable assets .				
b	Less accumulated depreciation				
11a	Depletable assets				
b	Less accumulated depletion				
12	Land (net of any amortization)				
13a	Intangible assets (amortizable only). . .				
b	Less accumulated amortization				
14	Other assets (attach schedule)				
15	Total assets				
	Liabilities and Shareholders' Equity				
16	Accounts payable				
17	Mortgages, notes, bonds payable in less than 1 year				
18	Other current liabilities (attach schedule)				
19	Loans from shareholders				
20	Mortgages, notes, bonds payable in 1 year or more				
21	Other liabilities (attach schedule) . . .				
22	Capital stock				
23	Paid-in or capital surplus				
24	Retained earnings				
25	Less cost of treasury stock		( )		( )
26	Total liabilities and shareholders' equity .				

Schedule M-1	**Reconciliation of Income (Loss) per Books With Income (Loss) per Return** (You are not required to complete this schedule if the total assets on line 15, column (d), of Schedule L are less than $25,000.)

1	Net income (loss) per books		5	Income recorded on books this year not included on Schedule K, lines 1 through 6 (itemize):	
2	Income included on Schedule K, lines 1 through 6, not recorded on books this year (itemize):			**a** Tax-exempt interest $	
	....		6	Deductions included on Schedule K, lines 1 through 11a, 15e, and 16a, not charged against book income this year (itemize):	
3	Expenses recorded on books this year not included on Schedule K, lines 1 through 11a, 15e, and 16a (itemize):			**a** Depreciation $	
a	Depreciation $			....	
b	Travel and entertainment $		7	Add lines 5 and 6	
	....		8	Income (loss) (Schedule K, line 23). Line 4 less line 7	
4	Add lines 1 through 3				

Schedule M-2	**Analysis of Accumulated Adjustments Account, Other Adjustments Account, and Shareholders' Undistributed Taxable Income Previously Taxed** (See instructions.)

		(a) Accumulated adjustments account	(b) Other adjustments account	(c) Shareholders' undistributed taxable income previously taxed
1	Balance at beginning of tax year . . .			
2	Ordinary income from page 1, line 21 . .			
3	Other additions			
4	Loss from page 1, line 21	( )		
5	Other reductions	( )	( )	
6	Combine lines 1 through 5			
7	Distributions other than dividend distributions .			
8	Balance at end of tax year. Subtract line 7 from line 6			

*U.S GPO:1994-375-315

SCHEDULE K-1 (FORM 1120S), SHAREHOLDER'S SHARE OF INCOME, CREDITS, DEDUCTIONS, ETC.

SCHEDULE K-1
(Form 1120S)

Department of the Treasury
Internal Revenue Service

Shareholder's Share of Income, Credits, Deductions, etc.
▶ See separate instructions.
For calendar year 1994 or tax year
beginning   , 1994, and ending   , 19

OMB No. 1545-0130

1994

Shareholder's identifying number ▶

Corporation's identifying number ▶

Shareholder's name, address, and ZIP code

Corporation's name, address, and ZIP code

A Shareholder's percentage of stock ownership for tax year (see Instructions for Schedule K-1) . . . . . . ▶ .... %
B Internal Revenue Service Center where corporation filed its return ▶ ....
C Tax shelter registration number (see Instructions for Schedule K-1) . . . . ▶ ....
D Check applicable boxes: **(1)** ☐ Final K-1   **(2)** ☐ Amended K-1

	(a) Pro rata share items		(b) Amount	(c) Form 1040 filers enter the amount in column (b) on:
Income (Loss)	1 Ordinary income (loss) from trade or business activities . . .	1		See Shareholder's Instructions for Schedule K-1 (Form 1120S).
	2 Net income (loss) from rental real estate activities	2		
	3 Net income (loss) from other rental activities	3		
	4 Portfolio income (loss):			
	a Interest	4a		Sch. B, Part I, line 1
	b Dividends	4b		Sch. B, Part II, line 5
	c Royalties	4c		Sch. E, Part I, line 4
	d Net short-term capital gain (loss).	4d		Sch. D, line 5, col. (f) or (g)
	e Net long-term capital gain (loss)	4e		Sch. D, line 13, col. (f) or (g)
	f Other portfolio income (loss) (attach schedule)	4f		(Enter on applicable line of your return.)
	5 Net gain (loss) under section 1231 (other than due to casualty or theft)	5		See Shareholder's Instructions for Schedule K-1 (Form 1120S)
	6 Other income (loss) (attach schedule)	6		(Enter on applicable line of your return.)
Deductions	7 Charitable contributions (see instructions) (attach schedule) . .	7		Sch. A, line 15 or 16
	8 Section 179 expense deduction	8		See Shareholder's Instructions for Schedule K-1 (Form 1120S).
	9 Deductions related to portfolio income (loss) (attach schedule) .	9		
	10 Other deductions (attach schedule)	10		
Investment Interest	11a Interest expense on investment debts	11a		Form 4952, line 1
	b (1) Investment income included on lines 4a, 4b, 4c, and 4f above	b(1)		See Shareholder's Instructions for Schedule K-1 (Form 1120S).
	(2) Investment expenses included on line 9 above	b(2)		
Credits	12a Credit for alcohol used as fuel	12a		Form 6478, line 10
	b Low-income housing credit:			
	(1) From section 42(j)(5) partnerships for property placed in service before 1990.	b(1)		Form 8586, line 5
	(2) Other than on line 12b(1) for property placed in service before 1990	b(2)		
	(3) From section 42(j)(5) partnerships for property placed in service after 1989	b(3)		
	(4) Other than on line 12b(3) for property placed in service after 1989	b(4)		
	c Qualified rehabilitation expenditures related to rental real estate activities (see instructions).	12c		See Shareholder's Instructions for Schedule K-1 (Form 1120S).
	d Credits (other than credits shown on lines 12b and 12c) related to rental real estate activities (see instructions)	12d		
	e Credits related to other rental activities (see instructions) . . .	12e		
	13 Other credits (see instructions)	13		
Adjustments and Tax Preference Items	14a Depreciation adjustment on property placed in service after 1986	14a		See Shareholder's Instructions for Schedule K-1 (Form 1120S) and Instructions for Form 6251
	b Adjusted gain or loss	14b		
	c Depletion (other than oil and gas)	14c		
	d (1) Gross income from oil, gas, or geothermal properties . . .	d(1)		
	(2) Deductions allocable to oil, gas, or geothermal properties . .	d(2)		
	e Other adjustments and tax preference items (attach schedule)	14e		

For Paperwork Reduction Act Notice, see page 1 of Instructions for Form 1120S.   Cat. No. 11520D   **Schedule K-1 (Form 1120S) 1994**

(a) Pro rata share items		(b) Amount	(c) Form 1040 filers enter the amount in column (b) on:
Foreign Taxes	**15a** Type of income ▶		Form 1116, Check boxes
	b Name of foreign country or U.S. possession ▶		
	c Total gross income from sources outside the United States *(attach schedule)*	**15c**	Form 1116, Part I
	d Total applicable deductions and losses *(attach schedule)* . .	**15d**	
	e Total foreign taxes (check one): ▶ ☐ Paid ☐ Accrued . .	**15e**	Form 1116, Part II
	f Reduction in taxes available for credit *(attach schedule)* . . .	**15f**	Form 1116, Part III
	g Other foreign tax information *(attach schedule)*	**15g**	See Instructions for Form 1116
Other	**16a** Total expenditures to which a section 59(e) election may apply	**16a**	See Shareholder's Instructions for Schedule K-1 (Form 1120S).
	b Type of expenditures ▶		
	17 Tax-exempt interest income	**17**	Form 1040, line 8b
	18 Other tax-exempt income	**18**	See Shareholder's Instructions for Schedule K-1 (Form 1120S).
	19 Nondeductible expenses	**19**	
	20 Property distributions (including cash) other than dividend distributions reported to you on Form 1099-DIV	**20**	
	21 Amount of loan repayments for "Loans From Shareholders" . .	**21**	
	22 Recapture of low-income housing credit:		
	a From section 42(j)(5) partnerships	**22a**	Form 8611, line 8
	b Other than on line 22a	**22b**	

Supplemental Information

23 Supplemental information required to be reported separately to each shareholder *(attach additional schedules if more space is needed)*:

....

....

....

....

....

....

....

....

....

....

....

....

....

....

....

....

....

....

INSTRUCTIONS FOR
SCHEDULE K-1 (FORM 1120S)

1994

Department of the Treasury
Internal Revenue Service

Shareholder's Instructions for Schedule K-1 (Form 1120S)

Shareholder's Share of Income, Credits, Deductions, etc.
(For Shareholder's Use Only)

Section references are to the Internal Revenue Code unless otherwise noted.

General Instructions

Purpose of Schedule K-1

The corporation uses Schedule K-1 (Form 1120S) to report your pro rata share of the corporation's income (reduced by any tax the corporation paid on the income), credits, deductions, etc. **Please keep it for your records. Do not file it with your tax return.** The corporation has filed a copy with the IRS.

Although the corporation may have to pay a capital gains tax (or built-in gains tax) and an excess net passive income tax, you, the shareholder, are liable for income tax on your share of the corporation's income, whether or not distributed, and you must include your share on your tax return if a return is required. **Your distributive share of S corporation income is not self-employment income and it is not subject to self-employment tax.**

You should use these instructions to help you report the items shown on Schedule K-1 on your tax return.

Where *(attach schedule)* appears next to a line on Schedule K-1, it means the information for these lines (if applicable) will be shown in the "Supplemental Information" space below line 23 of Schedule K-1. If additional space was needed, the corporation will have attached a statement to Schedule K-1 to show the information for the line item.

The notation "(see Instructions for Schedule K-1)" in items A and C at the top of Schedule K-1 is directed to the corporation. You, as a shareholder, should disregard these notations.

Schedule K-1 does not show the amount of actual **dividend** distributions the corporation made to you. The corporation must report to you such amounts totaling $10 or more for the calendar year on **Form 1099-DIV,** Dividends and Distributions. You report actual dividend distributions on Form 1040, line 9.

Basis of Your Stock

You are responsible for maintaining records to show the computation of the basis of your stock in the corporation. Schedule K-1 provides information to help you make the computation at the end of each corporate tax year. The basis of your stock (generally, its cost) is adjusted as follows and, except as noted, in the order listed. These rules generally apply for tax years of the S corporation beginning after 1993. For prior tax years, basis must be determined in a reasonable manner. Return positions consistent with these rules are reasonable. In addition, basis may be adjusted under other provisions of the Internal Revenue Code.

1. Basis is increased by **(a)** all income (including tax-exempt income) reported on Schedule K-1 and **(b)** the excess of the deduction for depletion (other than oil and gas depletion) over the basis of the property subject to depletion.

Note: *You must report the taxable income on your return (if you are required to file a return) for it to increase your basis.*

2. Basis is decreased by **(a)** nondeductible expenses and **(b)** the depletion deduction for any oil and gas property held by the corporation, but only to the extent your pro rata share of the property's adjusted basis exceeds that deduction.

3. Basis is decreased by all deductible losses and deductions reported on Schedule K-1.

4. Basis is decreased by property distributions (including cash) made by the corporation (excluding dividend distributions reported on Form 1099-DIV and distributions in excess of basis) reported on Schedule K-1, line 20.

You may elect to decrease your basis under **3** above prior to decreasing your basis under **2** above. If you make this election, any amount described under **2** that exceeds the basis of your stock and debt owed to you by the corporation is treated as an amount described under **2** for the following tax year. To make the election, attach a statement to your timely-filed original or amended return that states you agree to the carryover rule of Regulations section 1.1367-1(f) and the name of the S corporation to which the rule applies. Once made, the election applies to the year for which it is made and all future tax years for that S corporation, unless the IRS agrees to revoke your election.

The basis of each share of stock is increased or decreased (but not below zero) based on its pro rata share of the above adjustments. If the total decreases in basis attributable to a share exceed that share's basis, the excess reduces (but not below zero) the remaining bases of all other shares of stock in proportion to the remaining basis of each of those shares.

Inconsistent Treatment of Items

Generally, you must report subchapter S items shown on your Schedule K-1 (and any attached schedules) the same way that the corporation treated the items on its return. This rule does not apply if your corporation is within the small S corporation exception and does not elect to have the tax treatment of subchapter S items determined at the corporate level.

If the treatment on your original or amended return is inconsistent with the corporation's treatment, or if the corporation has not filed a return, you must file **Form 8082,** Notice of Inconsistent Treatment or Amended Return (Administrative Adjustment Request (AAR)), with your original or amended return to identify and explain any inconsistency (or to note that a corporate return has not been filed).

If you are required to file Form 8082 but fail to do so, you may be subject to the accuracy-related penalty. This penalty is in addition to any tax that results from making your amount or treatment of the item consistent with that shown on the corporation's return. Any deficiency that results from making the amounts consistent may be assessed immediately.

Errors

If you believe the corporation has made an error on your Schedule K-1, notify the corporation and ask for a corrected Schedule K-1. Do not change any items

Cat. No. 115210

on your copy. Be sure that the corporation sends a copy of the corrected Schedule K-1 to the IRS. If your corporation does not meet the small S corporation exception, and you are unable to reach agreement with the corporation regarding the inconsistency, you must file Form 8082.

International Boycotts

Every corporation that had operations in, or related to, a boycotting country, company, or national of a country, must file **Form 5713**, International Boycott Report.

If the corporation cooperated with an international boycott, it must give you a copy of its Form 5713. You must file your own Form 5713 to report the activities of the corporation and any other boycott operations that you may have. You may lose certain tax benefits if the corporation participated in, or cooperated with, an international boycott. See Form 5713 and the instructions for more information.

Elections

Generally, the corporation decides how to figure taxable income from its operations. For example, it chooses the accounting method and depreciation methods it will use.

However, certain elections are made by you separately on your income tax return and not by the corporation. These elections are made under:

● Section 59(e) (deduction of certain qualified expenditures ratably over the period of time specified in that section—see the instructions for lines 16a and 16b);

● Section 617 (deduction and recapture of certain mining exploration expenditures); and

● Section 901 (foreign tax credit).

Additional Information

For more information on the treatment of S corporation income, credits, deductions, etc., get **Pub. 589,** Tax Information on S Corporations; **Pub. 535,** Business Expenses; **Pub. 550,** Investment Income and Expenses; and **Pub. 925,** Passive Activity and At-Risk Rules.

These and other publications referenced throughout these instructions may be obtained at most IRS offices. To order publications and forms, call our toll-free number, 1-800-TAX-FORM (1-800-829-3676).

Limitations on Losses, Deductions, and Credits

Aggregate Losses and Deductions Limited to Basis of Stock and Debt

Generally, the deduction for your share of aggregate losses and deductions reported on Schedule K-1 is limited to the basis of your stock and debt owed to you by the corporation. The basis of your stock is figured at year end. See **Basis of Your Stock** on page 1. The basis of loans to the corporation is the balance the corporation now owes you, less any reduction for losses in a prior year. See the instructions for line 21. Any loss not allowed for the tax year because of this limitation is available for indefinite carryover, limited to the basis of your stock and debt, in each subsequent tax year. See section 1366(d) for details.

At-Risk Limitations

Generally, if you have:

1. A loss or other deduction from any activity carried on by the corporation as a trade or business or for the production of income, and

2. Amounts in the activity for which you are not at risk,

you will have to complete **Form 6198,** At-Risk Limitations, to figure your allowable loss.

The at-risk rules generally limit the amount of loss (including loss on the disposition of assets) and other deductions (such as the section 179 expense deduction) that you can claim to the amount you could actually lose in the activity. However, if you acquired your stock before 1987, the at-risk rules do not apply to losses from an activity of holding real property placed in service before 1987 by the corporation. The activity of holding mineral property does not qualify for this exception.

Generally, you are not at risk for amounts such as the following:

● The basis of your stock in the corporation or basis of your loans to the corporation if the cash or other property used to purchase the stock or make the loans was from a source **(a)** covered by nonrecourse indebtedness (except for certain qualified nonrecourse financing, as defined in section 465(b)(6)); **(b)** protected against loss by a guarantee, stop-loss agreement, or other similar arrangement; or **(c)** that is covered by indebtedness from a person who has an interest in the activity or from a related person to a person (except you) having such an interest, other than a creditor.

● Any cash or property contributed to a corporate activity, or your interest in the corporate activity, that is **(a)** covered by nonrecourse indebtedness (except for certain qualified nonrecourse financing,

as defined in section 465(b)(6)); **(b)** protected against loss by a guarantee, stop-loss agreement, or other similar arrangement; or **(c)** that is covered by indebtedness from a person who has an interest in such activity or from a related person to a person (except you) having such an interest, other than a creditor.

Any loss from a section 465 activity not allowed for this tax year will be treated as a deduction allocable to the activity in the next tax year.

To help you complete Form 6198, the corporation should specify on an attachment to Schedule K-1 your share of the total pre-1976 losses from a section 465(c)(1) activity (i.e., films or video tapes, and leasing section 1245, farm, or oil and gas property) for which there existed a corresponding amount of nonrecourse liability at the end of the year in which the losses occurred. Also, you should get a separate statement of income, expenses, etc., for each activity from the corporation.

Passive Activity Limitations

Section 469 provides rules that limit the deduction of certain losses and credits. The rules apply to shareholders who—

● Are individuals, estates, or trusts, and

● Have a passive activity loss or credit for the year.

Generally, passive activities **include:**

1. Trade or business activities in which you did not materially participate, and

2. Activities that meet the definition of rental activities under Temporary Regulations section 1.469-1T(e)(3) and Regulations section 1.469-1(e)(3).

Passive activities **do not** include:

1. Trade or business activities in which you materially participated.

2. Rental real estate activities in which you materially participated if you were a "real estate professional" for the tax year. You were a real estate professional only if you met both of the following conditions:

a. More than half of the personal services you performed in trades or businesses were performed in real property trades or businesses in which you materially participated, and

b. You performed more than 750 hours of services in real property trades or businesses in which you materially participated.

For purposes of this rule, each interest in rental real estate is a separate activity, unless you elect to treat all interests in rental real estate as one activity.

If you are married filing jointly, either you or your spouse must separately meet both of the above conditions, without taking into account services performed by the other spouse.

A real property trade or business is any real property development, redevelopment, construction, reconstruction, acquisition, conversion, rental, operation, management, leasing, or brokerage trade or business. Services you performed as an employee are not treated as performed in a real property trade or business unless you owned more than 5% of the stock (or more than 5% of the capital or profits interest) in the employer.

3. The rental of a dwelling unit any shareholder used for personal purposes during the year for more than the greater of 14 days or 10% of the number of days that the residence was rented at fair rental value.

4. Activities of trading personal property for the account of owners of interests in the activities.

5. Qualifying low-income housing activities.

The corporation will identify separately each activity that may be passive to you. If the corporation had more than one activity, it will report information in the line 23 Supplemental Information space, or attach a statement if more space is needed, that **(a)** identifies each activity (trade or business activity, rental real estate activity, rental activity other than rental real estate, etc.); **(b)** specifies the income (loss), deductions, and credits from each activity; and **(c)** provides other details you may need to determine if an activity loss or credit is subject to the passive activity limitations.

If you determine that you have a passive activity loss or credit, get **Form 8582,** Passive Activity Loss Limitations, to figure your allowable passive losses, and **Form 8582-CR,** Passive Activity Credit Limitations, to figure your allowable passive credit. See the instructions for these forms for more information.

Material participation.—You must determine if you materially participated **(a)** in each trade or business activity held through the corporation and **(b),** if you were a real estate professional (defined on page 2), in each rental real estate activity held through the corporation. All determinations of material participation are made with respect to your participation during the corporation's tax year.

Material participation standards for shareholders who are individuals are listed below. Special rules apply to certain retired or disabled farmers and to the surviving spouses of farmers. See the Instructions for Form 8582 for details.

Individuals.—If you are an individual, you are considered to materially participate in a trade or business activity only if one or more of the following apply:

1. You participated in the activity for more than 500 hours during the tax year.

2. Your participation in the activity for the tax year constituted substantially all of the participation in the activity of all individuals (including individuals who are not owners of interests in the activity).

3. You participated in the activity for more than 100 hours during the tax year, and your participation in the activity for the tax year was not less than the participation in the activity of any other individual (including individuals who were not owners of interests in the activity) for the tax year.

4. The activity was a significant participation activity for the tax year, and your aggregate participation in all significant participation activities (including those outside the corporation) during the tax year exceeded 500 hours. A significant participation activity is any trade or business activity in which you participated for more than 100 hours during the year and in which you did not materially participate under any of the material participation tests (other than this test **4**).

5. You materially participated in the activity for any 5 tax years (whether or not consecutive) during the 10 tax years that immediately precede the tax year.

6. The activity was a personal service activity and you materially participated in the activity for any 3 tax years (whether or not consecutive) preceding the tax year. An activity is a personal service activity if it involves the performance of personal services in the fields of health, law, engineering, architecture, accounting, actuarial science, performing arts, consulting, or any other trade or business, in which capital is not a material income-producing factor.

7. Based on all of the facts and circumstances, you participated in the activity on a regular, continuous, and substantial basis during the tax year.

Work counted toward material participation.—Generally, any work that you or your spouse does in connection with an activity held through an S corporation (in which you own stock at the time the work is done) is counted toward material participation. However, work in connection with an activity is not counted toward material participation if either of the following applies:

1. The work is not the sort of work that owners of the activity would usually do and one of the principal purposes of the work that you or your spouse does is to avoid the passive loss or credit limitations.

2. You do the work in your capacity as an investor and you are not directly involved in the day-to-day operations of the activity. Examples of work done as an investor that would not count toward material participation include:

a. Studying and reviewing financial statements or reports on operations of the activity;

b. Preparing or compiling summaries or analyses of the finances or operations of the activity; and

c. Monitoring the finances or operations of the activity in a nonmanagerial capacity.

Effect of determination.—If you determine that you materially participated in **(a)** a trade or business activity of the corporation, or **(b)** if you were a real estate professional (defined on page 2), in a rental real estate activity of the corporation, report the income (loss), deductions, and credits from that activity as indicated in either column (c) of Schedule K-1 or the instructions for your tax return.

If you determine that you **did not** materially participate in a trade or business activity of the corporation, or you have income (loss), deductions, or credits from a rental activity of the corporation (other than a rental real estate activity in which you materially participated, if you were a real estate professional), the amounts from that activity are passive. Report passive income (losses), deductions, and credits as follows:

1. If you have an overall gain (the excess of income over deductions and losses, including any prior year unallowed loss) from a passive activity, report the income, deductions, and losses from the activity as indicated on Schedule K-1 or in these instructions.

2. If you have an overall loss (the excess of deductions and losses, including any prior year unallowed loss, over income) or credits from a passive activity, you must report the income, deductions, losses, and credits from **all** passive activities following the Instructions for Form 8582 or Form 8582-CR, to see if your deductions, losses, and credits are limited under the passive activity rules.

Active participation in a rental real estate activity.—If you actively participated in a rental real estate activity, you may be able to deduct up to $25,000 of the loss from the activity from nonpassive income. This special allowance is an exception to the general rule disallowing losses in excess of income from passive activities. The special allowance is not available if you were married, file a separate return for the year, and did not live apart from your spouse at all times during the year.

Only individuals and qualifying estates can actively participate in a rental real estate activity. Estates (other than qualifying estates) and trusts cannot actively participate.

You are not considered to actively participate in a rental real estate activity if, at any time during the tax year, your interest (including your spouse's interest) in the activity was less than 10% (by value) of all interests in the activity.

Active participation is a less stringent requirement than material participation. You may be treated as actively participating if you participated, for example, in making management decisions or arranging for others to provide services (such as repairs) in a significant and bona fide sense.

Management decisions that can count as active participation include approving new tenants, deciding on rental terms, approving capital or repair expenditures, and other similar decisions.

An estate is a qualifying estate if the decedent would have satisfied the active participation requirement for the activity for the year the decedent died. A qualifying estate is treated as actively participating for tax years ending less than 2 years after the date of the decedent's death.

The maximum special allowance that single individuals and married individuals filing a joint return can qualify for is $25,000. The maximum is $12,500 for married individuals who file separate returns and who lived apart at all times during the year. The maximum special allowance for which an estate can qualify is $25,000 reduced by the special allowance for which the surviving spouse qualifies.

If your modified adjusted gross income (defined below) is $100,000 or less ($50,000 or less if married filing separately), your loss is deductible up to the amount of the maximum special allowance referred to in the preceding paragraph. If your modified adjusted gross income is more than $100,000 (more than $50,000 if married filing separately), the special allowance is limited to 50% of the difference between $150,000 ($75,000 if married filing separately) and your modified adjusted gross income. When modified adjusted gross income is $150,000 or more ($75,000 or more if married filing separately), there is no special allowance.

Modified adjusted gross income is your adjusted gross income figured without taking into account any passive activity loss, rental real estate losses allowed under section 469(c)(7) to real estate professionals (as defined on page 2), any taxable social security or equivalent railroad retirement benefits, any deductible contributions to an IRA or certain other qualified retirement plans under section 219, the deduction allowed under section 164(f) for one-half of self-employment taxes, or the exclusion from income of interest from Series EE U.S. Savings Bonds used to pay higher education expenses.

Special rules for certain other activities.—If you have net income (loss), deductions, or credits from any activity to which special rules apply, the corporation will identify the activity and

all amounts relating to it on Schedule K-1 or on an attachment.

If you have net income subject to recharacterization under Temporary Regulations section 1.469-2T(f) and Regulations section 1.469-2(f), report such amounts according to the Instructions for Form 8582.

If you have net income (loss), deductions, or credits from any of the following activities, treat such amounts as nonpassive and report them as instructed in column (c) of Schedule K-1 or in these instructions:

1. The rental of a dwelling unit any shareholder used for personal purposes during the year for more than the greater of 14 days or 10% of the number of days that the residence was rented at fair rental value.

2. Trading personal property for the account of owners of interests in the activity.

3. Qualified low-income housing projects.

Specific Instructions

Item C

If the corporation is a registration-required tax shelter or has invested in a registration-required tax shelter, it should have completed Item C. If you claim or report any income, loss, deduction, or credit from a tax shelter, you are required to attach **Form 8271,** Investor Reporting of Tax Shelter Registration Number, to your tax return. If the corporation has invested in a tax shelter, it is required to give you a copy of its Form 8271 with your Schedule K-1. Use the information on this Form 8271 to complete your Form 8271.

If the corporation itself is a registration-required tax shelter, use the information on Schedule K-1 (name of corporation, corporation identifying number, and tax shelter registration number) to complete your Form 8271.

Lines 1 Through 23

The amounts on lines 1 through 23 show your pro rata share of ordinary income, loss, deductions, credits, and other information from all corporate activities. These amounts do not take into account limitations on losses, credits, or other items that may have to be adjusted because of:

1. The adjusted basis of your stock and debt in the corporation,

2. The at-risk limitations,

3. The passive activity limitations, or

4. Any other limitations that must be taken into account at the shareholder level in figuring taxable income (e.g., the section 179 expense limitation).

The limitations of **1, 2,** and **3** are discussed above, and the limitations for

4 are discussed throughout these instructions and in other referenced forms and instructions.

If you are an individual, and your pro rata share items are not affected by any of the limitations, report the amounts shown in column (b) of Schedule K-1 as indicated in column (c). If any of the limitations apply, adjust the column (b) amounts for the limitations before you enter the amounts on your return. When applicable, the passive activity limitations on losses are applied after the limitations on losses for a shareholder's basis in stock and debt and the shareholder's at-risk amount.

Note: *The line number references in column (c) are to forms in use for tax years beginning in 1994. If you are a calendar year shareholder in a fiscal year 1994–95 corporation, enter these amounts on the corresponding lines of the tax form in use for 1995.*

Caution: *If you have losses, deductions, credits, etc., from a prior year that were not deductible or usable because of certain limitations, such as the basis rules or the at-risk limitations, take them into account in determining your income, loss, etc., for this year. However, except for passive activity losses and credits, do not combine the prior-year amounts with any amounts shown on this Schedule K-1 to get a net figure to report on your return. Instead, report the amounts on your return on a year-by-year basis.*

Income (Loss)

Line 1—Ordinary Income (Loss) From Trade or Business Activities

The amount reported on line 1 is your share of the ordinary income (loss) from trade or business activities of the corporation. Generally, where you report this amount on Form 1040 depends on whether the amount is from an activity that is a passive activity to you. If you are an individual shareholder, find your situation below and report your line 1 income (loss) as instructed after applying the basis and at-risk limitations on losses:

1. Report line 1 income (loss) from trade or business activities in which you materially participated on Schedule E (Form 1040), Part II, column (i) or (k).

2. Report line 1 income (loss) from trade or business activities in which you did not materially participate, as follows:

a. If income is reported on line 1, report the income on Schedule E, Part II, column (h).

b. If a loss is reported on line 1, follow the Instructions for Form 8582 to determine how much of the loss can be reported on Schedule E, Part II, column (g).

Line 2—Net Income (Loss) From Rental Real Estate Activities

Generally, the income (loss) reported on line 2 is a passive activity amount for all shareholders. However, the income (loss) on line 2 is not from a passive activity if (a) you were a real estate professional (defined on page 2) and you materially participated in the activity, or (b) you held an interest in the activity as a qualified investor in a qualified low-income housing project. The corporation should have attached a schedule identifying any amounts you held as a qualified investor in a qualified low-income housing project.

If you are filing a 1994 Form 1040, use the following instructions to determine where to enter a line 2 amount:

1. If you have a loss from a passive activity on line 2 and you meet **all** of the following conditions, enter the loss on Schedule E (Form 1040), Part II, column (g):

a. You actively participated in the corporate rental real estate activities. (See **Active participation in a rental real estate activity** on page 3.)

b. Rental real estate activities with active participation were your only passive activities.

c. You have no prior year unallowed losses from these activities.

d. Your total loss from the rental real estate activities was not more than $25,000 (not more than $12,500 if married filing separately and you lived apart from your spouse all year).

e. If you are a married person filing separately, you lived apart from your spouse all year.

f. You have no current or prior year unallowed credits from a passive activity.

g. Your modified adjusted gross income was not more than $100,000 (not more than $50,000 if married filing separately and you lived apart from your spouse all year).

2. If you have a loss from a passive activity on line 2 and you **do not** meet all of the conditions in **1** above, follow the Instructions for Form 8582 to determine how much of the loss can be reported on Schedule E (Form 1040), Part II, column (g).

3. If (a) you were a real estate professional and you materially participated in the activity, or (b) you held an interest in the activity as a qualified investor in a qualified low-income housing project, report line 2 income (loss) on Schedule E, Part II, column (i) or (k).

4. If you have income from a passive activity on line 2, enter the income on Schedule E, Part II, column (h).

Line 3—Net Income (Loss) From Other Rental Activities

The amount on line 3 is a passive activity amount for all shareholders. Report the income or loss as follows:

1. If line 3 is a loss, report the loss following the Instructions for Form 8582.

2. If income is reported on line 3, report the income on Schedule E (Form 1040), Part II, column (h).

Line 4—Portfolio Income (Loss)

Portfolio income or loss is not subject to the passive activity limitations. Portfolio income includes income not derived in the ordinary course of a trade or business from interest, dividends, annuities, or royalties, and gain or loss on the sale of property that produces these types of income or is held for investment.

Column (c) of Schedule K-1 tells shareholders where to report this income on Form 1040 and related schedules. Line 4f of Schedule K-1 is used to report income other than that reported on lines 4a through 4e. The type and the amount of income reported on line 4f will be listed in the line 23 Supplemental Information space of Schedule K-1. An example of the type of income that is reported on line 4f is income from a real estate mortgage investment conduit (REMIC) in which the corporation is a residual interest holder. Report your share of any REMIC income on Schedule E (Form 1040), Part IV.

Line 5—Net Gain (Loss) Under Section 1231 (Other Than Due to Casualty or Theft)

Section 1231 gain or loss is reported on line 5. The corporation will identify in the line 23 Supplemental Information space the activity to which the section 1231 gain (loss) relates.

If the amount on line 5 is from a rental activity, the section 1231 gain (loss) is generally a passive activity amount. Likewise, if the amount relates to a trade or business activity and you did not materially participate in the activity, the section 1231 gain (loss) is a passive activity amount.

However, an amount on line 6 from a rental real estate activity is not from a passive activity if (a) you were a real estate professional (defined on page 2) and you materially participated in the activity, or (b) you held an interest in the activity as a qualified investor in a qualified low-income housing project. The corporation should have attached a schedule identifying any amounts you held as a qualified investor in a qualified low-income housing project.

● If the amount is **not** from a passive activity, report it on line 2, column (g) or (h), whichever is applicable, of **Form 4797**, Sales of Business Property. You

do not have to complete the information called for in columns (b) through (f), Form 4797. Write "From Schedule K-1 (Form 1120S)" across these columns.

● If gain from a passive activity is reported on line 5, report the gain on line 2, column (h) of Form 4797.

● If a loss from a passive activity is reported on line 5, see **Passive loss limitations** in the Instructions for Form 4797. You will need to report the loss following the Instructions for Form 8582 to determine how much of the loss is allowed on Form 4797.

Line 6—Other Income (Loss)

Amounts on this line are other items of income, gain, or loss not included on lines 1 through 5. The corporation should give you a description and the amount of your share for each of these items.

Report loss items that are passive activity amounts to you following the Instructions for Form 8582.

Report income or gain items that are passive activity amounts to you as instructed below.

The instructions below tell you where to report line 6 items if such items are **not** passive activity amounts.

Line 6 items include the following:

● Income from recoveries of tax benefit items. A tax benefit item is an amount you deducted in a prior tax year that reduced your income tax. Report this amount on Form 1040, line 21, to the extent it reduced your tax.

● Gambling gains and losses.

1. If the corporation was not engaged in the trade or business of gambling:

a. Report gambling winnings on Form 1040, line 21.

b. Deduct gambling losses to the extent of winnings on Schedule A, line 28.

2. If the corporation was engaged in the trade or business of gambling:

a. Report gambling winnings in Part II of Schedule E.

b. Deduct gambling losses to the extent of winnings in Part II of Schedule E.

● Net gain (loss) from involuntary conversions due to casualty or theft. The corporation will give you a schedule that shows the amounts to be reported on **Form 4684**, Casualties and Thefts, line 34, columns (b)(i), (b)(ii), and (c).

● Net short-term capital gain or loss and net long-term capital gain or loss from Schedule D (Form 1120S) that is **not** portfolio income (e.g., gain or loss from the disposition of nondepreciable personal property used in a trade or business activity of the corporation). Report a net short-term capital gain or loss on Schedule D (Form 1040), line 5, column (f) or (g), and a net long-term capital gain or loss on Schedule D (Form 1040), line 13, column (f) or (g).

• Any net gain or loss from section 1256 contracts. Report this amount on line 1 of **Form 6781,** Gains and Losses From Section 1256 Contracts and Straddles.

Deductions

Line 7—Charitable Contributions

The corporation will give you a schedule that shows the amount of contributions subject to the 50%, 30%, and 20% limitations. For more details, see the Form 1040 instructions.

If property other than cash is contributed, and the claimed deduction for one item or group of similar items of property exceeds $5,000, the corporation is required to give you a copy of **Form 8283,** Noncash Charitable Contributions, and you must attach it to your tax return. Do not deduct the amount shown on Form 8283. It is the corporation's contribution. You should deduct the amount shown on line 7, Schedule K-1.

If the corporation provides you with information that the contribution was property other than cash and does not give you a Form 8283, see the Instructions for Form 8283 for filing requirements. A Form 8283 does not have to be filed unless the total claimed deduction of all contributed items of property exceeds $500.

Charitable contribution deductions are not taken into account in figuring your passive activity loss for the year. Do not enter them on Form 8582.

Line 8—Section 179 Expense Deduction

Use this amount, along with the total cost of section 179 property placed in service during the year from other sources, to complete Part I of **Form 4562,** Depreciation and Amortization. Part I of Form 4562 is used to figure your allowable section 179 expense deduction from all sources. Report the amount on line 12 of Form 4562 allocable to a passive activity from the corporation following the Instructions for Form 8582. If the amount is not a passive activity deduction, report it on Schedule E (Form 1040), Part II, column (j).

Line 9—Deductions Related to Portfolio Income (Loss)

Amounts on line 9 are deductions that are clearly and directly allocable to portfolio income reported on lines 4a through 4f (other than investment interest expense and section 212 expenses from a REMIC). Generally, you should enter line 9 amounts on Schedule A (Form 1040), line 22. See the instructions for Schedule A, lines 22 and 28, for more information.

These deductions are not taken into account in figuring your passive activity loss for the year. Do not enter them on Form 8582.

Line 10—Other Deductions

Amounts on this line are other deductions not included on lines 7, 8, 9, 15e, and 16a, such as:

• Itemized deductions that Form 1040 filers enter on Schedule A (Form 1040).

Note: *If there was a gain (loss) from a casualty or theft to property **not** used in a trade or business or for income-producing purposes, you will be notified by the corporation. You will have to complete your own Form 4684.*

• Any penalty on early withdrawal of savings.

• Soil and water conservation expenditures. See section 175 for limitations on the amount you are allowed to deduct.

• Expenditures for the removal of architectural and transportation barriers to the elderly and disabled that the corporation elected to treat as a current expense. The deductions are limited by section 190(c) to $15,000 per year from all sources.

• Interest expense allocated to debt-financed distributions. The manner in which you report such interest expense depends on your use of the distributed debt proceeds. See Notice 89-35, 1989-1 C.B. 675, for details.

If the corporation has more than one corporate activity (line 1, 2, or 3 of Schedule K-1), it will identify the activity to which the expenses relate.

The corporation should also give you a description and your share of each of the expense items. Associate any passive activity deduction included on line 10 with the line 1, 2, or 3 activity to which it relates and report the deduction following the Instructions for Form 8582 (or only on Schedule E (Form 1040), if applicable).

Investment Interest

If the corporation paid or accrued interest on debts properly allocable to investment property, the amount of interest you are allowed to deduct may be limited.

For more information on the special provisions that apply to investment interest expense, get **Form 4952,** Investment Interest Expense Deduction, and **Pub. 550,** Investment Income and Expenses.

Line 11a—Interest Expense on Investment Debts

Enter this amount on Form 4952, line 1, along with investment interest expense from Schedule K-1, line 10, if any, and from other sources to determine how

much of your total investment interest is deductible.

Lines 11b(1) and (2)—Investment Income and Investment Expenses

Use the amounts on these lines to determine the amounts to enter in Part II of Form 4952.

Caution: *The amounts shown on lines 11b(1) and 11b(2) include only investment income and expenses reported on lines 4a, 4b, 4c, 4f, and 9 of this Schedule K-1. If applicable, the corporation will have listed in the line 23 Supplemental Information space any other items of investment income and expenses reported elsewhere on this Schedule K-1. Be sure to take these amounts into account, along with the amounts on lines 11b(1) and 11b(2) and your investment income and expenses from other sources, when figuring the amounts to enter in Part II of Form 4952.*

Credits

Caution: *If you have credits that are passive activity credits to you, you must complete Form 8582-CR in addition to the credit forms named below. See the Instructions for Form 8582-CR for more information.*

*Also, if you are entitled to claim more than one general business credit (i.e., investment credit, jobs credit, credit for alcohol used as fuel, research credit, low-income housing credit, enhanced oil recovery credit, disabled access credit, renewable electricity production credit, Indian employment credit, credit for employer social security and Medicare taxes paid on certain employee tips, and credit for contributions to selected community development corporations), you must complete **Form 3800,** General Business Credit, in addition to the credit forms named below. If you have more than one credit, see the instructions for Form 3800 for more information.*

Line 12a—Credit for Alcohol Used as Fuel

Your share of the corporation's credit for alcohol used as fuel from all trade or business activities is reported on line 12a. Enter this credit on **Form 6478,** Credit for Alcohol Used as Fuel, to determine your allowed credit for the year.

Line 12b—Low-Income Housing Credit

Your share of the corporation's low-income housing credit is shown on lines 12b(1) through (4). Your allowable credit is entered on **Form 8586,** Low-Income Housing Credit, to determine your allowed credit for the year.

If the corporation invested in a partnership to which the provisions of section 42(j)(5) apply, it will report separately on lines 12b(1) and 12b(3) your share of the credit it received from the partnership.

Your share of all other low-income housing credits of the corporation is reported on lines 12b(2) and 12b(4). You must keep a separate record of the amount of low-income housing credit from these lines so that you will be able to correctly compute any recapture of the credit that may result from the disposition of all or part of your stock in the corporation. For more information, see the instructions for **Form 8611,** Recapture of Low-Income Housing Credit.

Caution: *You cannot claim the low-income housing credit on any qualified low-income housing project if you, or any person, were allowed relief from the passive activity limitations on losses from the project (section 502 of the Tax Reform Act of 1986).*

Line 12c—Qualified Rehabilitation Expenditures Related to Rental Real Estate Activities

The corporation should identify your share of rehabilitation expenditures from each rental real estate activity. Enter the expenditures on the appropriate line of **Form 3468,** Investment Credit, to figure your allowable credit.

Line 12d—Credits (Other Than Credits Shown on Lines 12b and 12c) Related to Rental Real Estate Activities

The corporation will identify the type of credit and any other information you need to compute credits from rental real estate activities (other than the low-income housing credit and qualified rehabilitation expenditures).

Line 12e—Credits Related to Other Rental Activities

If applicable, your share of any credit from other rental activities will be reported on line 12e. Income or loss from these activities is reported on line 3 of Schedule K-1. If more than one credit is involved, the credits will be listed separately, each credit identified as a line 12e credit, and the activity to which the credit relates will be identified. This information will be shown on the line 23 Supplemental Information space. The credit may be limited by the passive activity limitations.

Line 13—Other Credits

If applicable, your pro rata share of any other credit (other than on lines 12a through 12e) will be shown on line 13. If more than one credit is reported, the credits will be shown and identified in the line 23 Supplemental Information space. Expenditures qualifying for the **(a)** rehabilitation credit from other than

rental real estate activities, **(b)** energy credit, or **(c)** reforestation credit will be reported to you on line 23.

Line 13 credits include the following:

● Nonconventional source fuel credit. Enter this credit on a schedule you prepare yourself to determine the allowed credit to take on your tax return. See section 29 for rules on how to figure the credit.

● Unused investment credit from cooperatives. Enter this credit on Form 3468 to figure your allowable investment credit.

● Credit for backup withholding on dividends, interest income, and other types of income. Include the amount the corporation reports to you in the total that you enter on line 54, page 2, Form 1040. Be sure to check the box on line 54 and write "From Schedule K-1."

● Credit for increasing research activities and orphan drug credit (Form 6765).

● Jobs credit (Form 5884).

● Disabled access credit (Form 8826).

● Enhanced oil recovery credit (Form 8830).

● Qualified electric vehicle credit (Form 8834).

● Renewable electricity production credit (Form 8835).

● Empowerment zone employment credit (Form 8844).

● Indian employment credit (Form 8845).

● Credit for employer social security and Medicare taxes paid on certain employee tips (Form 8846).

● Credit for contributions to selected community development corporations (Form 8847).

Adjustments and Tax Preference Items

Use the information reported on lines 14a through 14e (as well as adjustments and tax preference items from other sources) to prepare your **Form 6251,** Alternative Minimum Tax—Individuals, or Schedule H of **Form 1041,** U.S. Income Tax Return for Estates and Trusts.

Lines 14d(1) and 14d(2)—Gross Income From, and Deductions Allocable to, Oil, Gas, and Geothermal Properties

The amounts reported on these lines include only the gross income from, and deductions allocable to, oil, gas, and geothermal properties included on line 1 of Schedule K-1. The corporation should have reported separately any income from or deductions allocable to such properties that are included on lines 2 through 10. This separate information is reported in the line 23 Supplemental Information space. Use the amounts reported on lines 14d(1) and 14d(2) and any amounts reported separately to help

you determine the net amount to enter on line 14f of Form 6251.

Line 14e—Other Adjustments and Tax Preference Items

Enter the line 14e adjustments and tax preference items shown in the line 23 Supplemental Information space, with other items from other sources, on the applicable lines of Form 6251.

Foreign Taxes

Use the information on lines 15a through 15g, and attached schedules, to figure your foreign tax credit. For more information, get **Form 1116,** Foreign Tax Credit—Individual, Estate, Trust, or Nonresident Alien Individual, and its instructions.

Other

Lines 16a and 16b

The corporation will show on line 16a the total qualified expenditures to which an election under section 59(e) may apply. It will identify the type of expenditures on line 16b. If there is more than one type of expenditure, the amount of each type will be listed on an attachment. Generally, section 59(e) allows each shareholder to elect to deduct certain expenses ratably over the number of years in the applicable period rather than deduct the full amount in the current year. Under the election, you may deduct circulation expenditures ratably over a 3-year period. Research and experimental expenditures and mining exploration and development costs qualify for a writeoff period of 10 years. Intangible drilling and development costs may be deducted over a 60-month period, beginning with the month in which such costs were paid or incurred. If you make this election, these items are not treated as adjustments or tax preference items for purposes of the alternative minimum tax. Make the election on Form 4562.

Because each shareholder decides whether to make the election under section 59(e), the corporation cannot provide you with the amount of the adjustment or tax preference item related to the expenses listed on line 16a. You must decide both how to claim the expenses on your return and how to compute the resulting adjustment or tax preference item.

Line 17—Tax-Exempt Interest Income

You must report on your return, as an item of information, your share of the tax-exempt interest received or accrued by the corporation during the year. Individual shareholders should include this amount on Form 1040, line 8b. Generally, you must increase the basis of your stock in the corporation by this amount.

Line 18—Other Tax-Exempt Income

Generally, you must increase the basis of your stock in the corporation by the amount shown on line 18, but do not include it in income on your tax return.

Line 19—Nondeductible Expenses

The nondeductible expenses paid or incurred by the corporation are not deductible on your tax return. Generally, you must decrease the basis of your stock in the corporation by this amount.

Line 20

Reduce the basis of your stock in the corporation by the distributions on line 20. If these distributions exceed the basis of your stock, the excess is treated as gain from the sale or exchange of property and is reported on Schedule D (Form 1040).

Line 21

If the line 21 payments are made on indebtedness with a reduced basis, the repayments result in income to you to the extent the repayments are more than the adjusted basis of the loan. See Regulations section 1.1367-2 for information on reduction in basis of a loan and restoration in basis of a loan with a reduced basis. See Rev. Rul. 64-162, 1964-1 (Part 1) C.B. 304 and Rev. Rul. 68-537, 1968-2 C.B. 372, for other information.

Lines 22a and 22b—Recapture of Low-Income Housing Credit

The corporation will report separately on line 22a your share of any recapture of a low-income housing credit from its investment in partnerships to which the provisions of section 42(j)(5) apply. All other recapture of low-income housing credits will be reported on line 22b. You must keep a separate record of recapture from line 22a and 22b so that you will be able to correctly figure any credit recapture that may result from the disposition of all or part of your corporate stock. Use the line 22a and 22b amounts to compute the low-income housing credit recapture on Form 8611. See the instructions for Form 8611 and section 42(j) for additional information.

Supplemental Information

Line 23

If applicable, the corporation should have listed in line 23, Supplemental Information, or on an attached statement to Schedule K-1, your distributive share of the following:

1. Taxes paid on undistributed capital gains by a regulated investment

company. (Form 1040 filers, enter your share of these taxes on line 59 of Form 1040, check the box for Form 2439, and add the words "Form 1120S." Also reduce the basis of your stock in the corporation by this tax.)

2. Gross income from the property, share of production for the tax year, etc., needed to figure your depletion deduction for oil and gas wells. The corporation should also allocate to you a proportionate share of the adjusted basis of each corporate oil or gas property. See Pub. 535 for how to figure your depletion deduction. Also, reduce the basis of your stock in the corporation by the amount of this deduction to the extent the deduction does not exceed your share of the adjusted basis of the property.

3. Recapture of the section 179 expense deduction. If the recapture was caused by a disposition of the property, include the amount on Form 4797, line 18. The recapture amount is limited to the amount you deducted in earlier years.

4. Recapture of certain mining exploration expenditures (section 617).

5. Any information or statements you need to comply with section 6111 (registration of tax shelters) or 6662(d)(2)(B)(ii) (regarding adequate disclosure of items that may cause an understatement of income tax).

6. Gross farming and fishing income. If you are an individual shareholder, enter this income, as an item of information, on Schedule E (Form 1040), Part V, line 41. Do not report this income elsewhere on Form 1040.

For a shareholder that is an estate or trust, report this income to the beneficiaries, as an item of information, on Schedule K-1 (Form 1041). Do not report it elsewhere on Form 1041.

7. Any information you need to figure the interest due under section 453(l)(3). If the corporation elected to report the dispositions of certain timeshares and residential lots on the installment method, your tax liability must be increased by the interest on tax attributable to your pro rata share of the installment payments received by the corporation during its tax year. If applicable, use the information provided by the corporation to figure your interest. Include the interest on Form 1040, line 53. Also write "453(l)(3)" and the amount of the interest on the dotted line to the left of line 53.

8. Any information you need to compute the interest due under section 453A(c) with respect to certain installment sales of property. If you are an individual, report the interest on Form 1040, line 53. Write "453A(c)" and the amount of the interest on the dotted line to the left of line 53. See the instructions

for **Form 6252,** Installment Sale Income, for more information. Also see section 453A(c) for details on making the computation.

9. Capitalization of interest under section 263A(f). To the extent certain production or construction expenditures of the corporation are made from proceeds associated with debt you incur as an owner-shareholder, you must capitalize the interest on this debt. If applicable, use the information on expenditures the corporation gives to you to determine the amount of interest you must capitalize. See Section XII of Notice 88-99, 1988-2 C.B. 422, for more information.

10. Any information you need to compute the interest due or to be refunded under the look-back method of section 460(b)(2) on certain long-term contracts. Use **Form 8697,** Interest Computation Under the Look-Back Method for Completed Long-Term Contracts, to report any such interest.

11. Your share of expenditures qualifying for the **(a)** rehabilitation credit from other than rental real estate activities, **(b)** energy credit, or **(c)** reforestation credit. Enter the expenditures on the appropriate line of Form 3468 to figure your allowable credit.

12. Investment credit properties subject to recapture. Any information you need to figure your recapture tax on **Form 4255,** Recapture of Investment Credit. See the Form 3468 on which you took the original credit for other information you need to complete Form 4255.

You may also need Form 4255 if you disposed of more than one-third of your stock in the corporation.

13. Preproductive period farm expenses. You may elect to deduct these expenses currently or capitalize them under section 263A. See **Pub. 225,** Farmer's Tax Guide, and Temporary Regulations section 1.263A-4T(c) for more information.

14. Any information you need to figure recapture of the qualified electric vehicle credit. See Pub 535 for details, including how to figure the recapture.

15. Any information you need to figure your recapture of the Indian employment credit. Generally, if the corporation terminated a qualified employee less than 1 year after the date of initial employment, any Indian employment credit allowed for a prior tax year by reason of wages paid or incurred to that employee must be recaptured. For details, see section 45A(d).

16. Any other information you may need to file with your individual tax return that is not shown elsewhere on Schedule K-1.

 Printed on recycled paper

*U.S. Government Printing Office: 1994 — 375-320

APPENDIX 31

EMPLOYER'S QUARTERLY FEDERAL TAX RETURN, FORM 941

Form **941**
(Rev. January 1992)
Department of the Treasury
Internal Revenue Service

4141

Employer's Quarterly Federal Tax Return

▶ **See Circular E for more information concerning employment tax returns.**

Please type or print.

OMB No. 1545-0029
Expires 5-31-93

Your name, address, employer identification number, and calendar quarter of return. (If not correct, please change.)

If address is different from prior return, check here ▶

Name (as distinguished from trade name)	Date quarter ended	
Trade name, if any	Employer identification number	
Address (number and street)	City, state, and ZIP code	

T	
FF	
FD	
FP	
I	
T	

IRS Use

If you do not have to file returns in the future, check here . ▶ ☐   Date final wages paid . . . ▶ _____

If you are a seasonal employer, see **Seasonal employers** on page 2 and check here . . ▶ ☐

1	Number of employees (except household) employed in the pay period that includes March 12th ▶	**1**

2	Total wages and tips subject to withholding, plus other compensation . . . . . . ▶	**2**	
3	Total income tax withheld from wages, tips, pensions, annuities, sick pay, gambling, etc. . ▶	**3**	
4	Adjustment of withheld income tax for preceding quarters of calendar year (see instructions) . ▶	**4**	
5	Adjusted total of income tax withheld (line 3 as adjusted by line 4—see instructions) . .	**5**	
6a	Taxable social security wages **(Complete line 7)** $ _____ · 12.4% (.124) =	**6a**	
b	Taxable social security tips $ _____ · 12.4% (.124) =	**6b**	
7	Taxable Medicare wages and tips . . . . $ _____ · 2.9% (.029) =	**7**	
8	Total social security and Medicare taxes (add lines 6a, 6b, and 7)	**8**	
9	Adjustment of social security and Medicare taxes (see instructions for required explanation) .	**9**	
10	Adjusted total of social security and Medicare taxes (line 8 as adjusted by line 9—see instructions) . ▶	**10**	
11	Backup withholding (see instructions)	**11**	
12	Adjustment of backup withholding tax for preceding quarters of calendar year	**12**	
13	Adjusted total of backup withholding (line 11 as adjusted by line 12)	**13**	
14	**Total taxes** (add lines 5, 10, and 13)	**14**	
15	Advance earned income credit (EIC) payments made to employees, if any . . . . . . ▶	**15**	
16	Net taxes (subtract line 15 from line 14). **This should equal line IV below** (plus line IV of Schedule A (Form 941) if you have treated backup withholding as a separate liability) .	**16**	
17	**Total deposits for quarter**, including overpayment applied from a prior quarter, from your records ▶	**17**	
18	**Balance due** (subtract line 17 from line 16). This should be less than $500. Pay to Internal Revenue Service . ▶	**18**	
19	**Overpayment**, if line 17 is more than line 16, enter excess here ▶ $ _____ and check if to be:		

☐ Applied to next return   **OR**   ☐ Refunded.

Record of Federal Tax Liability (You must complete if line 16 is $500 or more and Schedule B is not attached.) See instructions before checking these boxes.

If you made deposits using the 95% rule, check here ▶ ☐   If you are a first time 3-banking-day depositor, check here . . ▶ ☐

Show tax liability here, **not deposits**. The IRS gets deposit data from FTD coupons.

Date wages paid	First month of quarter		Second month of quarter		Third month of quarter	
1st through 3rd	A		I		Q	
4th through 7th	B		J		R	
8th through 11th	C		K		S	
12th through 15th	D		L		T	
16th through 19th	E		M		U	
20th through 22nd	F		N		V	
23rd through 25th	G		O		W	
26th through the last	H		P		X	
Total liability for month	I		II		III	

DO NOT Show Federal Tax Deposits Here

IV Total for quarter (add lines **I, II**, and **III**). **This should equal line 16 above** . . . . . . ▶

Sign Here

Under penalties of perjury, I declare that I have examined this return, including accompanying schedules and statements, and to the best of my knowledge and belief, it is true, correct, and complete.

Signature ▶   Print Your Name and Title ▶   Date ▶

For Paperwork Reduction Act Notice, see page 2.   Cat. No. 17001Z

Paperwork Reduction Act Notice.—We ask for the information on this form to carry out the Internal Revenue laws of the United States. You are required to give us the information. We need it to ensure that you are complying with these laws and to allow us to figure and collect the right amount of tax.

The time needed to complete and file this form will vary depending on individual circumstances. The estimated average time is: **Recordkeeping** 12 hr., 41 min.; **Learning about the law or the form** 34 min.; **Preparing the form** 1 hr., 43 min.; **Copying, assembling, and sending the form to the IRS** 16 min. If you have comments concerning the accuracy of these time estimates or suggestions for making this form more simple, we would be happy to hear from you. You can write to both the **Internal Revenue Service**, Washington, DC 20224, Attention: IRS Reports Clearance Officer, T:FP; and the **Office of Management and Budget**, Paperwork Reduction Project (1545-0029), Washington, DC 20503. DO NOT send the tax form to either of these offices. Instead, see **Where To File** below.

Important Reminder.—The wage bases for the two parts of the social security tax (social security and Medicare) now are different. Employers can no longer combine and report the withholding as a single amount. Social security wages must be reported on line 6a, social security tips must be reported on line 6b, and Medicare wages and tips must be reported on line 7. The wage bases are $55,500 for social security and $130,200 for Medicare.

The cost of group-term life insurance in excess of $50,000 provided former employees is subject to both the employer and employee portion of social security and Medicare taxes. Include the cost of the excess coverage on lines 6a and 7. Any uncollected social security and Medicare taxes must be reported as an adjustment on line 9.

Forms W-4.—Each quarter, send in with Form 941 copies of any Forms W-4 received during the quarter from employees: (1) claiming more than 10 withholding allowances, or (2) claiming exemption from income tax withholding if their wages will normally be more than $200 a week. For details, see section 10 of Circular E.

Circular E, Employer's Tax Guide, explains the rules for withholding, paying, depositing, and reporting Federal income tax, social security and Medicare taxes, and Federal unemployment (FUTA) tax on wages, fringe benefits, and sick pay paid by third-party payers. **Circular A,** Agricultural Employer's Tax Guide. explains different rules for employers who have farmworkers. These circulars are available free at IRS offices.

General Instructions

Purpose of Form.—To report:

● Income tax you withheld from wages, tips, annuities, supplemental unemployment compensation benefits, certain gambling winnings, and third-party payments of sick pay.

● Income tax withheld as backup withholding.

● Social security and Medicare taxes.

Who Must File.—Employers who withhold income tax, and both social security and Medicare taxes, must file Form 941 quarterly. Exceptions are:

● **Seasonal employers** no longer file for quarters when they regularly have no tax liability because they have paid no wages. To alert the IRS that you will not have to file a return for one or more quarters during the year, check the **Seasonal employer** box above line 1 on page 1. The IRS will mail two Forms 941 to the seasonal filer once a year after March 1. The preprinted label will not include the date the quarter ended. You must enter the date the quarter ended when you file the return. The IRS will generally not

inquire about unfiled returns if at least one taxable return is filed each year. However, you must check the **Seasonal employer** box on every quarterly return you file. Otherwise, the IRS will expect a return to be filed for each quarter.

● Employers who report payments not subject to social security, see **Form 941E,** Quarterly Return of Withheld Federal Income Tax and Medicare Tax, and Circular E.

● Employers who report wages on household employees, see **Form 942,** Employer's Quarterly Tax Return for Household Employees, and Circular E.

● Employers who report wages on farmworkers. see **Form 943,** Employer's Annual Tax Return for Agricultural Employees, and Circular A.

● Business Reorganization or Termination. If you sell or transfer your business, both you and the new owner must file a return for the quarter in which the change took place. Neither should report wages paid by the other. (An example of a transfer is when a sole proprietor forms a partnership or corporation.) If a change occurs. please attach to your return a statement that shows: new owner's name (or new name of the business); whether the business is now a sole proprietorship, partnership, or corporation; kind of change that took place (sale. transfer, etc.); and date of the change.

When a business is merged or consolidated with another, the continuing firm must file the return for the quarter in which the change took place. The return should show all wages paid for that quarter. The other firm should file a final return. The IRS will not mail you any Forms 941 after it receives your final return.

But if you go out of business or stop paying wages, file a final return. Be sure to fill in the entries above line 1. You may also file Form W-2 with the Social Security Administration now but not later than March 2, 1993.

When To File.—File starting with the first quarter in which you are required to withhold income tax or pay wages subject to social security and Medicare taxes.

Quarter	Ending	Due Date
Jan.-Feb.-Mar.	March 31	April 30
Apr.-May-June	June 30	July 31
July-Aug.-Sept.	Sept. 30	Oct. 31
Oct.-Nov.-Dec.	Dec. 31	Jan. 31

If you deposited all taxes when due for a quarter, you have 10 more days after the above due date to file. If the due date for filing a return falls on a Saturday, Sunday, or legal holiday, you may file the return on the next business day.

After you file your first return, we will send you a form every 3 months. Please use this form. If you don't have a form, get one from an IRS office in time to file the return when due.

Where To File.—

If your legal residence, principal place of business, office, or agency is located in:	Use the following Internal Revenue Service Center address:
Florida, Georgia, South Carolina	Atlanta. GA 39901
New Jersey, New York (New York City and counties of Nassau, Rockland, Suffolk, and Westchester)	Holtsville, NY 00501
New York (all other counties), Connecticut, Maine, Massachusetts, New Hampshire, Rhode Island, Vermont	Andover, MA 05501
Illinois, Iowa, Minnesota, Missouri, Wisconsin	Kansas City, MO 64999
Delaware, District of Columbia, Maryland, Pennsylvania, Virginia	Philadelphia, PA 19255
Indiana, Kentucky, Michigan, Ohio, West Virginia	Cincinnati, OH 45999
Kansas, New Mexico, Oklahoma, Texas	Austin, TX 73301

Alaska, Arizona, California (counties of Alpine, Amador, Butte. Calaveras, Colusa, Contra Costa, Del Norte, El Dorado, Glenn, Humboldt. Lake. Lassen, Marin, Mendocino, Modoc. Napa. Nevada. Placer. Plumas. Sacramento, San Joaquin, Shasta, Sierra. Siskiyou. Solano, Sonoma Sutter, Tehama, Trinity, Yolo. and Yuba). Colorado, Idaho. Montana, Nebraska, Nevada. North Dakota, Oregon. South Dakota. Utah, Washington. Wyoming	Ogden. UT 84201
California (all other counties). Hawaii	Fresno, CA 93888
Alabama, Arkansas, Louisiana, Mississippi, North Carolina. Tennessee	Memphis TN 37501
If you have no legal residence or principal place of business in any state	Philadelphia, PA 19255

Employer Identification Number (EIN).—If you have not asked for a number, apply for one on **Form SS-4,** Application for Employer Identification Number. Get this form from the IRS or the Social Security Administration (SSA). If you do not have a number by the time a return is due, write "Applied for" and the date you applied in the space shown for the number.

Note: *Always make certain that the EIN on the form you file matches the EIN assigned to your business by the IRS. Filing a Form 941 with an incorrect EIN or using another business' EIN may result in penalties and delays in processing your return.*

Penalties and Interest.—There are penalties for filing a return late and paying or depositing taxes late, unless there is reasonable cause. If you are late, please attach an explanation to your return. There are also penalties for willful failure to file returns and pay taxes when due, furnish Forms W-2 to employees and file copies with the SSA, keep records, deposit taxes when required, and for filing false returns or submitting bad checks. See Circular E for additional information.

Caution: *A 100% penalty may apply where income, social security, and Medicare taxes that should be withheld are not withheld or are not paid to the IRS. Under this penalty, certain officers or employees of a corporation, or certain members or employees of a partnership become personally liable for the payments of the taxes and are penalized an equal amount.*

Interest is charged on taxes paid late at the rate set by law.

Depositing Taxes.—Use Form 8109, Federal Tax Deposit Coupon, to deposit your taxes. See Circular E, section 13, for information and rules concerning Federal tax deposits.

Do not use the deposit coupons to pay delinquent taxes for which you have received a notice from the IRS. These payments should be sent directly to your Internal Revenue Service Center along with a copy of any related notice the IRS sent you.

Specific Instructions

Reconciliation of Forms 941 and W-3.— Certain amounts reported on the four quarterly Forms 941 for 1992 should agree with the **Forms W-2,** Wage and Tax Statement, totals reported on **Form W-3,** Transmittal of Income and Tax Statements, or with information filed on equivalent magnetic media reports filed with the SSA. The amounts that should agree are: social security wages, social security tips, Medicare wages and tips, and the advance earned income credit. If the totals do not agree, the IRS will require you to explain any differences and correct any errors. You can avoid this by making sure that correct amounts (including adjustments) are reported on Forms 941 and W-3.

(continued on page 4)

Line 1—Number of employees.—Complete for the January-March calendar quarter only. Do not include household employees. persons who received no pay during the pay period. pensioners. or members of the Armed Forces. If you have only household employees in the pay period. enter zero. An entry of 250 or more on line 1 indicates a need to file wage reports on magnetic media. You should immediately request Publication TIB-4 from SSA if not already a magnetic media filer. Call 1-800-772-1213 for more information.

Line 2.—Enter the total of all wages paid. tips reported. taxable fringe benefits provided. and other compensation paid to your employees. even if you do not have to withhold income or social security and Medicare taxes on it. Do not include pensions. annuities. supplemental unemployment compensation benefits. or gambling winnings. even if you withheld income tax on them.

When an employer receives timely notice from its insurance carrier concerning the amount of third-party sick pay paid. the employer should include the third-party sick pay on this line. In these cases. an insurance company should not include third-party sick pay that it paid to the employees of policy holders. See section 19 of Circular E for more details.

Line 3.—Enter the income tax you withheld on wages. tips. taxable fringe benefits. annuities. supplemental unemployment compensation benefits. and gambling winnings. An insurance company should enter the income tax it withheld on third-party sick pay here.

Line 4—Adjustment of withheld income tax.— Use line 4 to correct errors in income tax withheld from wages paid in earlier quarters of the same calendar year. Explain any amount on **Form 941c**, Statement to Correct Information. or attach a statement that shows (a) what the error was. (b) quarter in which the error was made. (c) the amount of the error for each quarter. (d) quarter in which you found the error. and (e) how you and your payees have settled any overcollection or undercollection. Do not use this line to adjust income tax withholding for earlier years.

Line 5—Adjusted total of income tax withheld.—Add line 4 to line 3 if you are reporting additional income tax withheld for an earlier quarter in this calendar year. Subtract line 4 from line 3 if you are reducing the amount of income tax withheld. If there is no entry on line 4. the entry will be the same as line 3.

Line 6a—Taxable social security wages.— Enter the total wages subject to social security taxes that you paid your employees during the quarter. Also include any sick pay and taxable fringe benefits subject to social security taxes. Enter the amount before deductions. Do not include tips on this line. Stop reporting when an employee's wages (including tips) reach $55.500 for 1992. However. continue to withhold income tax for the whole year on wages and tips even when the social security wage base of $55.500 is reached. See line 7 below for Medicare tax. If none of the payments are subject to social security tax. enter zero and attach a statement explaining why the wages are not subject to social security tax.

Line 6b—Taxable tips.—Enter all tips your employees reported during the quarter. until tips and wages for each employee reach $55.500 in 1992. Do this even if you were not able to withhold the employee tax (6.2%). However. see line 9 instructions below.

An employee must report to you cash tips. including tips you paid the employee for charge customers. totaling $20 or more in a month by the 10th of the next month. The employee may use **Form 4070**, Employee's Report of Tips to Employer. or a written statement.

Do not include allocated tips on this line. Instead. report them on **Form 8027**, Employer's Annual Information Return of Tip Income and Allocated Tips. Allocated tips are not reportable on Form 941 and are not subject to withholding of income. social security. or Medicare taxes.

Line 7—Taxable Medicare wages and tips.— Use this line to report all wages and tips subject to the Medicare portion of social security. Stop reporting when an employee's wages and tips reach $130.200 for 1992. If none of the payments are subject to Medicare tax. enter zero and attach a statement explaining why the wages are not subject to the Medicare tax.

Include all tips your employees reported during the quarter. even if you were not able to withhold the employee tax (1.45%). However. see line 9 instructions below.

Line 9—Adjustment of social security and Medicare taxes.—Use line 9 to correct errors in social security and Medicare taxes reported on an earlier return. If you report both an underpayment and an overpayment. show only the difference. Except for fractions of cents or third-party sick pay. explain any amount on line 9 on Form 941c. If you do not have a Form 941c. attach a statement that shows (a) what the error was. (b) ending date of each quarter in which the error was made and the amount of the error. (c) quarter in which you found the error. (d) that you repaid the employee tax or got each affected employee's written consent to this refund or credit. if the entry corrects an overcollection. and (e) if the entry corrects social security and Medicare taxes overcollected in an earlier year. that you got from the employee a written statement that he or she has not claimed and will not claim a refund or credit for the amount. If you are adjusting an employee's social security wages. tips. Medicare wages. Medicare tips. or tax withheld for a prior year. you must also file **Form W-2c**, Statement of Corrected Income and Tax Amounts. and **Form W-3c**, Transmittal of Corrected Income and Tax Statements. with the Social Security office where you filed Forms W-2. You can get these from the IRS.

Enter on Form 941c or include in the statement the total social security wages. social security tips. and Medicare wages and tips for all your employees as previously reported and as corrected. However. if you are correcting wage amounts for years prior to 1990 you need not show separate entries for Medicare wages and tips. If some or all of your wages are not subject to both social security and Medicare. you must attach a statement explaining why all your wages are not subject to social security and Medicare tax. You can get Form 941c from the IRS or by calling 1-800-829-3676.

Adjustments of tax on tips and group-term life insurance premiums paid for former employees.—Include on line 9 the total uncollected employee social security and Medicare taxes. Attach a statement explaining each adjustment. (See Circular E for details.)

Adjustment of tax on third-party sick pay.— Deduct on line 9 the social security and Medicare taxes on third-party sick pay for which you are not responsible. and write "Sick pay" in the margin.

Fraction of cents.—If there is a difference between the total tax on line 8 and the total deducted from your employees' wages or tips plus the employer's contribution because of fractions of cents added or dropped in collecting the tax. report the difference on line 9. If this difference is the only entry. write "Fractions only" in the margin.

Line 10—Adjusted total of social security and Medicare taxes.—Add line 9 to line 8 if you are

reporting additional taxes for an earlier quarter. Subtract line 9 from line 8 if you are reducing the amount of taxes reported for an earlier quarter.

Line 11—Backup withholding.—Enter the income tax withheld as backup withholding.

Line 12.—Use line 12 to correct errors in backup withholding tax for earlier quarters of this year. You must attach a statement explaining your adjustment.

Line 17—Total deposits for quarter.—Enter the total deposits for the quarter including backup withholding reported on Schedule A (Form 941) and any overpayment applied from the previous quarter from your records.

Line 18—Balance due.—If you deposited all taxes when due. any balance will be less than $500. Enter your EIN. "Form 941." and the tax period to which the payment applies on your check or money order.

Line 19—Overpayment.—If you deposited more than the correct amount for a quarter. you can have the overpayment refunded or applied to your next return. Also. the IRS may apply your overpayment to any past due tax account that we have under your EIN.

Completing the Record of Federal Tax Liability (ROFT).—Note: *This is a record of when you were liable for taxes. NOT a record of when you made a deposit.*

(a) Line 16 is less than $500.—You do not have to complete the ROFT.

(b) Your tax liability is $500 or more but less than $3,000 for each month of the quarter.— Only enter your total liability for each month on the **Total liability for month** lines (I. II. and III). No entries are required in A through X.

(c) Your tax liability is $3,000 or more for at least one month during the quarter.—Each month is divided into eight deposit periods (called eighth-monthly periods) that end on the 3rd. 7th. 11th. 15th. 19th. 22nd. 25th. and last day of the month as shown in the record. Find the eighth-monthly period(s) during the quarter in which you had a payday. Make entries only on the lines next to these periods. (For example. if you pay wages on the 1st and 15th of each month. complete lines A. D. I. L. Q. T. and the monthly Total lines.) Enter your tax liability (income tax withheld plus both the employee and employer social security and Medicare taxes minus any advance earned income credit payments) for each eighth-monthly period during which you had a payday.

(d) Your tax liability is $100,000 or more during any eighth-monthly period.—You **DO NOT** have to complete the ROFT. Instead. you must complete and attach **Schedule B (Form 941)**, Supplemental Record of Federal Tax Liability. You must enter the total of Column 2 from Schedule B (Form 941) on line IV of the ROFT.

DO NOT show Federal tax deposits here. This information is obtained from the deposit coupon.

The total of the tax liability column. line IV (plus line IV on Schedule A (Form 941) if you treat backup withholding as a separate liability) should equal "Net taxes" (line 16). Otherwise. you may be charged a penalty. based on your average tax liability. for not making deposits of taxes.

Check the first box at the top of the ROFT only if you are making deposits using the 95% rule. This is explained in Circular E.

Check the second box at the top of the ROFT only if you qualify for the exception under Rule 4 explained in Circular E and attach a statement showing your net taxes for each of the preceding 4 calendar quarters.

U.S. PARTNERSHIP RETURN OF INCOME, FORM 1065

| Form **1065**
Department of the Treasury
Internal Revenue Service | **U.S. Partnership Return of Income**
For calendar year 1994, or tax year beginning ...., 1994, and ending ...., 19 ....
▶ See separate instructions. | OMB No. 1545-0099
1994 |

A Principal business activity	Use the IRS label. Otherwise, please print or type.	Name of partnership	D Employer identification number
B Principal product or service		Number, street, and room or suite no. (If a P.O. box, see page 9 of the instructions.)	E Date business started
C Business code number		City or town, state, and ZIP code	F Total assets (see Specific Instructions) $

G Check applicable boxes: (1) ☐ Initial return (2) ☐ Final return (3) ☐ Change in address (4) ☐ Amended return
H Check accounting method: (1) ☐ Cash (2) ☐ Accrual (3) ☐ Other (specify) ▶ ....
I Number of Schedules K-1. Attach one for each person who was a partner at any time during the tax year ▶ ....

Caution: *Include only trade or business income and expenses on lines 1a through 22 below. See the instructions for more information.*

Income

1a	Gross receipts or sales	1a	
b	Less returns and allowances	1b	1c
2	Cost of goods sold (Schedule A, line 8)	2	
3	Gross profit. Subtract line 2 from line 1c	3	
4	Ordinary income (loss) from other partnerships, estates, and trusts *(attach schedule)* . .	4	
5	Net farm profit (loss) *(attach Schedule F (Form 1040))*	5	
6	Net gain (loss) from Form 4797, Part II, line 20	6	
7	Other income (loss) (see instructions) *(attach schedule)*	7	
8	**Total income (loss).** Combine lines 3 through 7	8	

Deductions *(see instructions for limitations)*

9	Salaries and wages (other than to partners) (less employment credits) . . .	9	
10	Guaranteed payments to partners	10	
11	Repairs and maintenance	11	
12	Bad debts	12	
13	Rent	13	
14	Taxes and licenses	14	
15	Interest	15	
16a	Depreciation (see instructions)	16a	
b	Less depreciation reported on Schedule A and elsewhere on return	16b	16c
17	Depletion **(Do not deduct oil and gas depletion.)**	17	
18	Retirement plans, etc.	18	
19	Employee benefit programs	19	
20	Other deductions *(attach schedule)*	20	
21	**Total deductions.** Add the amounts shown in the far right column for lines 9 through 20 .	21	
22	**Ordinary income (loss)** from trade or business activities. Subtract line 21 from line 8 .	22	

Please Sign Here

Under penalties of perjury, I declare that I have examined this return, including accompanying schedules and statements, and to the best of my knowledge and belief, it is true, correct, and complete. Declaration of preparer (other than general partner) is based on all information of which preparer has any knowledge.

▶ _____ ▶ _____
Signature of general partner or limited liability company member   Date

Paid Preparer's Use Only	Preparer's signature ▶	Date	Check if self-employed ▶ ☐	Preparer's social security no.
	Firm's name (or yours if self-employed) and address ▶		E.I. No. ▶	
			ZIP code ▶	

For Paperwork Reduction Act Notice, see page 1 of separate instructions.   Cat. No. 11390Z   Form **1065** (1994)

Form 1065 (1994)

Page **2**

Schedule A — Cost of Goods Sold

1	Inventory at beginning of year	1
2	Purchases less cost of items withdrawn for personal use	2
3	Cost of labor	3
4	Additional section 263A costs (see instructions) *(attach schedule)*	4
5	Other costs *(attach schedule)*	5
6	**Total.** Add lines 1 through 5	6
7	Inventory at end of year	7
8	**Cost of goods sold.** Subtract line 7 from line 6. Enter here and on page 1, line 2	8

9a Check all methods used for valuing closing inventory:

   (i) ☐ Cost

   (ii) ☐ Lower of cost or market as described in Regulations section 1.471-4

   (iii) ☐ Writedown of "subnormal" goods as described in Regulations section 1.471-2(c)

   (iv) ☐ Other (specify method used and attach explanation) ▶ ....

   b Check this box if the LIFO inventory method was adopted this tax year for any goods *(if checked, attach Form 970)* . . ▶ ☐

   c Do the rules of section 263A (for property produced or acquired for resale) apply to the partnership? . . ☐ Yes ☐ No

   d Was there any change in determining quantities, cost, or valuations between opening and closing inventory? ☐ Yes ☐ No
   If "Yes," attach explanation.

Schedule B — Other Information

		Yes	No
1	What type of entity is filing this return? Check the applicable box ▶ ☐ General partnership ☐ Limited partnership ☐ Limited liability company		
2	Are any partners in this partnership also partnerships?		
3	Is this partnership a partner in another partnership?		
4	Is this partnership subject to the consolidated audit procedures of sections 6221 through 6233? If "Yes," see **Designation of Tax Matters Partner** below		
5	Does this partnership meet **ALL THREE** of the following requirements?		
a	The partnership's total receipts for the tax year were less than $250,000;		
b	The partnership's total assets at the end of the tax year were less than $600,000; **AND**		
c	Schedules K-1 are filed with the return and furnished to the partners on or before the due date (including extensions) for the partnership return. If "Yes," the partnership is not required to complete Schedules L, M-1, and M-2; Item F on page 1 of Form 1065; or Item J on Schedule K-1		
6	Does this partnership have any foreign partners?		
7	Is this partnership a publicly traded partnership as defined in section 469(k)(2)?		
8	Has this partnership filed, or is it required to file, **Form 8264,** Application for Registration of a Tax Shelter? . .		
9	At any time during calendar year 1994, did the partnership have an interest in or a signature or other authority over a financial account in a foreign country (such as a bank account, securities account, or other financial account)? (See the instructions for exceptions and filing requirements for Form TD F 90-22.1.) If "Yes," enter the name of the foreign country. ▶		
10	Was the partnership the grantor of, or transferor to, a foreign trust that existed during the current tax year, whether or not the partnership or any partner has any beneficial interest in it? If "Yes," you may have to file Forms 3520, 3520-A, or 926		
11	Was there a distribution of property or a transfer (e.g., by sale or death) of a partnership interest during the tax year? If "Yes," you may elect to adjust the basis of the partnership's assets under section 754 by attaching the statement described under **Elections Made By the Partnership**		

Designation of Tax Matters Partner (See instructions.)

Enter below the general partner designated as the tax matters partner (TMP) for the tax year of this return:

Name of
designated TMP ▶

Identifying
number of TMP ▶

Address of
designated TMP ▶ _____

SCHEDULE K (FORM 1065), PARTNERS' SHARES OF INCOME, CREDITS, DEDUCTIONS, ETC.

Form 1065 (1994)   Page **3**

Schedule K   **Partners' Shares of Income, Credits, Deductions, etc.**

	(a) Distributive share items		(b) Total amount
Income (Loss)	**1** Ordinary income (loss) from trade or business activities (page 1, line 22)	**1**	
	2 Net income (loss) from rental real estate activities *(attach Form 8825)*	**2**	
	3a Gross income from other rental activities **3a**		
	b Expenses from other rental activities *(attach schedule)* **3b**		
	c Net income (loss) from other rental activities. Subtract line 3b from line 3a	**3c**	
	4 Portfolio income (loss) (see instructions): **a** Interest income	**4a**	
	b Dividend income	**4b**	
	c Royalty income	**4c**	
	d Net short-term capital gain (loss) *(attach Schedule D (Form 1065))*	**4d**	
	e Net long-term capital gain (loss) *(attach Schedule D (Form 1065))*	**4e**	
	f Other portfolio income (loss) *(attach schedule)*	**4f**	
	5 Guaranteed payments to partners	**5**	
	6 Net gain (loss) under section 1231 (other than due to casualty or theft) *(attach Form 4797)*	**6**	
	7 Other income (loss) *(attach schedule)*	**7**	
Deductions	**8** Charitable contributions (see instructions) *(attach schedule)*	**8**	
	9 Section 179 expense deduction *(attach Form 4562)*	**9**	
	10 Deductions related to portfolio income (see instructions) (itemize)	**10**	
	11 Other deductions *(attach schedule)*	**11**	
Investment Interest	**12a** Interest expense on investment debts	**12a**	
	b **(1)** Investment income included on lines 4a, 4b, 4c, and 4f above	**12b(1)**	
	(2) Investment expenses included on line 10 above.	**12b(2)**	
Credits	**13a** Credit for income tax withheld	**13a**	
	b Low-income housing credit (see instructions):		
	(1) From partnerships to which section 42(j)(5) applies for property placed in service before 1990	**13b(1)**	
	(2) Other than on line 13b(1) for property placed in service before 1990	**13b(2)**	
	(3) From partnerships to which section 42(j)(5) applies for property placed in service after 1989	**13b(3)**	
	(4) Other than on line 13b(3) for property placed in service after 1989	**13b(4)**	
	c Qualified rehabilitation expenditures related to rental real estate activities *(attach Form 3468)*	**13c**	
	d Credits (other than credits shown on lines 13b and 13c) related to rental real estate activities (see instructions)	**13d**	
	e Credits related to other rental activities (see instructions)	**13e**	
	14 Other credits (see instructions)	**14**	
Self-Employment	**15a** Net earnings (loss) from self-employment	**15a**	
	b Gross farming or fishing income	**15b**	
	c Gross nonfarm income	**15c**	
Adjustments and Tax Preference Items	**16a** Depreciation adjustment on property placed in service after 1986	**16a**	
	b Adjusted gain or loss	**16b**	
	c Depletion (other than oil and gas)	**16c**	
	d **(1)** Gross income from oil, gas, and geothermal properties	**16d(1)**	
	(2) Deductions allocable to oil, gas, and geothermal properties	**16d(2)**	
	e Other adjustments and tax preference items *(attach schedule)*	**16e**	
Foreign Taxes	**17a** Type of income ▶ .... **b** Foreign country or U.S. possession ▶		
	c Total gross income from sources outside the United States *(attach schedule)*.	**17c**	
	d Total applicable deductions and losses *(attach schedule)*	**17d**	
	e Total foreign taxes (check one): ▶ ☐ Paid ☐ Accrued	**17e**	
	f Reduction in taxes available for credit *(attach schedule)*	**17f**	
	g Other foreign tax information *(attach schedule)*	**17g**	
Other	**18a** Total expenditures to which a section 59(e) election may apply	**18a**	
	b Type of expenditures ▶...		
	19 Tax-exempt interest income	**19**	
	20 Other tax-exempt income	**20**	
	21 Nondeductible expenses	**21**	
	22 Other items and amounts required to be reported separately to partners (see instructions) *(attach schedule)*		

Analysis	**23a** Income (loss). Combine lines 1 through 7 in column (b). From the result, subtract the sum of lines 8 through 12a, 17e, and 18a **23a**				
	b Analysis by type of partner:	**(a) Corporate**	**(b) Individual**	**(c) Partnership**	**(d) Exempt organization**	**(e) Nominee/Other**

		(a) Corporate	(b) Individual		(c) Partnership	(d) Exempt organization	(e) Nominee/Other
			i. Active	ii. Passive			
	(1) General partners						
	(2) Limited partners						

Form 1065 (1994)   Page **4**

Note: If Question 5 of Schedule B is answered "Yes," the partnership is not required to complete Schedules L, M-1, and M-2.

Schedule L — Balance Sheets

Assets	Beginning of tax year (a)	(b)	End of tax year (c)	(d)
1 Cash				
2a Trade notes and accounts receivable				
b Less allowance for bad debts				
3 Inventories				
4 U.S. government obligations				
5 Tax-exempt securities				
6 Other current assets (attach schedule)				
7 Mortgage and real estate loans				
8 Other investments (attach schedule)				
9a Buildings and other depreciable assets				
b Less accumulated depreciation				
10a Depletable assets				
b Less accumulated depletion				
11 Land (net of any amortization)				
12a Intangible assets (amortizable only)				
b Less accumulated amortization				
13 Other assets (attach schedule)				
14 Total assets				
Liabilities and Capital				
15 Accounts payable				
16 Mortgages, notes, bonds payable in less than 1 year				
17 Other current liabilities (attach schedule)				
18 All nonrecourse loans				
19 Mortgages, notes, bonds payable in 1 year or more				
20 Other liabilities (attach schedule)				
21 Partners' capital accounts				
22 Total liabilities and capital				

Schedule M-1 — Reconciliation of Income (Loss) per Books With Income (Loss) per Return (see instructions)

1 Net income (loss) per books
2 Income included on Schedule K, lines 1 through 4, 6, and 7, not recorded on books this year (itemize): ....
3 Guaranteed payments (other than health insurance)
4 Expenses recorded on books this year not included on Schedule K, lines 1 through 12a, 17e, and 18a (itemize):
  a Depreciation $ ....
  b Travel and entertainment $ ....
5 Add lines 1 through 4

6 Income recorded on books this year not included on Schedule K, lines 1 through 7 (itemize):
  a Tax-exempt interest $ ....
7 Deductions included on Schedule K, lines 1 through 12a, 17e, and 18a, not charged against book income this year (itemize):
  a Depreciation $ ....
8 Add lines 6 and 7
9 Income (loss) (Schedule K, line 23a). Subtract line 8 from line 5

Schedule M-2 — Analysis of Partners' Capital Accounts

1 Balance at beginning of year
2 Capital contributed during year
3 Net income (loss) per books
4 Other increases (itemize): ....
5 Add lines 1 through 4

6 Distributions: a Cash
                 b Property
7 Other decreases (itemize): ....
8 Add lines 6 and 7
9 Balance at end of year. Subtract line 8 from line 5

Printed on recycled paper

*U.S.GPO:1994-375-264

SCHEDULE K-1 (FORM 1065), PARTNER'S SHARE OF INCOME, CREDITS, DEDUCTIONS, ETC.

SCHEDULE K-1
(Form 1065)
Department of the Treasury
Internal Revenue Service

Partner's Share of Income, Credits, Deductions, etc.
▶ See separate instructions.

For calendar year 1994 or tax year beginning _____ , 1994, and ending _____ , 19 ___

OMB No. 1545-0099

1994

Partner's identifying number ▶

Partnership's identifying number ▶

Partner's name, address, and ZIP code

Partnership's name, address, and ZIP code

A This partner is a ☐ general partner ☐ limited partner
☐ limited liability company member

B What type of entity is this partner? ▶ ....

C Is this partner a ☐ domestic or a ☐ foreign partner?

D Enter partner's percentage of:

	(i) Before change or termination	(ii) End of year
Profit sharing	.... %	.... %
Loss sharing	.... %	.... %
Ownership of capital	.... %	.... %

E IRS Center where partnership filed return:

F Partner's share of liabilities (see instructions):
- Nonrecourse . . . . $ ....
- Qualified nonrecourse financing . $ ....
- Other . . . . $ ....

G Tax shelter registration number . ▶ ....

H Check here if this partnership is a publicly traded partnership as defined in section 469(k)(2) . . . . ☐

I Check applicable boxes: **(1)** ☐ Final K-1 **(2)** ☐ Amended K-1

J Analysis of partner's capital account:

(a) Capital account at beginning of year	(b) Capital contributed during year	(c) Partner's share of lines 3, 4, and 7, Form 1065, Schedule M-2	(d) Withdrawals and distributions	(e) Capital account at end of year (combine columns (a) through (d))
			( )	

	(a) Distributive share item		(b) Amount	(c) 1040 filers enter the amount in column (b) on:
Income (Loss)	**1** Ordinary income (loss) from trade or business activities . . .	**1**		} See Partner's Instructions for Schedule K-1 (Form 1065).
	2 Net income (loss) from rental real estate activities	**2**		
	3 Net income (loss) from other rental activities	**3**		
	4 Portfolio income (loss):			
	a Interest	**4a**		Sch. B, Part I, line 1
	b Dividends	**4b**		Sch. B, Part II, line 5
	c Royalties	**4c**		Sch. E, Part I, line 4
	d Net short-term capital gain (loss)	**4d**		Sch. D, line 5, col. (f) or (g)
	e Net long-term capital gain (loss).	**4e**		Sch. D, line 13, col. (f) or (g)
	f Other portfolio income (loss) *(attach schedule)*	**4f**		Enter on applicable line of your return.
	5 Guaranteed payments to partner	**5**		} See Partner's Instructions for Schedule K-1 (Form 1065).
	6 Net gain (loss) under section 1231 (other than due to casualty or theft)	**6**		
	7 Other income (loss) *(attach schedule)*	**7**		Enter on applicable line of your return.
Deductions	**8** Charitable contributions (see instructions) *(attach schedule)* .	**8**		Sch. A, line 15 or 16
	9 Section 179 expense deduction.	**9**		} See Partner's Instructions for Schedule K-1 (Form 1065).
	10 Deductions related to portfolio income *(attach schedule)* . .	**10**		
	11 Other deductions *(attach schedule)*.	**11**		
Investment Interest	**12a** Interest expense on investment debts	**12a**		Form 4952, line 1
	b (1) Investment income included on lines 4a, 4b, 4c, and 4f above	**b(1)**		} See Partner's Instructions for Schedule K-1 (Form 1065).
	(2) Investment expenses included on line 10 above	**b(2)**		
Credits	**13a** Credit for income tax withheld	**13a**		See Partner's Instructions for Schedule K-1 (Form 1065).
	b Low-income housing credit:			
	(1) From section 42(j)(5) partnerships for property placed in service before 1990	**b(1)**		
	(2) Other than on line 13b(1) for property placed in service before 1990	**b(2)**		
	(3) From section 42(j)(5) partnerships for property placed in service after 1989	**b(3)**		} Form 8586, line 5
	(4) Other than on line 13b(3) for property placed in service after 1989	**b(4)**		
	c Qualified rehabilitation expenditures related to rental real estate activities (see instructions)	**13c**		
	d Credits (other than credits shown on lines 13b and 13c) related to rental real estate activities (see instructions)	**13d**		} See Partner's Instructions for Schedule K-1 (Form 1065).
	e Credits related to other rental activities (see instructions) . . .	**13e**		
	14 Other credits (see instructions)	**14**		

For Paperwork Reduction Act Notice, see Instructions for Form 1065.

Cat. No. 11394R

Schedule K-1 (Form 1065) 1994

	(a) Distributive share item		(b) Amount	(c) 1040 filers enter the amount in column (b) on:
Self-employment	**15a** Net earnings (loss) from self-employment	15a		Sch. SE, Section A or B
	b Gross farming or fishing income.	15b		See Partner's Instructions for Schedule K-1 (Form 1065).
	c Gross nonfarm income.	15c		
Adjustments and Tax Preference Items	**16a** Depreciation adjustment on property placed in service after 1986	16a		
	b Adjusted gain or loss	16b		See Partner's Instructions for Schedule K-1 (Form 1065) and Instructions for Form 6251.
	c Depletion (other than oil and gas)	16c		
	d (1) Gross income from oil, gas, and geothermal properties . .	d(1)		
	(2) Deductions allocable to oil, gas, and geothermal properties	d(2)		
	e Other adjustments and tax preference items *(attach schedule)*	16e		
Foreign Taxes	**17a** Type of income ▶			Form 1116, check boxes
	b Name of foreign country or U.S. possession ▶			
	c Total gross income from sources outside the United States *(attach schedule)*	17c		Form 1116, Part I
	d Total applicable deductions and losses *(attach schedule)* . .	17d		
	e Total foreign taxes (check one): ▶ ☐ Paid ☐ Accrued . .	17e		Form 1116, Part II
	f Reduction in taxes available for credit *(attach schedule)* . . .	17f		Form 1116, Part III
	g Other foreign tax information *(attach schedule)*	17g		See Instructions for Form 1116.
Other	**18a** Total expenditures to which a section 59(e) election may apply	18a		See Partner's Instructions for Schedule K-1 (Form 1065).
	b Type of expenditures ▶			
	19 Tax-exempt interest income	19		Form 1040, line 8b
	20 Other tax-exempt income.	20		See Partner's Instructions for Schedule K-1 (Form 1065).
	21 Nondeductible expenses	21		
	22 Recapture of low-income housing credit:			
	a From section 42(j)(5) partnerships	22a		Form 8611, line 8
	b Other than on line 22a.	22b		

23 Supplemental information required to be reported separately to each partner *(attach additional schedules if more space is needed):*

(blank lines for supplemental information)

INDEX